PENGUIN

Civ   ide

Civil Liberty:

The Liberty/NCCL Guide

MALCOLM HURWITT and
PETER THORNTON

FOURTH EDITION

liberty

National Council for Civil Liberties

PENGUIN BOOKS

Published by the Penguin Group
27 Wrights Lane, London W8 5TZ, England
Viking Penguin Inc., 40 West 23rd Street, New York, New York 10010, USA
Penguin Books Australia Ltd, Ringwood, Victoria, Australia
Penguin Books Canada Ltd, 2801 John Street, Markham, Ontario, Canada L3R 1B4
Penguin Books (NZ) Ltd, 182–190 Wairau Road, Auckland 10, New Zealand

Penguin Books Ltd, Registered Offices: Harmondsworth, Middlesex, England

First published as a Penguin Special 1972
Second edition 1973
Third edition published as a Penguin Handbook 1978
Fourth edition 1989
10 9 8 7 6 5 4 3 2 1

Made and printed in Great Britain by
Richard Clay Ltd, Bungay, Suffolk

Filmset in Monophoto Photina

Contents

List of contributors

ROBIN ALLEN is a barrister. He is a founder member of the Free Representation Unit and was previously the employment law consultant to the Legal Action Group. He is author of the Equal Opportunities Commission guide *How to Prepare a Case for an Industrial Tribunal for Claims under the Sex Discrimination and Equal Pay Acts*.

BARBARA COHEN is a solicitor with particular interest in policing, public order and discrimination law. She was NCCL legal officer from 1982 to 1985.

JEAN COUSSINS was women's rights officer at NCCL from 1975–80. She is author of several publications on a wide range of topics related to equal rights and discrimination, and is the director of Housing and Education Services at the Commission for Racial Equality.

FIONA FAIRWEATHER is a solicitor and senior lecturer in law at the Polytechnic of East London. She is co-author of *A Practitioner's Guide to Police Powers* and lectures throughout the country on police procedure.

EDWARD FITZGERALD is a practising barrister specializing in criminal law, prisoners' law, mental health law and international human rights law. He is the author of numerous articles on prisoners' rights and mental patients' rights.

BILL FORRESTER is Gypsy Liaison Officer for Essex County Council. He has been involved with the issues of travellers since 1973, including while working for NCCL and for the Minority Rights Group, and is an active member of Haringey Travellers' Support Group and several other organizations. He is author of *The Travellers' Handbook*.

ALISON HANNAH is a solicitor currently working in private practice in East London. She was previously employed as a community lawyer in a Citizens' Advice Bureau.

SARA HUEY is director of the Civil Liberties Trust.

MALCOLM HURWITT is a solicitor and a president of Mental Health Review Tribunals. He has been a member of the executive committee of NCCL since 1958 and has twice been chair of NCCL. He was formerly a part-time adjudicator under the Immigration Act, and is now a Trustee and Honorary Secretary of the Civil Liberties Trust.

HOWARD LEVENSON is a practising solicitor and lecturer in law at the Polytechnic of East London. He was formerly legal officer for NCCL and was co-editor of the third edition of *Civil Liberty: The NCCL Guide to Your Rights*. He is co-author of *A Practitioner's Guide to Police Powers* and has written a number of books on criminal procedure.

JEREMY MCBRIDE is a lecturer at the University of Birmingham, specializing in constitutional and international law with particular reference to the protection of human rights. He is the co-author of *Civil Liberties and a Bill of Rights, Human Rights in Pakistan After Martial Law* and *Legality and Local Politics*. He was a co-founder of Interights and is a member of its executive committee.

JEREMY MCMULLEN is a barrister specializing in employment law. He has written and broadcast widely on workers' rights and lectures at the London School of Economics. He is a member of the ACAS panel of independent experts set up to assess equal pay claims.

TERRY MUNYARD is a practising barrister. He has been involved in campaigning for lesbian and gay rights over the past decade. He is a former executive committee member of NCCL and co-author of their publication *Gay Workers, Trade Unions and the Law*.

ANDREW NICOL is a barrister practising in London. He previously taught law at the London School of Economics. He is the co-author of *Media Law: the Rights of Journalists and Broadcasters*.

CATHY NICHOLES is a barrister specializing in family and children's work.

HEATHER ROGERS is a barrister practising in London.

SUE SHUTTER has been an adviser at the Joint Council for the Welfare of Immigrants for the last twelve years. She is co-author and editor of *Worlds Apart: Women under immigration and nationality law.*

PETER THORNTON is a barrister specializing in criminal and civil liberty cases. He is a trustee of the Civil Liberties Trust and a past chairman of NCCL. He is the author of a number of NCCL's publications, including: *The Rights of Suspects, Trial or Error, We Protest – The Public Order Debate, The Civil Liberties of the Zircon Affair* and *Decade of Decline: Civil Liberties in the Thatcher Years.* He is also author of *Public Order Law.*

ALASTAIR WILSON QC is a barrister practising in the fields of trade mark, copyright and patent law.

Preface to the fourth edition

The National Council for Civil Liberties (NCCL) was founded in 1934 to defend civil and political rights. The need to establish an independent watchdog had resulted from the observation of police handling of the hunger marches in 1932. Amongst its founding members were Harold Laski, Vera Brittain, Kingsley Martin, Edith Summerskill and Claud Cockburn. E. M. Forster was NCCL's first President. Clement Attlee, Nye Bevan, J. B. Priestley, A. P. Herbert and Bertrand Russell lent their support. For more than fifty years NCCL, a non-party, non-denominational voluntary organization, has fought for the liberty of the subject. It has taken up test cases, led campaigns, briefed legislators and politicians, researched and reported, published the views of experts, advised and defended.

One of the key roles of the NCCL has always been to encourage and spread a greater awareness of an individual's rights under the law. It is to this aspect of NCCL's work that the guide is especially directed. Rights cannot be enjoyed without knowledge of their existence. Justice cannot be obtained without awareness of the remedies available to correct injustice.

The need for such a guide and for an organization like NCCL is greater than ever. Attacks upon civil liberties are on the increase: restrictions on press freedom, greater public secrecy, censorship in the name of national security, less freedom of information, increased detention without charge, reductions in the right to trial by jury, longer prison sentences and less use of alternatives to prison, internal exile without trial under the Prevention of Terrorism Act, intolerance against travellers and homosexuals, discrimination against immigrants, wider police controls on demonstrations, more public order offences, restrictions on trade unionists.

The boundaries of civil liberty are the subject of continual debate. They shift with the demands and political dictates of a developing

society. To crystallize its current objectives NCCL has adopted as a
working statement the Charter of Civil Liberties, which can be
found at the back of the guide.

It is necessary to repeat the warning, given in earlier editions,
that this book is a guide and not an exhaustive treatise on any of
the subjects with which it deals. It is intended to help the general
reader to understand the basic law involved and to know where to
find expert help when it is required. We have included only a brief
section on Scotland, since the Scottish Council for Civil Liberties is
currently preparing a separate work for publication and because
the work of NCCL does not generally extend to Scotland. It does,
however, extend to Wales, which has the same laws as England,
and especially to Northern Ireland.

The law in this guide is stated with best endeavours at accuracy
as at 14 February 1989. Some Acts of Parliament which are due to
become law shortly thereafter, such as the Prevention of Terrorism
(Temporary Provisions) Act 1989 and the Employment Act 1989,
have been incorporated into the text as if they were in force.

Finally, we would like to thank all the contributors for their hard
work and generous cooperation. The services of the contributors
and the editors have been provided free of charge so that the profits
from the guide can go to furthering the work of NCCL. Our thanks
also go to Sarah Spencer, general secretary of NCCL for her helpful
advice, to Richard Kinsey for help on the law of Scotland, to Diana
Shelley and Phil Jeffries for use of the map on p. 10 which is taken
from the Legal Advice Pack for Nuclear Disarmers published by
CND, and to Andrew Franklin and Keith Taylor at Penguin.

Malcolm Hurwitt
Peter Thornton
February 1989

Introduction

In the absence of a written constitution or a modern Bill of Rights, our law, made up of statutes and judge-made common law, provides for precious few positive rights. Parliament has never decreed that there should be, for example, rights of free speech, of assembly, or of privacy. Such rights as there are can only be found in the negative: if the law does not prohibit it you can do it. A public protest along the streets of London is legal not because a statute permits it but simply because the common law allows everyone to pass and repass along the highway as long as no unreasonable obstruction is caused.

This negative approach has three principal consequences. First, positive rights are not enshrined in the law. They cannot be invoked to protect the individual from police or other controls. The controls exist but not the rights. Secondly, the boundaries of civil liberties are uncertain: because they are not written down they are open to interpretation, to the expression of political will, and often to police discretion. Thirdly, the undoubted existence in generally accepted terms of certain basic freedoms, of speech, for example, and of movement, or of protest, can be established only by reference to tradition and accepted practice.

It is not the task of this guide to direct the reader to areas of reform. The case for a Bill of Rights is fully argued elsewhere. To some extent the United Kingdom has already taken tentative steps in that direction by deciding to ratify the European Convention for the Protection of Human Rights and Fundamental Freedoms (which is discussed in chapter 5). But the procedures for enforcing rights under the Convention are cumbersome and slow, and legal aid to bring a case is limited. The Convention is not incorporated into our law and it is not enforceable in our courts. Its value to an aggrieved individual or organization is, therefore, limited.

Earlier editions of this guide set out three main objectives: to explain in simple terms the legal rights of people in the United Kingdom; to suggest ways of putting these rights into practice; and to highlight aspects of the law which adversely affect civil liberties. These objectives have been largely retained for the fourth edition. The main departure from earlier editions is the concentration on the type of civil liberty areas which are the primary concern of NCCL, at the expense of more general rights, such as the rights of motorists, consumer rights and welfare rights. These subjects are important but they are adequately dealt with in other publications, notably the *Penguin Guide to the Law*.

1 The right of peaceful protest

This chapter deals with:

- Freedom of assembly   1
- The right to use the highway (and other public places)   16
- Public order offences   20
- More information   27

1.1   Freedom of assembly

There is no specific law which confers a legal right to demonstrate. The fact that Parliament has passed legislation which explicitly restricts the rights of people to march or to assemble suggests, however, that there is an implicit assumption that such rights exist. Senior judges have often referred to the right of peaceful protest. Lord Denning has said: 'The right to demonstrate and the right to protest on matters of public concern ... are rights which it is in the public interest that individuals should possess; and indeed, that they should exercise without impediment so long as no wrongful act is done.' A Government circular on the Public Order Act 1986 states: 'The right to assemble, demonstrate and protest peacefully within the law is fundamental to our democratic way of life.'

The Public Order Act 1986 substantially increased the powers of the police to impose conditions on both marches and assemblies (i.e. 'static' demonstrations such as a rally, a picket or a vigil) which could severely limit their impact. Police powers arise not only to prevent 'disorder' but also to prevent disruption to the normal life of the community – leaving it to the police to balance freedom of expression against traffic flow, the rights of traders, shoppers, etc. Following mass support for pickets in several industrial disputes, the Act also allows the police to intervene if they believe the demonstration is intended to be intimidating.

PROCESSIONS AND MARCHES

A procession is simply defined as people moving together along a route; the law does not provide a minimum number to constitute a procession. Most processions are lawful. The participants are exercising their right to pass along the highway (see 1.2, p. 16). A procession may become an obstruction of the highway (see 1.2, p. 16) if the use of the highway is unreasonable.

The Public Order Act 1986 considerably extends the previous police controls over processions. Organizers of most processions must now give seven days' advance notice to the police. The police may also impose conditions on processions and, in limited circumstances, have them banned. Failure to comply with these provisions is a criminal offence.

Advance notice of processions

Prior to 1986, in some areas there were local laws which required organizers of processions to give advance notice to the police, but in most areas this was not required. Now, under the Public Order Act 1986, the *organizer* of most processions must give *advance notice* to the police. It is a criminal offence to fail to give proper notice (see below).

Who is the organizer?

There is no legal definition. For a big procession an official organizer will probably have been selected well in advance of the date. For a spontaneous event or one which is collectively planned the organizer could be anyone who takes the lead.

Notice

Advance notice is required if the procession is intended to:

- demonstrate support for or opposition to the views or actions of any person or group;

- publicize a cause or campaign; or
- mark or commemorate an event.

The notice must be in writing and must include:

- the date of the procession;
- the time it will start;
- the proposed route;
- the name and address of the organizer.

The written notice must be delivered to a police station in the area where the procession is planned to start (or the first police area in England on the route if it starts in Scotland) either *by hand* or by *recorded delivery six clear days* in advance. 'Six clear days' means, effectively, a full week in advance, e.g. on Saturday for a procession the following Saturday.

If a procession is planned at short notice (less than one week) then the organizer is required to deliver written notice *by hand* as soon as reasonably practicable.

No notice

No notice need be given:

- if it is *not reasonably practicable to give notice* in advance. This is intended to allow for a completely spontaneous procession, for example when a meeting turns itself into a march or, as Christian CND put it, when it is necessary 'to call acts of witness or protest at short notice'. If a prosecution is brought it will be for the magistrates' court to decide whether notice could have been given. A last minute telephone call to the police – a record should be kept of the call – is advisable to show you are prepared to follow the spirit of the law.
- if it is a *funeral procession* or a *procession commonly or customarily held*. This will include the Lord Mayor's show in the City of London, the Notting Hill Carnival, the Durham Miners' Gala and other annual local parades including those organized by the Scouts or religious groups. If a protest march

occurs regularly (weekly, annually) at the same time along the same route then no notice should be required.

It is always good practice to inform the police of a march or procession and to discuss the route and other details, such as the carrying of banners and the use of loud-speakers.

Offences connected with notice

The organizer commits an offence (maximum penalty fine at level 3, currently £400) if:

- notice was not given as required; *or*
- the date, starting time or route differs from that given in the notice.

There is no power of arrest, but the police could rely on their general power of arrest (see 6.3, p. 137). It is not an offence merely to take part in a procession where notice has not been given.

It is a defence if you can prove:

- you were not aware that notice had not been given or not given in time; *or*
- the different date, starting time or route was due to circumstances beyond your control or was changed with the agreement of the police or by direction of the police.

Therefore, you should always make a careful record of any last minute negotiations with the police.

Police conditions on processions

Even if you give advance notice there is no guarantee that the police will allow your proposed procession to take place as planned. In advance, the Chief Constable (or the Commissioner in London) can impose conditions relating to the route, number of marchers, types of banners, duration, or restrict entry to a public place. These conditions must be in writing. However, when the procession has begun the most senior officer on the spot can impose similar conditions, which do not need to be in writing.

The test for imposing conditions

Conditions can only be imposed if the senior officer reasonably believes that

- the procession may result in:
  - serious public disorder; or
  - serious damage to property; or
  - serious disruption to the life of the community; *or*
- the purpose of the organizers is to intimidate others 'with a view to compelling them not to do an act they have a right to do, or to do an act they have a right not to do'.

The conditions must be ones which the officer believes are *necessary* to prevent the disorder, damage, disruption or intimidation.

Failure to comply with a condition is a criminal offence (see below).

Banning processions

The Public Order Act 1986 leaves unchanged the power of the police to ban all or a 'class' of processions in a local area for up to three months. If a Chief Constable (or the Commissioner in London) is satisfied that the powers to impose conditions will not be sufficient to prevent serious public disorder if the procession takes place, then he must apply for a banning order.

Outside London, the Chief Constable applies to the district council for a banning order. The district council is not obliged to make an order, but it must have the Home Secretary's consent to any banning order it makes. In London, the Commissioner of Police makes the order with the Home Secretary's consent.

A banning order can cover all or part of a district (or all or part of the Metropolitan Police area or the City of London) and can ban all processions or all processions within a certain class (for example, processions marking the death of a political terrorist). A blanket ban of all processions is often imposed, even though it is designed to prevent one march only. The standard formula is to ban 'all public processions other than those of a traditional or ceremonial character'.

Failure to comply with a banning order is a criminal offence (see below).

ASSEMBLIES, STATIC DEMONSTRATIONS AND RALLIES

In addition to the powers which the police have used effectively for many years (breach of the peace, obstruction of the highway, local by-laws etc, (see 1.2, p. 16 and 1.3, p. 25)) to move or disperse a crowd which has assembled for a common purpose, the Public Order Act 1986 gives the police specific powers to control public assemblies. These are similar to the powers which the police have to impose conditions on processions (see above). It should be noted that there is no power to ban an assembly, and no advance notice need be given to the police of an assembly.

A 'public assembly' is twenty or more people gathered together in a public place which is at least partly open air. A public place is any highway (including the pavement) and any other place to which the public or a section of the public can have access and therefore includes parks and gardens, shopping precincts, shops and offices, restaurants and pubs, cinemas, football stadia, rights of way etc. A public assembly could be twenty people spaced across a wide entrance, but probably not four sets of five pickets at different factory gates.

Police conditions on assemblies

Conditions may be imposed on a public assembly which restrict:

- the place – e.g., forcing pickets to move from the factory gates;
- the duration – e.g., reducing a twenty-four hour vigil to four hours;
- the numbers – e.g., reducing a mass picket from thousands to twenty.

Similar to the powers concerning processions, the Chief Constable (Commissioner in London) can impose conditions in advance, in writing, or the most senior officer on the spot can impose conditions as soon as twenty people have assembled.

Conditions may only be imposed if the senior police officer reasonably believes that:

- the public assembly may result in
  - serious public disorder;
  - serious damage to property; or
  - serious disruption to the life of the community; *or*
- the purpose of the organizers is to intimidate others 'with a view to compelling them not to do an act they have a right to do, or to do an act they have a right not to do'.

Whilst Parliament's intention was clearly to give the police greater control over picketing in particular, the courts have said it was not intimidation when the conduct complained of was 'abuse, swearing and shouting' as workers crossed a picket line, and that causing 'discomfort' to guests entering South Africa House did not amount to intimidation.

It is an offence to defy a condition or a banning order

If you *know* that a condition has been imposed on either a procession or a public assembly or that a procession has been banned, it is an offence to organize, to take part or to incite others to take part or not to comply with the condition or to ignore the banning order. The police can arrest organizers or demonstrators, which in a large gathering gives them extremely wide discretion as to whom they choose to remove from the scene. The maximum penalty for organizers or inciters is three months' imprisonment or a fine at level 4 (currently £1,000) and for participants a fine at level 3 (currently £400). It is a defence to prove that any failure to comply with a condition was beyond your control.

Challenging conditions on marches or assemblies – judicial review

If you are the organizer of a demonstration, then your first concern will be that the demonstration should take place as planned with the maximum effect. You may, therefore, want to enter into negotiations with the police about the plans for the event. If you do so, you should be fully prepared with details of arrangements for stewarding and crowd control, first aid and access by emergency vehicles, maps and plans, a detailed time schedule and an estimate of numbers. Relying on your own knowledge of the community and any other events likely to take place on the same date, try to anticipate police objections. Keep a full note of any objections they raise.

If the police decide to impose conditions in advance of the event then you could apply for judicial review to challenge the decision. You would need to be able to argue that either:

- the decision was improperly reached (for example, because the proper procedure was not followed or improper considerations were taken into account); or
- the decision was so unreasonable or arbitrary that no reasonable chief officer could have reached that conclusion.

It would be relevant to show that negotiations were still open. Cases brought to challenge banning orders under the 1936 Act show that courts are very unwilling to interfere in operational police decisions of this kind. They are reluctant to substitute their own assessment of the facts and the possible prospects of disorder, damage, disruption or intimidation for the assessment made by senior police officers.

Applications for judicial review must be made to the Divisional Court of the High Court in London. Urgent applications can be heard quickly. In very many instances, however, you will be informed of conditions to restrict processions or assemblies far too late to apply to the court. There is no one with immediate power to overrule the senior officer on the spot if he decides to impose conditions.

If there are prosecutions for defying conditions on a march or demonstration then the lawfulness of the conditions can be raised as a defence. If there was not a proper reason for imposing the conditions then they would be invalid and no offence committed.

Demonstrations near the Houses of Parliament

At the beginning of each Parliamentary session the Metropolitan Police Commissioner is instructed by Parliament to give directions under the Metropolitan Police Act to police officers 'to disperse all assemblies or processions of persons causing or likely to cause an obstruction, disorder or annoyance' within a specified area around Westminster whenever Parliament is sitting (see map overleaf).

The police must rely on their general powers of arrest or powers to prevent a breach of the peace (see 1.3, p. 25). You commit an offence (maximum sentence, a fine at level 2) if you fail to disperse after you are made aware of the Commissioner's directions, which normally means that the police must read them to you before they can arrest you. It is a defence to show that the free passage of MPs would not have been obstructed by you. The directions do not affect processions or meetings on a day when Parliament is not sitting.

Additional powers to control demonstrations in London and other towns

There are several nineteenth-century statutes (Metropolitan Police Act 1839, City of London Police Act 1839, Town Police Clauses Act 1847) which enable the Commissioner of Police in London and the City or local councils outside London to make regulations and give directions to prevent obstruction and to keep order. Directions are given to constables and are not required to be made public. There are no conditions which must be satisfied before directions can be given, and, therefore, little scope to challenge them as excessive or unjustified. When directions have been given, if you do not comply with police instructions (for example, not to continue down a particular street), you commit an offence or you could be charged with obstructing the police (see p. 16). Police directions are often used to restrict protest events. For example, when a 'Stop the City' demonstration was planned, the City of London Commissioner issued directions under which the police arrested people who distributed leaflets or gathered in groups of three or more. During the News International dispute at Wapping the Metropolitan Commissioner's directions, which were renewed monthly throughout the dispute, gave the police authority to close streets and stop any person walking or driving in any street in Tower Hamlets. In Salisbury the district council made an order which banned 'hippies' from the town centre for two days and restricted them to a designated route.

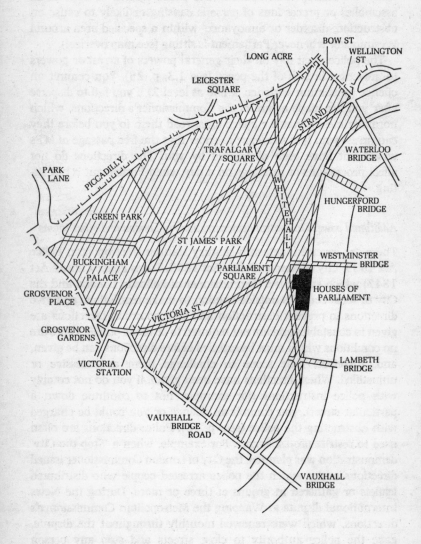

MEETINGS

Private meetings

A meeting is private if the public are not free to attend, in payment or otherwise (for example, the meeting of a trade union branch or a political party). A private meeting remains private even though it is held in a public building like a town hall. Organizers can refuse entry or require someone to leave. Private meetings are governed by the rules of the organization involved, or by conditions specified by the organizers together with any requirements, e.g., as to maximum numbers which apply to the premises where the meeting takes place. Unless the police are invited by the organizers they have no right to enter a private meeting and can be asked to leave unless they are present to prevent crime or an imminent breach of the peace.

Public meetings

A public meeting is a meeting which is open to the public, with or without payment, to attend and is held in a public place (a place to which the public have access on payment or otherwise). Many private premises, including town halls and council buildings, church halls, football stadia, pubs, etc., become 'public places' when public meetings are held there. A meeting could be any number of people and there is no duty to advertise it or to offer tickets widely. Local council meetings are public (except for confidential parts of the agenda).

If you are the organizer of a public meeting on private premises you must ensure that you comply with the terms and conditions for the use of the hall etc., including all fire and safety regulations, and that the meeting is conducted in an orderly manner. *Stewards* should be easily identifiable but they should not wear a uniform to promote a political object or to signify membership of a political organization. They must not try to take over the functions of the police or use force to promote a political object. They can assist in the admission and seating of members of the public and in the control of disorder. They are entitled to use reasonable force to prevent crime or disorder or to remove members of the public who go too far in their heckling.

It is an *offence* under the Public Meeting Act 1908 to try to break up a lawful public meeting by acting in a disorderly manner or to incite others to do so. The maximum penalty is six months' imprisonment and/or a fine on level 5. If a police officer is present and reasonably suspects you of trying to disrupt the meeting then, at the chairperson's request, he can ask you for your name and address and it is an offence if you fail to give these details or give a false name or address (maximum penalty a fine on level 1). These offences do not carry a power of arrest, although the police could rely on their general powers of arrest (see 6.3, p. 138).

If there is serious disruption or aggressiveness, and if the police believe that you are involved then, relying on their common law powers to prevent a breach of the peace, the police could ask you to leave the meeting, threatening you with arrest if you refused, or they could arrest you for an offence under section 4 or section 5 of the Public Order Act 1986 (see 1.3, p. 22).

It appears to be the law that the police are entitled to be present at a public meeting held on private premises if they reasonably believe a breach of the peace is likely to occur. Organizers who do not want police officers to be present can challenge the police to justify their presence. Organizers should also be aware that plain clothes police officers may attend political meetings without authority for the purpose of collecting information.

Remember, any meeting of twenty or more people which is wholly or partly in the open air is a 'public assembly' and subject to conditions being imposed by the police under the Public Order Act 1986 (see p. 6).

Election meetings

The Representation of the People Act 1983 makes special provision for public meetings held at the time of local or national elections. All candidates are entitled to use rooms in local schools and other publicly owned meeting halls, free of charge, for election meetings *provided that* the meetings are open to the public and are intended to further the candidate's prospects by discussion of election issues.

Some local authorities have refused permission to the National

Front to use their premises for election meetings on the grounds that they did not intend their meetings to be genuinely open to the public or because damage was likely to be caused to the premises. In 1986 the Court of Appeal upheld the right of a British National Party candidate to be allowed to use a schoolroom for an election meeting, and ruled that a candidate who was refused such access could sue the local authority to enforce his rights under the election law.

The Representation of the People Act makes it an *offence*, punishable with a fine at level 3 (see p. 27), to disrupt, or to incite others to disrupt, an election meeting. If a police officer reasonably suspects you of trying to disrupt the meeting, then, at the chairperson's request, he can ask you for your name and address and it is an offence if you fail to give these details. Police powers for public meetings also apply to election meetings.

PICKETING

For more than a century, trade unions and organized groups of workers have used picketing as a powerful means of protecting their employment rights and improving the conditions in which they have been expected to work. In recent years, picketing has been used by campaigning and protest groups as an effective way of bringing their views to public attention. But there is no legal right to picket. The law gives some special status to picketing when it is related to an industrial dispute but no special exemption under the criminal law. However, most picketing is lawful unless it causes an obstruction of the highway (see 1.2, p. 16).

You are protected under the civil law if you picket in connection with an *industrial dispute* at or near your own workplace for the purpose of 'peacefully obtaining or communicating information or peacefully persuading any person to work or abstain from working' (Trade Union and Labour Relations Act 1974, as amended by the Employment Acts 1980 and 1982). Employers have increasingly used the civil courts to get injunctions in order to limit severely the effectiveness of picketing. Injunctions have been granted on the basis that it was not the workplace of some or all of the pickets or that the picketing was not peaceful. Unions who continue to picket in breach of an injunction are in contempt of court and liable to pay very heavy fines. By injunction the court can limit the location and number of pickets and impose conditions on their conduct.

In a *non-industrial situation*, the court granted an injunction to a firm of estate agents whose premises were being picketed by local people protesting against the firm's alleged involvement in the eviction of tenants. The court was satisfied that the pickets, although peaceful, were interfering with the firm's trade.

No legal case has been decided which specifies that a particular *number of pickets* at a location will always be lawful. But the Code of Practice under the 1980 Employment Act suggests that the number of pickets at any entrance to a workplace should not generally exceed *six* and the courts may refer to the Code. In applications for injunctions, the civil courts have tended to use six as the upper limit. Other cases have given the police a very wide discretion to limit the number of pickets if they believed this was necessary to prevent a breach of the peace or an obstruction of the highway.

Secondary picketing, picketing at a workplace or premises where you do not work, is not a criminal offence and it is not the job of the police to enforce the civil law on picketing, even if an injunction is in force.

Police powers and picketing

Giving the police greater powers to control and restrict picketing was a primary object of the Public Order Act 1986. Any picket of twenty or more people is a 'public assembly' and therefore subject to police conditions under the Act (see p. 6).

The police are likely to be present at a picket of whatever size. In addition to the power to impose conditions, the police possess a wide range of public order powers to restrict and control picketing and to arrest pickets for various offences, including:

- obstruction of the highway (see 1.2, p. 16): on the basis of too many pickets, even if they were moving, or a single picket trying to compel a driver to stop and listen;

- obstruction of the police (see 1.3, p. 24): for example, refusing to comply with directions when the police are acting to prevent a breach of the peace, as happened at the police road-blocks during the 1984/5 miners' strike;
- using threatening, abusive or insulting words or behaviour (Section 4 Public Order Act 1986 – 1.3, p. 22);
- disorderly conduct likely to cause harassment, alarm or distress (Section 5 Public Order Act 1986 – 1.3, p. 23);
- intimidation, including watching and besetting (Section 7 Conspiracy and Protection of Property Act 1875, maximum penalty six months' imprisonment and/or a fine on level 5 – for fine levels see 1.3, p. 26). Specifically, it is an offence of intimidation if you unlawfully:
  - use violence to intimidate someone or his family or damage property;
  - persistently follow someone;
  - hide someone's tools or clothes;
  - 'watch and beset' or picket someone's home or place of work or the approach to that place (NB it is not unlawful to picket peacefully at your own place of work);
  - with two others, follow someone in the street in a disorderly manner;

but *only if* you do any of these acts with the intention of *compelling* the person either not to do something he has a legal right to do (e.g. the right to use the highway to go to work) or to do something he has a legal right not to do (e.g. the right not to join the picket). This offence carries a power of arrest.

The police often rely on their powers of arrest (incliuding the use of reasonable force) to remove people who are taking part in a mass picket and then, when cases come to court, consent to *bindovers* being offered and the charges dismissed (see 1.3, p. 26).

If you decide to defend a charge which relates to picketing, you should be aware that the police or Crown Prosecution Service may try to persuade the court that it should be a *condition of your bail* that you stay away from the picket line until your trial, which could be several months away.

1.2   The right to use the highway (and other public places)

THE RIGHT TO PASS AND REPASS ALONG THE HIGHWAY

Although the law fails to recognize the right of assembly in any
positive form (see 1.1, p. 1), it does provide a specific right
to use the public highway. It is the right to pass and repass along
the highway (including the pavement), the right to make ordinary
and reasonable use of the highway, which includes processions
along the highway. Lord Denning said in one case that the right to
meet together, to go in procession, to demonstrate and to protest on
matters of public concern was an undoubted right of Englishmen.
But the use of the highway must be reasonable; any unreasonable
obstruction of the highway is a criminal offence (see below).

RESTRICTIONS ON THE RIGHT TO USE THE HIGHWAY

Obstruction of the highway

You commit an offence if, without lawful authority or excuse, you
wilfully obstruct the free passage of the highway.

This is a widely drawn offence. It is often seen in practice as a
police licensing power over public gatherings. The police use it to
remove sit-down demonstrators, to prevent protestors outside South
Africa House in Trafalgar Square from straying outside the barrier
positions agreed with the police, to keep marchers from leaving the
agreed police route, to control pickets, and in every conceivable
public order context on the highway.

The offence does not require violence or threat of violence, and
when cases reach court, prosecutors commonly agree to offer no
evidence if the defendant agrees to be bound over (see 1.3, p. 26).
Often, the police will give a warning to move before making an
arrest, although there is no legal requirement to do so. Nevertheless,
a failure to give a warning may be relevant to the reasonableness
or otherwise of the use of the highway.

The test of reasonableness is an objective test. Was there any
actual obstruction? If there was, how long did it last? Where was it?
What was its purpose? The police often decide to make an arrest on
the basis that other people are prevented from passing along the

highway or going into shops or business premises. But it is a question of fact in each case, and the test of reasonableness can often be argued successfully in demonstration cases, particularly where the police have taken no action in the past, or where the place of protest is a regular spot or where the obstruction was trivial.

The offence can only be tried in the magistrates' court. The maximum penalty is a fine of £400.

By-laws

Many activities on the highway and in other public places such as parks and gardens and on common land are restricted by local by-laws. A copy of the by-laws should be on sale at the local town hall and also available for inspection.

By-laws may, for example, prohibit indecent language or behaviour, or behaving in a disorderly or offensive manner whereby a breach of the peace may be occasioned, or riotous and violent behaviour. By-laws for parks may prohibit public meetings, bill-posting, the erection of notices, stalls and booths, and the sale or distribution of pamphlets and leaflets. They will usually give the police and local authority officials the power to remove anybody who breaches the by-laws.

Ministry of Defence by-laws are used, for example, to keep trespassers out of United States Air Force bases. The RAF Greenham Common by-laws list twelve prohibited activities, beginning with entering the Protected Area except by way of an authorized entrance, and including affixing posters to perimeter fences.

It is an offence to breach a by-law. The penalty is set out in the particular by-law or, if not, is a fine up to £100. When a charge is brought, by-laws may be challenged on the basis that they are *ultra vires*, that is, beyond the scope of the Act of Parliament which creates them, or that they are obviously unreasonable or inconsistent with or repugnant to the general law.

Motor vehicles

The highway authority can close or restrict a road for roadworks or if there is a danger to the public or a risk of serious damage to the highway.

A police officer in uniform may stop a motor vehicle (or a bicycle). He may ask the driver to supply his name and address and that of the owner. He may also check the vehicle for roadworthiness. He cannot ask the driver to give a breath test unless he suspects him of having alcohol in his body, of having committed a moving traffic offence, or if he has been in an accident. The police may also stop and search a vehicle if they reasonably suspect that it contains drugs, firearms, offensive weapons or stolen goods (see 6.1, p. 124).

A police officer may control the traffic. He can make vehicles turn back if he suspects that a breach of the peace is imminent (see 1.3, p. 25), even several miles away. He can make motorists disobey traffic regulations only if life and property are at risk.

The police have no specific power to create *road-blocks* (see 6.1, p. 128). Apart from the above powers the police have limited powers to conduct road checks in a locality in order to search for wanted criminals or escaped prisoners. In towns and cities the police may make regulations and give directions for keeping order and preventing the obstruction of the highway (see 1.2, p. 16 above). The use of these powers for creating road-blocks (for example, at Wapping during the print dispute) is uncertain and untested in the courts.

For the right to use the highway for industrial and consumer picketing see 1.1, p. 13 above.

STREET COLLECTIONS, LEAFLETING, PETITIONS AND NEWS-PAPERS

The law relating to these subjects is confused and inconsistently applied by the police. If in doubt, check with the local authority *and* the police beforehand.

Street collections

The collection of *money for charitable purposes* may take place at open-air meetings in public places and at private meetings with the permission of the organizers without infringing the law, as long as there is no obstruction of the highway (see p. 16), for example, by causing a crowd to gather on the pavement outside the hall, and as long as there is no by-law to prohibit it. The collection must be within a reasonable distance of the meeting, but it may be taken from passers-by and onlookers as well as from members of the audience.

Otherwise (for example, taking a collection alongside a procession), a licence is required from the local authority or, in London, from the police. When a licence is granted the collectors must comply with detailed regulations. For example, no collector may be under sixteen and all collectors must wear a badge of identity and carry a collection box. If the licence is refused, an appeal can be made to the Home Secretary.

Charitable purposes means any charitable, benevolent or philanthropic purpose. It includes the relief of poverty and the advancement of religion or education at home or abroad, but it does not include collections to raise funds for a political party or political campaign, like CND or animal liberation.

Making a street collection without a licence or failing to comply with the regulations is a criminal offence.

Similar considerations apply to the *sale of articles for charitable purposes*. Where a licence is required (for example, for a stall in a market), selling goods without one constitutes the offence of street trading.

Food and household items may be collected *for charitable purposes* as long as the collection does not create an obstruction of the highway, for example, by the position of a stall.

Collecting *money for non-charitable purposes* is the offence of begging. Collecting for workers on strike and their families does not constitute begging.

Door-to-door collections: A licence is required from the district council or, in London, from the police, for going from door-to-door asking for donations of money or goods. It is an offence under the House to House Collections Act 1939 to collect without a licence, although the collection of jumble for a good cause is unlikely to lead to prosecution.

Door-to-door salesmen (with certain exceptions) for non-charitable purposes require a pedlar's certificate from the local police.

Leaflets and petitions

There is no need to obtain a licence or certificate for handing out leaflets or collecting signatures for a petition. A leaflet must have on it the name and address of the printer. Some by-laws contain restrictions on the places where leafleting may take place; check the by-laws at the local town hall. The police may also move leafleters on if they appear to be causing an obstruction. It may be an offence to hand out leaflets which are threatening, abusive or insulting or which are intended to stir up racial hatred.

Sticking up posters in public places is illegal without planning permission. An exception is made for posters (no more than six foot square) advertising non-commercial events, including political, educational, social and religious meetings. However, you commit a criminal offence unless you have the permission of the owners of the hoarding, fence, window etc., (maximum penalty a fine on level 2, see p. 27).

A petition to Parliament is governed by special rules and must conform to special wording. Copies of the rules can be obtained from:

> House of Commons
> Westminster
> London SW1A 0AA (01–219 3000)

Selling newspapers

Persons over eighteen may sell newspapers in the street or from door-to-door, as long as the sale is *for campaigning purposes.* If the sale is for profit it becomes street-trading or peddling (if door-to-door), both of which are illegal without a licence (see above). Sometimes difficulty is caused because the police believe that the newspaper or magazine is less of a campaigning document and more of a charitable collection – which requires a licence. Also, the sale of newspapers may obstruct the highway, which is a criminal offence (see p. 19).

1.3   Public order offences

The right of protest may only be exercised peaceably. Otherwise, a variety of offences may be committed. The Public Order Act 1986 introduced sweeping changes into the law. In particular, it created a number of new offences like disorderly conduct, as well as updating some old offences like riot. But there are many offences elsewhere in the law which may be used against activities in public, such as assault, criminal damage, and having an offensive weapon.

SERIOUS OFFENCES OF VIOLENCE

The three main offences in the Public Order Act 1986 for group violence are riot, violent disorder and affray.

Riot

You are guilty of riot if you use violence where at least twelve people are together using or threatening violence for a common purpose and in such a way that a person 'of reasonable firmness' witnessing the events would fear for his or her personal safety.

This is the most serious of the public order offences. Prosecutions are becoming less common because of the difficulty of proving a 'common purpose'. The offence can only be tried in the Crown Court and the Director of Public Prosecutions must consent to the case being brought. The maximum penalty is ten years' imprisonment.

Violent disorder

You are guilty of violent disorder if you use or threaten violence where at least three people are together using or threatening violence and in such a way that a person 'of reasonable firmness' would fear for his or her personal safety.

This offence is used especially for group violence, such as disturbances commonly associated with football hooliganism, or where weapons are used. It can be tried in either the Crown Court or the magistrates' court. The maximum penalty is five years' imprisonment.

Affray

You are guilty of affray if you use or threaten violence to somebody else in such a way that a person 'of reasonable firmness' would fear for his or her personal safety (*effrayer* is the French word meaning *to frighten*).

Street fighting, with or without weapons or missiles, is an affray. It can be tried in either the Crown Court or in the magistrates' court. The maximum penalty is three years' imprisonment.

Grievous bodily harm and actual bodily harm

Serious assaults on individuals include the offences of inflicting grievous bodily harm and assault occasioning actual bodily harm. These offences are set out in the Offences against the Person Act 1861.

If you cause or inflict grievous bodily harm on somebody or wound them (i.e. cut the skin), the maximum penalty is life imprisonment. If the person dies, the charge may be murder or manslaughter. If the injury is less serious, such as bruising or grazes, the charge may be assault occasioning actual bodily harm, with a maximum penalty of five years' imprisonment.

LESS SERIOUS OFFENCES

Threatening, abusive or insulting words or behaviour

You are guilty of an offence under section 4 of the Public Order Act 1986 if you use any one, or any combination of, the above words or actions towards somebody else, *and*

- you intend the other person to believe that violence is going to be used; *or*
- you intend to provoke violence; *or*
- the other person is likely to expect violence; *or*
- violence may well be provoked.

This rather complicated offence is normally used where threats, abuse or insults are likely to cause a breach of the peace: rival football supporters hurling abuse, threats at the picket line, abusive language by rival demonstrators. The charge is often used against protesters who, in the view of the police, go beyond the bounds of ordinary protest. It is an offence if the words are on a banner or placard or even a T-shirt or badge.

This offence can only be tried in the magistrates' court; there is no right to trial by jury. The maximum penalty is six months' imprisonment and/or a fine of £2,000.

Disorderly conduct

You are guilty of an offence under section 5 of the Public Order Act 1986 if you use threatening, abusive or insulting words or behaviour or disorderly behaviour within the hearing or sight of a person likely to be caused harassment, alarm or distress. There must be a victim (a 'person likely to be caused harassment', etc.) present at the scene of the crime. That person must be identified but need not be brought to court. Police officers are unlikely to be victims of this offence.

This is the lowest-level public order offence. It is intended to cover minor acts of hooliganism, especially behaviour directed at the elderly and other vulnerable groups. It was much criticized when it was introduced in the Public Order Act because it covered behaviour which was generally not considered before to be criminal. In particular, it covers behaviour which falls short of violence or the threat or fear of violence.

The offence carries a two-stage power of arrest, not dissimilar to the arrest power for the repealed offence of 'sus' (being a suspected person), although the police may also make an arrest for this offence under the Police and Criminal Evidence Act (see 6.3, p. 135) or under their breach of the peace powers (see p. 25). The offence can only be tried in the magistrates' court. The maximum penalty is a fine of £400; there is no power to send a person convicted of this offence to prison.

Assault

You are guilty of common assault (under the common law) if you engage in an act which intentionally or recklessly causes another person to expect immediate personal violence, anything from a punch or a push or a kick to throwing something at somebody. If injury is caused a more serious charge of assault may be brought (see above). The offence can only be tried in the magistrates' court. The maximum penalty is six months' imprisonment.

You are guilty of a separate offence with a similar penalty if you assault a police officer in the execution of his duty (see p. 15).

Criminal damage

You are guilty under the Criminal Damage Act 1971 if you damage or destroy property or threaten to do so intentionally or recklessly and without lawful excuse. There is a full range of offences from arson with intent to endanger life (maximum penalty life imprisonment), to damage of property under £2,000 in value (magistrates' courts only with a maximum penalty of three months' imprisonment and/or a fine up to £1,000). The damage need not be permanent. Even graffiti designed to wash away with the rain may be criminal damage.

Offensive weapons

You are guilty under the Prevention of Crime Act 1953 if you have an offensive weapon in a public place without lawful authority or reasonable excuse. There are three types of weapon: one made for causing injury such as a knuckleduster, dagger or flick-knife; one adapted for causing injury like a broken bottle; and one intended for use to cause injury, such as an ordinary knife or a spanner. The offence can be tried in the Crown Court (maximum penalty two years' imprisonment) or in the magistrates' court (maximum penalty three months' imprisonment and/or a fine up to £2,000).

Under the Criminal Justice Act 1988 it is an offence to have, in a public place, a knife, but not a folding pocket knife with a blade of not more than 3 inches. Mere possession of a knife or other article with a blade is an offence (maximum penalty a fine of £400 in the magistrates' court), unless you can prove you had a good reason for carrying it, for example, for use at work, for religious reasons or as part of a national costume (for stop and search powers, see 6.1, p. 124 below).

OFFENCES CONNECTED WITH PROCESSIONS, ASSEMBLIES AND MEETINGS

You commit an offence if you *breach a condition* imposed by the police on a procession or an assembly or if you *breach an order* banning processions in your locality (see 1.1, p. 7).

You commit an offence if you *wilfully obstruct the highway* (see 1.2, p. 16) or if you *wilfully obstruct a police officer* in the execution of his duty. Both offences are widely-used by the police at demonstrations and in other public order contexts. Wilful obstruction of a police officer means simply doing any act which makes it more difficult for the police to carry out their duty (magistrates' courts only, maximum penalty one month's imprisonment and/or a fine up to £400). It is used against those who refuse to move on or to keep back, or against those who interfere with police work, for example, by objecting to an arrest or a search. No warning need be given before an arrest can be made.

You may commit an offence if you *wear a uniform* in public signifying association with any political organization or with the promotion of any political object (trial in the magistrates' court, maximum penalty three months' imprisonment and/or a fine up to £1,000). You commit an offence if you organize or train members of a *quasi-military organization* (maximum penalty in the Crown Court two years' imprisonment, and in the magistrates' court six months' imprisonment and/or a fine of £2,000).

For offences connected with *picketing* see 1.1, p. 14.

For offences connected with *meetings* see 1.1, p. 12.

For offences of *stirring up racial hatred* see 2.5, p. 40.

BREACH OF THE PEACE

There is no offence of breach of the peace (except in Scotland, see 15.2, p. 327). But if a police officer sees a breach of the peace, or reasonably believes that a breach of the peace is about to be committed or that a renewal of a breach of the peace is threatened, he may arrest, disperse or detain those involved and, if necessary, take them before a magistrates' court to be bound over.

There is a breach of the peace whenever harm is actually done, or is likely to be done to a person, or in his presence to his property, or a person is in fear of being so harmed. If a breach of the peace occurs, one or more of the public order offences of threatening behaviour, disorderly conduct, assault or criminal damage (see above for these offences) is likely to have been committed. In such a case, the police can choose whether to charge an offence or go before the magistrates for a bind-over order.

Bind-overs

The magistrates' court may bind you over to keep the peace or to be of good behaviour in a number of different circumstances:

- you may be brought before the court for a breach of the peace (under the Justices of the Peace Act 1361);
- you may be brought before the court on a complaint made by any person at the court;
- in a criminal case, a witness or a defendant (even if acquitted) may be bound over.

A bind-over order is not a conviction nor a penalty. It is an undertaking as to future conduct. Its purpose is to prevent offences being committed in the future. The order will bind you over to keep the peace for a period of time in a specified sum, say £200 for twelve months. Sometimes sureties are taken. If you breach the order and are brought back to court, you will have to pay up to the whole amount. If you refuse to be bound over in the first place, you can be sent to prison or detention (if over sixteen) for up to six months. You should always be given the opportunity to say in court why you should not be bound over, if you wish to, or why you are not in breach of the order.

Bind-over orders are often used against demonstrators and protesters. Sometimes a charge, such as obstruction of the highway, is dropped by the prosecution if the defendant agrees to be bound over and the court also agrees. In some cases, unions will advise their members who have been picketing not to accept bind-overs if they wish to return to the picket line. A bind-over cannot of itself prevent someone from returning to the picket line (see the right to bail, p. 167), but it is an inhibiting factor.

Some people believe that the bind-over order is an outdated form of justice and that it is wrong to give the courts the power to send somebody to prison for refusing to be bound over, particularly when no offence has been committed.

FINE LEVELS

Fine levels for offences tried in magistrates' courts are updated from time-to-time. The current amounts of maximum fines for adults were set in 1984:

Level	£
1	50
2	100
3	400
4	1,000
5	2,000

Where the statute gives no specific level the maximum fine is £400.
The maximum fines for juveniles are:

young person (14–16)	£400
child (10–13)	£100

For offences which can be tried either in the Crown Court or in the magistrates' court the maximum fine in the magistrates' court is £2,000.

For offences which are tried in the Crown Court there is no limit on the fine which can be imposed.

In fixing the amount of the fine the court must take into account the means of the offender. The court may give the offender time to pay, for example, within three months, or at so much a week. If the court imposes a sentence of imprisonment in default and the fine is not paid, the court may send the offender to prison, but only after a careful means inquiry (for criminal compensation orders see 5.8, p. 119).

1.4　　More information

BIBLIOGRAPHY

A. T. H. Smith, *Offences against Public Order*, Sweet and Maxwell, 1987.
P. Thornton, *Public Order Law*, Blackstone Press, 1987.
P. Thornton, *We Protest: The Public Order Debate*, NCCL, 1985.

2 The right of free expression

This chapter deals with:

2.1 The right to speak freely?

Surely we can say what we like? It's a free country, isn't it? American lawyers can answer these inquiries with reasonable confidence by pointing to their Bill of Rights. Its first clause (and the First Amendment to the US Constitution) prohibits the US Congress from making any law which would infringe freedom of speech or the press. The English Parliament passed a Bill of Rights after the 1688 revolution. It guaranteed freedom of speech – but only for Members of Parliament. There was not then, and there has never been since, a British equivalent of the First Amendment promising freedom of expression for all.

THE RIGHT OF FREE EXPRESSION IN THE EUROPEAN CONVEN-
TION ON HUMAN RIGHTS

The closest that Britain has come to a constitutional guarantee of
free speech is in ratifying the European Convention on Human
Rights. Article 10 of the Convention provides:

1. Everyone has the right of free expression. This right shall include
freedom to hold opinions and to receive and impart information and ideas
without interference by public authority and regardless of frontiers. This
Article shall not prevent States from requiring the licensing of broadcasting,
television or cinema enterprises.

2. The exercise of these freedoms, since it carries with it duties and
responsibilities, may be subject to such formalities, conditions, restrictions
or penalties as are prescribed by law and necessary in a democratic society,
in the interests of national security, territorial integrity or public safety, for
the prevention of disorder or crime, for the protection of health or morals,
for the protection of the reputation or rights of others, for preventing the
disclosure of information received in confidence, or for maintaining the
authority and impartiality of the judiciary.

Even here then, the initial promise of free expression is hedged and
circumscribed by exceptions and provisos, but the European Court
of Human Rights (see generally 5.7, p. 101), which is the ultimate
arbiter on disputes as to the Convention's meaning, has not
allowed paragraph 2 to drain paragraph 1 of all meaning. It has
given the right of free expression a special status to which only
limited restrictions are permissible.

British restrictions on free speech have often failed the European
test. The law on contempt of court (see 2.6, p. 41), for instance, has
had to be changed twice because it did not match up to Article
10.

Yet the European Convention is still a very inferior means of
protecting free expression by comparison with the American First
Amendment. The Convention is a treaty. It binds the government
in international law. It has a better system of enforcement than
many treaties in that the European Court was created to decide
disputes, and individuals can make use of the complaint procedure.
In addition, English judges should use the Convention in resolving

ambiguities in English law. But these are the limits of its usefulness.
The Convention has not been adopted by Parliament in a British
statute. British judges cannot use it to override an unambiguous
British law. The victim of an unjustified restriction on freedom of
expression must start the European complaint procedure and have
the patience to wait several years before reaching the European
Court and, if successful, before UK law is changed to bring it into
line with the Court's decision.

The negative approach

Without a First Amendment, without Article 10 as part of British
law, 'the right of free expression' has only the limited legal
meaning that a person is free to say anything which is not
prohibited. Hence, this chapter will largely be concerned with
things that cannot be said. However, the position is not quite as
bleak as this statement suggests. Thankfully, the popular understanding of the right of free speech, however ill-defined or shifting,
expects more than a purely negative proposition. This matters
because many of the restrictions which we examine are only
brought into play if the government takes the initiative. It may
choose not to do so if it perceives such action being criticized as
contrary to the popular notion of 'free speech'. Of course, on other
occasions (for instance, the *Spycatcher* litigation) it will carry on
regardless, but whatever the courts say such obduracy may carry a
political price.

The role of the jury in 'free speech' cases

In other respects, as well, the principle of free speech has more
than purely negative connotations. The conflicts between the
government and the press in the seventeenth and eighteenth
centuries demonstrated the importance of the jury. The right of the
jury to acquit – whatever the weight of the evidence in favour of
the Crown – was established in 'free speech' cases. That right has
not been altered even though it has meant in recent years that the
government's ability to successfully prosecute under the Official
Secrets Act has been severely curtailed.

In libel cases, both criminal and civil, it is for the jury to decide whether the publication was against the law. In turn this means that juries have been preserved in libel cases although they have been abolished in almost all other types of civil litigation. This has not always been to the advantage of the press who have been ordered to pay huge sums in damages by libel juries. More importantly, the courts are extremely reluctant to issue an injunction to prevent publication of something that is said to be libellous. If the publisher (or broadcaster) swears an affidavit that it is true, the judges regard it as a matter for the jury at the trial to decide the dispute and will not prevent publication in advance. Unfortunately, this judicial self-restraint does not apply outside libel, and injunctions are all too readily granted against the media to prevent disclosure of something which is said to be in breach of confidence.

The following sections give an outline of the principal restrictions that limit the right of free expression.

2.2   Defamation – libel and slander

Libel and slander are intended to protect reputations and provide compensation for injury to them. 'Libel' is used if the damaging words take a permanent form (books, magazines, films etc., and broadcasts have been included in this category by Parliament); 'slander' if they do not. We refer to 'words', but pictures, signs and any other expression can be defamatory. Collectively these wrongs are known as 'defamation'. The distinction between libel and slander is largely historical, but a difference of continuing importance is that a plaintiff must show financial loss to succeed in slander: this is not necessary for libel. For certain types of slander even this distinction dissolves: accusations of imprisonable crime; that the plaintiff carries a contagious disease; that the victim is unfit for his or her office, business or profession; slanders on the credit of tradespeople; and the imputation of unchastity or adultery to a woman or a girl. Here, as with all libels, damage is presumed and need not be proved.

MEANING OF DEFAMATION

Words are defamatory if they damage the reputation of the victim in the eyes of 'right-thinking' members of society. This definition has the ring of ancient clubland quarrels and indeed this type of litigation is still the prerogative of the rich since, uniquely, legal aid is not available to bring (or defend) actions for defamation. However, the definition does also contain important limitations. Mere vulgar abuse is not defamatory because no one would think the worse of its object. The words may be untrue or hurtful, but still not defamatory if they do not impinge on a person's reputation. In addition, damage to a person's credibility amongst the more heretical members of society is immaterial. In one case a person wrongly accused of being a police informer failed in a defamation action for this reason.

There are two remedies which might help a person who is angered by a false publication which is not defamatory. Firstly, 'false attribution of authorship' may be relied on when a publisher fabricates quotations. Secondly, if it can be shown that the words were spoken or written maliciously and that they have caused financial loss, then, even though they are not defamatory, the victim can claim damages for 'malicious falsehood'.

In addition, complaints about the unethical behaviour of news-papers and magazines can be made to the Press Council. The behaviour need not have resulted in a libel or any of the other legal wrongs considered above: the Council is not a court but a body voluntarily set up by the newspaper industry. It cannot award damages or any redress other than a decision vindicating (or rejecting) the complaint. Its decisions are usually well publicized.

Publication

To return to defamation, the words must have been 'published' by the person sued. This expression has a much wider meaning than its colloquial one. It covers any means of communication even if to only one other person.

Because 'publish' is defined so broadly, distributors and even shops can find themselves sued for libel. They do have a special defence that, having taken all reasonable care, they had no reason to believe that their wares contained defamatory material. For this reason, distributors will sometimes insist that magazines obtain an opinion from a barrister that nothing defamatory is included in the publication. On the other hand, publishers, printers, writers, editors and broadcasters are all responsible for what they put out and cannot argue for immunity because they took every precaution. They are responsible also in the sense that they will be liable for repeating what others have said. Untrue allegations in a published reader's letter can cost a magazine dear. For the same reason it is usually no help to attribute a defamatory remark to a source, or to put it in quotation marks or to preface it by 'allegedly', if the net effect of the publication is still to damage the reputation of the person spoken of in the eyes of 'right-thinking' readers.

Identification

At least one person to whom the words are published must be able to identify the victim as the object of the attack. However, direct identification is not essential and the anonymous victim of an attack can sue if there are sufficient clues in the piece pointing to his or her identity. Sometimes the reference to the victim is unintentional, for instance, the character in a novel who, unwittingly, is given the name of a real person. Publishers have a defence in these circumstances, although the conditions which surround it mean that it is rarely relied upon.

Who can sue?

This is not to say that defamation actions can be brought only by individuals. Companies can and do sue if their trading reputation is damaged. This principle has even been extended to allow local authorities to complain of damage to their governing reputation. However, groups without a legal identity cannot complain of libel. Thus blacks or Jews can get no help from the law of libel for the outrageous lies published about them. For the same reason an unincorporated club cannot sue for libel, whatever the damage to its reputation. The same rule applies to trade unions. There are some cases though where the words can be read as libelling every member of the group: all the crime reporters who covered the Old Bailey once obtained damages for a story which implied they were all drunk.

Only the living can sue for defamation. Thus, historians have considerably greater freedom of expression than current commentators, but even they must be careful that the things they write about the dead do not in some way damage the reputations of the living.

The defences of truth, fair comment and privilege

The law does not elevate the protection of reputations above all else. There are three important defences which limit the incursion which actions for defamation make on free speech: truth; fair comment; and privilege.

Truth (or justification) is simple to state. If a publisher can show that the words were true, the plaintiff's claim fails. The adage 'the greater the truth the greater the libel' is dangerously misleading.

The only exception to this principle concerns defendants whose convictions have become 'spent' under the Rehabilitation of Offenders Act 1974. Publication of the details of these old convictions can lead to damages for libel, but only if the plaintiff can show that the publisher acted 'maliciously' (see 7.7, p. 173).

The position is less clear-cut when a criminal prosecution for libel is brought. These are rare: the libel (slanders are not criminal) must be serious and, in the case of a newspaper or periodical, permission to bring the action must first be obtained from a High Court judge, who must be persuaded that the evidence is strong and that criminal charges are in the public interest. Historically, the crime was intended to prevent breaches of the peace (for example, caused by speakers at public meetings) and it was in this context that truth was recognized as being an aggravating feature of the publication. Justification *is* a defence, but here the defendant must show that the words were true and that their publication was in the public interest. Criminal libel is an anachronism; the Law Commission has recommended that it ought to be abolished.

In civil actions for damages, these complications are stripped away and truth on its own is a complete defence. The simplicity is beguiling. The court assumes that the plaintiff is of good character. The publisher has to prove, by admissible evidence, that the words were true. This can be difficult if there are 'reliable sources' but they are not prepared to testify in court. Like all other aspects of libel litigation, this defence will also only benefit the publisher who can afford to do battle through the courts. There are insurers who will cover such legal costs as well as any damages which are ultimately ordered, but the premiums are considerable and the insurance company will insist on taking over or reviewing closely the progress of the litigation.

Critics and reviewers do not have to prove the truth of their opinions in order to defend a libel action: they have the easier defence of *fair comment*. This covers any comment on a matter of public importance, however trenchantly expressed or misguided, as long as it is honestly held. The plaintiff can undermine the defence only by showing that the comment was written with 'malice'. This is not the same as spite or ill-will, but means rather abusing the commentator's position. Honestly held expressions are safe.

Privilege is the general name given to the wide variety of occasions on which the law thinks it preferable that people should be able to speak freely even though reputations may suffer. No distinction is made between fact and comment. There is, though, an important difference between occasions which carry 'qualified privilege' and those where the privilege is absolute. When the privilege is qualified, it is lost if the speaker or publisher acts through malice (as with fair comment, above). If the privilege is absolute, the speaker is protected from a libel action even if he or she has acted maliciously.

Absolute privilege is relatively unusual. It is confined to cases such as proceedings in Parliament or the courts where, such is the priority given to free speech, it is considered undesirable to allow even the possibility of a libel action. Reports in newspapers or court reports are absolutely privileged if they are fair, accurate and contemporaneous.

Qualified privilege is more common. It covers not only reports of parliamentary proceedings and (non-contemporaneous) court reports, but a wide range of other official sources. These include fair and accurate reports of: Commonwealth Parliaments, conferences of international organizations of which Britain is a member or is represented, proceedings of international courts, proceedings of British court-martials outside Britain, and of any Commonwealth courts, public inquiries set up by Commonwealth governments, extracts from public registers and notices published by judges or court officers.

Fair and accurate reports of the following are also subject to qualified privilege, but only if the victim is granted, on request, a reasonable right of reply: findings or decisions of any association or committee of associations formed in the UK and empowered by its constitution to exercise control over or adjudicate on matters relating to art, religion or learning; any trade, business, industry or profession, or persons connected with games, sports or pastimes and who are contractually subject to the association; proceedings at any lawful public meeting (whether or not admission is restricted) which is called to discuss any matter of public concern; proceedings of any meeting open to the public within the UK of a local authority or its committees; Justices of the Peace acting in non-judicial capacities; committees of inquiry appointed by statute or the government, local authority inquiries, bodies constituted under Acts of Parliament, general meetings of public companies and associations, and any notices or other matter issued for the information of the public by or on behalf of any government department, officer of state, local authority or Chief Constable.

Qualified privilege also applies where the person who publishes the words has a duty or interest in communicating them and his or her audience has a duty or interest in receiving them. The press argued unsuccessfully that they had such a duty in informing their readers of matters of public interest. The courts would not extend the privilege that far, but it does protect, for instance, employers providing references or complaints made to the proper authority.

2.3   Obscenity and indecency

Commercial dealings in obscene items, or possession of them for these purposes, is an offence. With or without a prosecution, the items can be seized under a magistrate's warrant and, after a hearing to determine whether they contravene the statute, can be forfeited. The statute is the Obscene Publications Act 1959 (as amended in 1964).

THE TEST OF OBSCENITY – 'DEPRAVE OR CORRUPT'

The 1959 Act adopted as the core of its test of obscenity the famous phrase of Lord Chief Justice Cockburn in 1868: does the article have a tendency to deprave or corrupt the persons who are likely to read, see or hear it? Courts have since interpreted 'deprave or corrupt' as implying a powerful and corrosive effect. There must be more than an immoral suggestion or persuasion or depiction: it must constitute a serious menace. Despite this, the deprave and corrupt test is essentially nebulous. It is difficult to predict in advance whether juries or magistrates will be persuaded that it has been satisfied. This in turn can lead to incompatible decisions in different parts of the country. The film *The Evil Dead* was found to be obscene in some parts of the country but not others.

However, the 1959 Act did not simply mimic the common law. There had been a tendency for earlier prosecutors to focus on purple passages and to invite juries to consider them in isolation. The statute now requires courts to have regard to the effect of the item taken as a whole (where the article, for instance a magazine, consists of two or more distinct items, they can be viewed separately). Again, what matters is the likely reader or audience and a publisher is entitled to rely on circumstances of distribution which will restrict those into whose hands the article might fall. The prosecution's case is not made out by showing that the odd stray copy might be read by a more impressionable person; it is necessary to show that it would have the tendency to deprave or corrupt a *significant proportion* of the likely audience.

The law of obscenity controls the viler expressions of pornography. It is not designed to, nor can it, control the everyday degradation and devaluation of women. Pictures of naked women on page three are not caught by the Obscene Publications Act. A Private Member's bill was introduced recently to prohibit such pictures but it was unable to overcome the twin problems of male blindness to the problem and the difficulty of framing the prohibition in such a way that it did not create unintended and unacceptable restrictions on press freedom.

Defence of merit

The most important change introduced by the 1959 Act was a new defence that publication (in the case of magazines and books) is in the interests of science, literature, art or learning or of other objects of general concern. A similar but rather narrower defence (interests of drama, opera, ballet or any other art, or of literature or learning) applies to plays and films. The use of this defence was demonstrated in the first major case under the 1959 Act when the publishers of D. H. Lawrence's *Lady Chatterley's Lover* were acquitted at the Old Bailey.

Obscenity – drugs and violence

Obscenity cases do not necessarily involve sex. There have been occasional prosecutions and forfeitures of books which advocated the taking of prohibited drugs. In 1968, while allowing the appeal of the publishers of *Last Exit to Brooklyn*, the Court of Appeal said that the encouragement of brutal violence could come within the test of obscenity and in recent years video 'nasties' have been dealt with under the Act.

Children

There are special and much more rigorous offences to try and stop the taking or distributing of indecent photographs of children.

INDECENCY OFFENCES

Obscenity is concerned with the harmful effect of the article on its reader or audience; another group of offences regulates *indecency* where the complaint is more that the material is offensive to public susceptibilities – a nuisance rather than a danger. No easy definition of indecency exists. The courts have said that it is something that 'offends against the modesty of the average man . . . offending against recognized standards of propriety at the lower end of the scale'. It depends on the circumstances and current (and in some cases, local) standards. This vagueness is dangerous. Posters for causes such as animal rights which are deliberately intended to shock their audience have sometimes had to contend with indecency prosecutions.

There is no general crime of trading in indecent articles (as there is with obscene ones), but a number of specific offences incorporate the indecency test. Thus, it is a crime to send indecent matter through the post, or to put it on public display unless entry is restricted to persons over eighteen and payment is required, or the display is in a special part of a shop with an appropriate warning notice. The indecency offences do *not* apply to television broadcasts (although, as we shall see, both the BBC and private TV companies operate under internal prohibitions on indecent matter – see 2.9, p. 53), to exhibitions inside art galleries or museums, exhibitions arranged by or in premises occupied by the Crown or local authorities, performances of a play or films in licensed cinemas.

In addition to these offences, local councils can now adopt powers to regulate sex shops and sex cinemas in their areas. Council licences always prohibit the public display of indecent material and licences can be revoked for breaches of these conditions. Similarly, the music and entertainment licences granted by local authorities will often be conditional on the licensee ensuring that no indecent display takes place. Breach of this condition is both an offence and a ground for withdrawing the licence.

Customs regulations also prohibit the importation of indecent articles. The bookshop Gay's the Word was prosecuted under these provisions for importing books concerned with homosexuality. However, these restrictions have been substantially undermined by an unlikely source – the EEC provisions on free trade. A cardinal principle of the EEC is that one member State should not set up trade barriers to goods from another member State if there is a legitimate internal market in the same goods. In the case of the UK there is a legitimate market in indecent (but not obscene) articles as long as the traders observe the restrictions noted above. Consequently, Britain cannot discriminate against the importation of the same, indecent, goods from other EEC countries: European law prevails over the British Customs regulations. For these reasons the Gay's the Word prosecution was dropped.

2.4   Blasphemy

Blasphemy is another anachronistic relic of the common law of libel. It applies to outrageous comment or immoderate or offensive treatment of the Christian faith. More particularly, it protects only the sensibilities of the followers of the Church of England. The intentions of the publisher are irrelevant. Moderate or reasoned criticism of Anglican doctrine is not a crime and the court must consider the likely audience in order to decide whether the publication would produce the necessary outrage.

For newspapers and periodicals there are the same procedural protections as with criminal libel. Consequently, the prosecutor must first get permission to bring the case from a High Court judge who must be persuaded that the evidence is clear 'beyond argument', that the offence is a serious one and that the public interest would justify a prosecution.

There has only been one prosecution for blasphemy since 1922, and that a private one (brought by Mrs Mary Whitehouse), of the magazine *Gay News* for a poem on the homoerotic musings of the centurion guarding the body of Christ. It has been argued that the crime can no longer be justified in our pluralistic society, and that the alternative of extending the offence to all religions (a suggestion made by Lord Scarman in the *Gay News* case) would seriously curtail freedom to criticize and ridicule some of the more bizarre cults which style themselves religions.

2.5   Racial hatred

The offences of inciting or stirring up racial hatred have been progressively enlarged since they were first introduced in 1965 (see also 9.1, p. 193). They are currently contained in the Public Order Act 1986 (see 1.3, p. 20). In brief, they prohibit the use of threatening, abusive or insulting words, behaviour or displays with the intention of stirring up racial hatred or where racial hatred is likely to be stirred up.

The acts do not have to be done in public, but they are not crimes if done in a private dwelling and cannot be seen or heard from the outside. The inadvertent use of words which are threatening, abusive or insulting is not an offence. Only since the Public Order Act 1986 have the police had a limited power of arrest without warrant for the main offence. There are other offences of publishing or distributing material, presenting or directing a play, distributing, showing or playing visual images or sounds, broadcasting a TV programme (except programmes transmitted by the BBC or IBA; for further controls on broadcasting see 2.9, p. 53) or distributing a cable programme with the same characteristics (i.e. threatening, abusive or insulting) and which is either intended to stir up race hatred or which is likely to have this effect. In addition, it is an offence to possess racially inflammatory material unless ignorant of its contents. The police can obtain a search warrant for such material and magistrates can order its forfeiture.

Very few prosecutions have been brought for racial hatred offences. One of the reasons for this is that no prosecution can be brought without the consent of the Attorney-General and successive Attorneys-General have expressed their reluctance to authorize prosecutions giving the reason that unsuccessful prosecutions do more harm than good to racial equality.

2.6   Contempt of court

Contempt of court covers a multitude of sins, but all of them share the common feature that they are regarded by the courts as a threat to the administration of justice.

The most obvious example is disobedience to a court's order or the failure to observe an undertaking given to the court. Publication of a secret document in defiance of an injunction prohibiting its disclosure would thus be punishable as contempt. Until 1987 it was thought that orders of this kind only affected the immediate person to whom they were directed (and their servants or agents). Third parties, it was thought, would only be in contempt if they aided the defendant to break the court's order. However, one of the most serious encroachments on press freedom in the *Spycatcher* litigation was the decision of the Court of Appeal that other publishers, acting on their own behalf, could be in contempt of court by publishing the same material. Because this would frustrate the court's intention to keep the material secret it was a contempt.

JUDGE-MADE LAW

The *Spycatcher* litigation further illustrates a general problem of the law of contempt: it has been developed almost exclusively by the judges who have tended to pay only nodding respect to other values (such as freedom of expression) which have to be balanced against the preservation of the administration of justice. Thus, by using this branch of contempt, the courts have invented offences of disclosing the identity of blackmail victims who had remained anonymous in court, day-by-day re-enactments on television of court hearings, and (in certain circumstances) of disclosing details of a jury's deliberations. These were matters more properly left to Parliament. Parliament did subsequently enact restrictions on jury disclosures, ironically much more severe than the judge-made law. It is now an offence to disclose any details of a jury's deliberations or votes taken, other than to give their verdict at the end of the trial.

Another type of contempt is the *deliberate interference with current proceedings*. Understandably, there is no freedom to intimidate or threaten reprisals against witnesses. A more controversial question is whether it is impermissible to put pressure on a party to abandon a law suit. *Private Eye* in its own special way castigated Sir James Goldsmith for his various suits against the magazine. The magazine was held not to be guilty of contempt because none of what they published was likely to have any effect on the outcome of the proceedings. In the early 1970s the *Sunday Times* campaigned for compensation on behalf of the victims of the drug thalidomide and urged Distiller's, its UK distributor, to reach a generous settlement with the plaintiffs. The Attorney-General successfully obtained an injunction to stop further stories on the grounds that they would be in contempt of court. The principal basis for the decision has now been reversed by legislation, but two of the Law Lords suggested that it was contempt to pressurize a party into settling. The current position is probably that fair and temperate appeals are not prohibited, but that abusive or misrepresented articles would run the risk of contempt proceedings.

It is still said that it is contempt to do any act or publish anything which is *calculated to bring a court or judge into contempt or lower his authority*. 'Scandalizing the court' was one of the whips fashioned for John Wilkes, the eighteenth-century radical. It was revived in the early twentieth century to punish various affronts to judicial dignity, including a communist paper which dared to suggest that the judges were class biased. This type of contempt has been used occasionally in Commonwealth countries but it has lain dormant in the UK for the last fifty years. The present attitude is that judges must tolerate even misplaced criticism and that only serious allegations of corruption or other impropriety could possibly prompt a prosecution.

STRICT LIABILITY — THE *SUB JUDICE* RULE

The manifestation of contempt which most frequently restricts what the papers can say is that known as 'strict liability contempt'. For specified periods before and during the time that a case is going through the courts, the media are liable if they publish anything which would cause a substantial risk of serious prejudice to the proceedings. During these periods the case is 'active' although the older phrase *sub judice* is still used.

Criminal proceedings are active from the time an arrest takes place, or a warrant or summons is issued. Civil proceedings do not become active until a date is fixed for the hearing. The degree of restriction that this imposes depends on the court or tribunal which will hear the case. If it will be tried by a jury, nothing should be written or broadcast which might prejudice the jury against the defendant, in particular, no past misdeeds should be referred to, and care should be taken that reports do not assume the defendant's guilt. At the other end of the spectrum are cases on appeal. These will be heard by professional judges who are trained to exclude extraneous considerations such as press reports. Consequently, it will be very rare for a publication to be in contempt of such proceedings. However, the Court of Appeal banned Channel 4 from broadcasting a dramatic re-enactment of the appeal of the Birmingham 6 until after the case was over.

Defences to strict liability contempt

There are two important special defences to charges of strict liability contempt. The first is that a *discussion in good faith of public affairs* or other matters of general public importance will not be contempt if the risk of prejudice is merely incidental to the discussion. Thus, Malcolm Muggeridge was free to write about the issues of terminating medical support to deformed babies even though a doctor was on trial at the same time for the killing of a Down's Syndrome child. Muggeridge focused on a by-election in which the issues of principle had been raised and did not mention the trial. The House of Lords held that the newspaper could rely on the public interest defence.

A second important defence is that it is not generally contempt to publish a *fair, accurate, good faith and contemporaneous report of legal proceedings held in public*. This is important because things are sometimes said in trials which might reflect adversely on either participants in those proceedings or in other active cases. However, the media's freedom to report is subject to the power of the court to make a postponement order. These can delay full reporting until the end of either the proceedings in question or the others which are at risk of prejudice. Postponement orders are a real headache for the media who are not allowed to address the court on why they should not be made. Usually, none of the parties has any interest in full publicity and too often, it is felt, orders are made with insufficient regard to the principles of open justice of which the ability of the press to carry full reports is an integral part. A limited right of appeal against such orders was introduced in 1989.

OTHER RESTRICTIONS ON COURT REPORTING

These powers are in addition to restrictions on reporting which apply without the need for a specific order. Only very attenuated reports can be carried, for instance, of, proceedings in a magistrates' court of a case which might eventually be sent to trial by a judge and jury at a Crown Court. Newspapers can name the parties, their lawyers, whether bail was granted, but very little else until the trial is over.

A defendant has the right to have these restrictions lifted, but if co-accused differ in their attitude to publicity, the bench decides.

In rape cases the victim must remain anonymous unless the court orders otherwise. Until 1988 the defendant was given the same protection (unless convicted). The press (unlike the rest of the public) have a right to attend juvenile court hearings, but are prohibited from identifying defendants or witnesses, or from publishing their photographs. Young people do not have automatic anonymity in other courts, but the courts can make orders in specific cases.

In *civil cases* the problem is not so much that reporting is prohibited (though this is so in certain cases involving children and others to do with trade secrets), but that journalists (and other members of the public) frequently do not have the right to be present and so cannot learn what has transpired unless one of the parties is willing to talk. This may be acceptable in disputes over custody or access to children. It is wholly unjustifiable in a large and important category of cases heard in the judge's private chambers.

Before a civil dispute comes to trial it is common for there to be initial skirmishes or interlocutory applications. The most important are where one party wants a court order pending trial. Classic examples are injunctions against the press to prevent disclosure of an allegedly secret document, or orders prohibiting industrial action. If the plaintiff has chosen to bring the case in the Chancery Division of the High Court, these applications are heard by a judge in public (subject to any special orders to preserve legitimate confidences). However, if the case is brought in the Queen's Bench Division of the High Court, the applications are heard in chambers and the press are excluded. Plaintiffs are generally free to choose in which division to bring their case, and can thus effectively select the degree of publicity they prefer.

These cases apart, it is very unusual for courts to depart from the principle of open justice. There is a statutory power to do so in particular cases (e.g., official secrets prosecutions) and a general power where the public's presence would defeat the ends of justice. The courts have repeatedly stressed that it is only exceptional circumstances which will justify excluding the public or restricting reporting.

The public may be present in court, but sketching and photography is prohibited. In 1981 Parliament permitted the limited use of tape recorders in court with the judge's leave. There are administrative directions that applications should be treated sympathetically. Taping can be used only as an aid in compiling an accurate record of what was said: public reproduction is banned.

TRIBUNALS

In addition to the regular criminal and civil courts, there is a bewildering array of 'courts', tribunals and inquiries. It is impossible to generalize about when the public have a right of access. If they do, there will usually be a qualified privilege to protect the publisher of a fair and accurate report from libel actions. The 'strict liability contempt' provisions will only apply if the body is 'exercising the judicial power of the state'. By way of example, licensing authorities act administratively and therefore their proceedings are never 'active' (see above); industrial tribunals, on the other hand, do exercise a statutory judicial jurisdiction – their proceedings will be active from the time a hearing date is set, but of course there will be no contempt unless the publication poses a serious threat to the integrity of the proceedings.

ENFORCEMENT

Prosecutions under the strict liability rule can be brought only with the Attorney-General's consent. This was intended to ensure that some consideration was given to the public interest before prosecutions were brought. However, while private parties cannot prosecute, they can, if they would suffer particularly from a publication which offended against the rule, seek an injunction to stop it. This development has therefore considerably undermined such protection as the Attorney-General's veto had offered.

2.7   Secrets and confidentiality

Secrecy, it is sometimes said, is the British disease. The scope of the law for preventing and punishing the disclosure of private and governmental confidences represents one of the most important restrictions on free speech. We will look at the criminal and civil dimensions in turn.

THE OFFICIAL SECRETS ACTS

The Official Secrets Act 1911 slipped on to the statute book in a single day, borne along on a wave of anti-German spy fever (although its gestation had been much longer). While it does provide punishment for spies, it has become notorious for its section 2 which was intended to curb civil service leaks and their publication in the press. On one occasion in 1978 the government did try to turn the big guns of section 1 (the spying charge, carrying a maximum of fourteen years' imprisonment) on journalists investigating signals intelligence and its disturbing implications. This trial, known as the ABC case (after the initials of the defendants), was notable for the judge's round denunciation of the section 1 charges as 'oppressive'. The defendants were convicted under section 2, but the journalists were given conditional discharges. While the government has on rare occasions (e.g., Tisdall and Ponting) prosecuted their sources, it has not, since the ABC case, tried again to prosecute the media itself under these Acts.

Section 2

In theory and on paper the Official Secrets Acts 1911 and 1939 are awesome in their breadth. Section 2 of the 1911 Act, with its multiple subordinate clauses and alternatives, creates literally hundreds of variants which are prohibited by law (with a maximum penalty of two years' imprisonment). The courts have said repeatedly that notwithstanding the name of the statute it does not apply only to secret information. The unauthorized communication of almost any information learnt by a civil servant in the course of his or her job is an offence. (Hence the half-serious joke that it is a crime for an official in the Ministry of Defence to disclose the colour of the lavatory paper.) Section 2 also makes it an offence to receive such unauthorized leaks and to pass them on to others. There is no defence in the Act that communication (or receipt) was in the public interest.

The right to jury trial

The critical fact that anyone charged with an official secrets offence can elect jury trial has a real effect in curbing the impact of the Act. Whatever the law may say, if the information leaked was already public knowledge or if its disclosure is in the public interest (as in the case of Clive Ponting's memorandum on the government's policy on the sinking of the *Belgrano*), convictions are far from certain. Even if a conviction is achieved, it will be at the price of attracting considerable press attention to the prosecution and the 'secret' at its centre will attract substantial press coverage. By now the reputation of the Acts has become so tarnished that the government cannot be certain of convictions in any case outside their proper espionage sphere. The very width of their application has become their weakness.

Reform

No one seriously disputes that the scope of the Acts should be narrowed, but the shape of new restrictions has been highly controversial. In 1988 Richard Shepherd proposed, in a Private Member's Bill, the introduction of a 'public interest' defence. This would have had the merit of bringing out into the open a debate which must inevitably take place in the jury room. The Bill was defeated.

In 1988 a government Bill proposed that disclosure relating to certain activities (e.g., telephone tapping) should always be an offence; that in other specified areas the prosecution should have to prove their disclosure was harmful; and that for other types of information disclosure should not attract criminal penalties. While ostensibly narrowing the law, the Bill proposes significant extensions (e.g., a new category of disclosing information that would prejudice international relations); the burden of proving harm would not apply to the kind of disclosures which have prompted recent controversies (e.g., the *Spycatcher* disclosures about the security services), and the government still resists a public interest defence.

Other secrecy offences

Apart from the Official Secrets Acts, there are dozens of specific statutory offences of disclosing information in the hands of the government. Frequently, they are imposed where a government department has powers to acquire information under compulsion. These 'mini' Official Secrets Acts also lack a public interest defence.

THE CIVIL LAW OF CONFIDENCE

Increasingly, the government has abandoned the use of the criminal law to protect its secrets in favour of the civil law of breach of confidence (see also 3.1, p. 59). This law was originally intended to protect trade secrets (such as the formula for Coca-Cola), or the business development plans of companies. It was extended to afford some privacy to an individual's confidential documents or papers. This was first done for Prince Albert and Queen Victoria whose sketchings were about to be published without their permission.

Unlike the criminal law, the civil law of confidence will generally only protect material which is still confidential. It was the wide-spread publication of *Spycatcher* which powerfully influenced the House of Lords to refuse a final injunction to the government.

In the public interest

None of the civil law was thought relevant to public secrets until the Labour government tried to use the law of confidence to stop the publication of Richard Crossman's diaries. It failed because the Cabinet meetings and other private encounters which Crossman described had happened too long ago. Yet the principle was established that the government could rely on the law of confidence to stop a publication if it could show a public interest that still needed protection. The public interest is also material as a defence. It used to be said that only crime or iniquity would justify the breach of a confidence, but now the test is more open and the court must strike a balance between the interest in preserving confidence and the interest in publication.

Pre-trial injunctions

If the plaintiff can find out in advance that publication of a leak or other alleged breach of confidence is planned, and is willing to go to court, then the inevitable first step will be an application for an injunction to stop publication until trial. The test which the courts apply in deciding whether to grant such injunctions is extremely favourable to plaintiffs. Usually the judges will grant an injunction, unless there is clear evidence of public interest, and in the case of the *Spycatcher* pre-trial injunction even that was not sufficient. The argument for this 'balance of convenience test' is that at the pre-trial stage the evidence is incomplete and the court is often required to make a hasty decision because publication is imminent. The objection is that the time between injunction and trial is usually so great that the story will have gone cold by the time that full argument on the merits is heard. This in turn means that the defence is not pursued and there never is a full hearing of the case.

2.8   Copyright

Writers, broadcasters and artists have an ambivalent attitude towards copyright law. On the one hand it grants them the exclusive use to exploit (and thus profit from) their works. On the other hand it can seriously hamper the creative process by giving other copyright owners a power of veto over the incorporation of their words or images in some new work. The use of 'sampling' technology to produce highly original and very profitable 'hit' records has led to copyright litigation between record companies. The collage artist, the scratch video-maker, the popular songwriter, the cartoonist, the journalist in possession of a leaked memorandum, can all encounter copyright obstacles in creating their work, yet none of them would want others to be free to plagiarize their final product.

MEANING OF COPYRIGHT

Copyright, in brief, gives the owner of the work the right to stop others reproducing it without his or her consent. The Copyright Act 1956 is one of the most bewildering statutes (which its recent revamping by Parliament in 1988 has done little to simplify). It creates several different categories of 'work' in which copyright can exist: the most important are original (but not necessarily distinguished) literary, dramatic, musical and artistic works (including photographs); sound recordings (notably records and tapes); films; television and sound broadcasts; and cable programmes.

Copyright does not exist in ideas as such, although the law of confidence has recently been developed to protect those who provide well worked out and practicable suggestions for others to develop and exploit. The law of copyright does not operate until the ideas have been reduced to some material form and then it is generally the reproduction of that form which is restricted. This means, for instance, that newspapers do not have a monopoly even in their 'exclusive' news stories. They can stop others using their photographs, their text (or a substantial part of it) or a colourable imitation of their work, but the information conveyed is not theirs to control.

DEFENCES

Copyright is not infringed if the owner *consents* to the copying. This sounds simple, but it can be a complicated business finding out who the owner is. In some works (a television play, for instance) it is possible for different people to own the copyright in the script, the photographs, the sound-track, the dramatic screenplay, the film recording the play and the broadcast. Even if the owners can be identified there is generally no obligation on them to sell reproduction rights.

In the absence of the owner's licence, the media have two important defences to a claim for infringement of copyright. The first is *fair dealing*. This includes the fair use of another's work for the purpose of criticism or review, or the reporting of current events. The originator of the work must be acknowledged in a criticism or review and in the print media's news reporting. In an important case concerning a critical book about Scientology which made use of unpublished internal Scientology documents, the courts confirmed that the fair dealing defence could apply, even though the work had not previously been published and even though the criticism was directed at the contents of the work rather than its style.

The second important defence is *public interest*. This does not appear in the statute, but the courts have said that, just as they will not stop publication of confidential information which is in the public interest (see 2.7, p. 49), so, too, they would not prohibit the infringement of another's copyright where the public interest in publication outweighed the private right of property.

CUT-PRICE COPIES

The purpose of many of the recent changes in the law of copyright has been to strengthen the rights of copyright owners. The making of unauthorized copies of films, cassettes and videos for sale at cut-rate prices has been perceived as a major threat to the industry and led to substantial increases in the penalties that can be imposed for the criminal offences that are involved. The civil courts have also been prepared enthusiastically to grant to copyright owners what in practice are private search warrants.

'MORAL RIGHTS'

The 1988 Act introduced new 'moral' rights for the authors of copyright works. Subject to complex limitations and qualifications, authors of copyright works have the right to be identified as such and the right not to have their works subjected to derogatory treatment. A new right of privacy was also introduced to limit the use of photographs commissioned for private and domestic purpose.

PASSING OFF

In addition to copyright protection, the law will prevent one trader passing off its goods as those of another. These commercial disputes often have little to do with free speech, but their over-zealous application (or the minimal investigation of a plaintiff's claim on an application for an interlocutory injunction) can lead to the suppression of parody, spoof and satire.

2.9   Controls on broadcasting, films, videos and cable

Milton campaigned against 'prior restraint', the suppression or censorship of material in advance of publication. Court injunctions can still prevent the press from adopting a 'publish and be damned' posture, but, these apart, the press is generally free of prior restraint. For broadcasters the position is very different.

The Independent Broadcasting Authority (IBA) by statute and the British Broadcasting Corporation (BBC) by its charter, are intended and expected to 'censor' the programmes they transmit. Unlicensed broadcasters are prohibited. A radio transmitter is still one of the cheapest ways to reach a large audience, but the radio pirates have to keep one step ahead of the Department of Trade Inspectors, who can forfeit equipment as well as prosecute for infringements. The government has a residual power to direct that certain matters should not be broadcast. It used this power in 1988 to ban spoken comment by or in support of Sinn Fein, the UDA or any of the organizations proscribed under the anti-terrorism laws.

The IBA is under a duty to see as far as possible that nothing is included in its programmes which offends against good taste or decency or is likely to encourage or incite to crime or lead to disorder or be offensive to public feeling. Its news programmes must be presented with due accuracy and impartiality. Due impartiality must be preserved on the part of persons providing programmes on matters of political or industrial controversy or relating to current public policy. Unlike newspapers, which can openly propagate their own views, neither the TV companies nor the IBA can editorialize on matters (other than broadcasting) which are of political or industrial controversy or relate to current public policy. Subliminal messages are prohibited and religious broadcasting is specifically controlled.

There are limits to these duties. Thus, the Court of Appeal has accepted that in judging whether all the constituent parts of a programme satisfy the 'good taste' canon, the IBA can take account of the purpose and character of the programme as a whole. The duties set out above have also to be reconciled with the Authority's other duties, for instance, to secure a wide showing of programmes of merit. Channel 4 was deliberately created to provide programmes 'calculated to appeal to tastes and interests not generally catered for by ITV' and 'to encourage innovation and experimentation in the form and content of programmes'. Inevitably, this can only be done in some cases at the risk of causing offence to those with mainline tastes. The requirement of impartiality in non-news programmes can be satisfied over a series of programmes and a tradition has developed of allowing more latitude to 'personal view' programmes that are 'balanced' by others.

The courts have discouraged legal challenges to the exercise of these powers. Both the systems established by the IBA for vetting programmes and their decisions on individual programmes can (generally) only be quashed if they are so perverse as to be unreasonable. The BBC has accepted similar restraints to those imposed on the IBA but they are not legally enforceable. The Obscene Publications Act (see 2.3, p. 37) does not apply to television or radio programmes, although in response to pressure from MPs to change this, the government has established a Broadcasting Standards Council to monitor sex and violence on television.

THE BROADCASTING COMPLAINTS COMMISSION

Radio or television programmes put out by the IBA or the BBC can be reviewed by the Broadcasting Complaints Commission. This was created by Parliament in 1981 to consider complaints of unjust or unfair treatment or unwarranted infringements of privacy in, or in connection with, the obtaining of material included in sound or television broadcasts. Any complaint must be made by a person affected. Complaints cannot be made in connection with someone who has died more than five years previously, but within this period a member of the family, a personal representative or someone closely connected can complain.

The Commission cannot order the payment of any money to the complainant, but they can insist on the responsible body publishing the Commission's findings and, more significantly, can insist on an approved summary being broadcast at a stipulated time.

THE BRITISH BOARD OF FILM CLASSIFICATION

The British Board of Film Classification (BBFC) is a hybrid system. There is no general requirement that a *film* must have a BBFC certificate before being shown, but this position is achieved indirectly by the power of local councils to licence cinemas. Most licences have a condition attached that only films with a BBFC certificate will be shown. Unlike television and radio programmes, films can be prosecuted under the Obscene Publications Act (see 2.3, p. 37) although feature films (not less than 16 mm) can only be prosecuted or forfeited with the approval of the Director of Public Prosecutions.

The BBFC has been given an enlarged role in relation to video cassettes. Here, it is a censor in law as well as in practice and it is an offence to supply an unclassified video or to breach any restrictions which have been imposed by the BBFC (as to minimum age, type of supplier etc.). Videos concerned with sport, religion, music and education are exempt, but not if they show or are designed to encourage human sexual activity (or force or restraint associated with it), or mutilation, torture or other gross acts of violence towards humans or animals. Videos are not exempt either if they show human genitalia or human urinary or excretory functions. The BBFC has to consider whether videos are suitable for viewing in the home. There is an appeal structure for those who submit videos to the BBFC, but the sizeable fees charged by the Board and the delays that the process necessarily entails can cause grave difficulties for producers.

THE CABLE AUTHORITY

Cable programming is still in its infancy but the regulatory framework has been established on a similar model to that for broadcasting. Thus, the Cable Authority has the power to licence operators. It must do all that it can to see that its licensees do not include in their programmes material which offends against good taste or decency or is likely to encourage or incite to crime or lead to public disorder or to be offensive to public feeling. Subliminal images are, again, banned. News must be presented with due accuracy and impartiality, but only if it originates in the UK. Non-news programmes are considerably less inhibited than broadcasts: instead of a requirement of 'balance' there is only the duty to see that undue prominence is not given to the views and opinions of particular persons or bodies on religious matters or matters of public controversy or relating to current public policy. Editorializing on religious, political, industrial controversy or current public policy is, as with broadcasting, prohibited.

The Cable Authority has the ultimate sanction of withdrawing an operator's licence if these or the other conditions are broken. Unlike television and radio, cable programmers are not immune from the Obscene Publications Act.

2.10   Whose freedom?

It might be thought that the restrictions we have examined are of relevance only to the wealthy, for surely only they have the practical and legal freedom to publish what they will. But publishers or media organizations are not necessarily large, wealthy and dependent on large audiences. A radical bookshop, a community radio station and a local video project could be as much affected by the restrictions of free expression discussed here as the multinational media organization.

It is, though, true that the laws we have examined are concerned mostly with what cannot be said, not with what must be said. There are generally no rights to be heard, broadcast or published. The exceptions are few.

A RIGHT OF REPLY

We saw, for instance, that certain types of qualified privilege were dependent on the victim being given a right of reply. During election time, one candidate cannot appear in a programme about the constituency without the other candidates' consent (so that, in effect, all have the right to appear or to veto the programme). The broadcaster's duty of balance can again effectively mean that one party to a current controversy can insist on the opportunity to put

their view. Under threat of a libel action, some publishers will prefer
to offer a reply to the person they attacked. This, though, like
readers' letters columns or the television 'video box' is a matter of
negotiation or marketing policy rather than a legal right of access.

On several occasions MPs have introduced private members' bills
to give a legal right of reply to correct mis-statements of fact or to
offer alternative views. These attempts have been generated by the
blithe indifference to truth or any notion of journalistic standards
in some parts of the media. Yet the problems of a legal right of
reply would be formidable. Resolving whether a statement is true
or false can be no easy task. As long as the press (unlike
broadcasters) are free to be partisan, there are real difficulties in
insisting that equal – and as prominent – space be given to the
papers' adversaries.

THE RIGHT TO RECEIVE INFORMATION AND IDEAS

Accepting the inequality of access to the media, the rights and
restrictions considered in this chapter are still important for those
unable to be publishers themselves. The corollary of freedom to
communicate, as the European Convention recognizes, is the
freedom to receive information and ideas. The Peter Wright and
Spycatcher litigation is not just about the right of the *Sunday Times*
to serialize the book or of the *Independent* and other papers to print
its allegations, but also, and more importantly, of the public to read
them.

2.11   More information

USEFUL ORGANIZATIONS

Campaign for Freedom of Information, 3 Endsleigh Street, London
WC1H 0DD (01-278 9686).

Campaign for Press and Broadcasting Freedom, 9 Poland Street,
London W1V 3DG (01-437 2795).

National Union of Journalists, 314 Gray's Inn Road, London WC1X
8PD (01-278 7916).

Newspaper Society, Bloomsbury House, Bloomsbury Square, 74–77 Great Russell Street, London WC1 3DA (01-636 7014).

BIBLIOGRAPHY

G. J. Borrie and N. V. Lowe, *Law of Contempt*, 2nd edn, Butterworth, 1983.

D. Hooper, *Official Secrets: The Use and Abuse of the Act*, Secker and Warburg, 1987.

J. Michael, *The Politics of Secrecy: The Case for a Freedom of Information Law*, Penguin, 1982.

Report of the Committee on Obscenity and Film Censorship (the Williams Report), Cmnd 7772, HMSO, 1979.

G. Robertson, *Obscenity*, Weidenfeld and Nicolson, 1979.

G. Robertson and A. Nicol, *Media Law: The Rights of Journalists and Broadcasters*, Oyez Longman, 1984.

3   The right of privacy

This chapter deals with:

There is no general right of privacy recognized in English law. For example, there is no law to forbid your neighbour gossiping about you (unless what he says is defamatory); there is no general right to prevent people, such as private detectives or the police, gathering information about you behind your back; nor is there any right to prevent the press taking sneak photographs of you when you do not expect it.

All that can be said is that in certain specific circumstances the law does forbid acts which most would regard as intrusions into their privacy.

3.1   The protection of confidential information

English law forbids anyone to whom confidential information has been entrusted from misusing it to the detriment of the person who entrusted it (see also 2.7, p. 49). There are three ingredients of the 'tort' of misuse of confidential information:

- a collection of confidential information;
- a relationship which imposes an obligation of confidence on the person who receives the information; *and*
- misuse of the information by the person who receives it.

Most court cases have been about industrial secrets, such as ex-employees who have stolen secret formulae or lists of customers. In such cases there is no particular difficulty in applying the above principles to the facts. It is also well established that the law applies not merely to the person who stole or was entrusted with the information but to anyone who is subsequently given it (at least once he has been told or ought to have realized the position).

There is, however, a great deal of uncertainty about the extent to which the law can be exploited outside the field of industrial secrets. It is certainly true that the law is not confined to industrial cases.

In a recent case, the plaintiff claimed that the police were bugging his telephone. Most would regard this as an invasion of his privacy, but in the absence of any law against invasions of privacy, he had to rely on the law of confidential information. The court held, perhaps surprisingly, that if you choose to tell your secrets on the telephone, you run the risk of a crossed line, and therefore you must be taken to have abandoned your right to have the information treated as confidential. (The law relating to telephone tapping has changed since then – see below – but not in a way which alters the law of confidential information.)

Another limitation on the use of the law of confidential information to protect privacy is that the duty of confidence has to be owed to the plaintiff. Take, for example, police records. Although the records of people's convictions are not, individually, confidential information (because each conviction has taken place in open court), the police have a *collection* of such information. This collection probably can be regarded as confidential information, in the same way as a manufacturer's list of customers is protected. But only the police could enforce this duty of confidence should one of their employees start handing out the information to third parties: the victim of such a disclosure is owed no duty of confidence so far as the contents of the Police National Computer are concerned (see 4.2, p. 78).

3.2   Telephone tapping and the interception of mail

The Interception of Communications Act 1985 makes it an offence intentionally to 'intercept a communication in the course of its transmission by post or by means of a public telecommunications system'.

There are two important defences:

- If the interceptor is acting with the consent either of the person sending the communication *or* of the person receiving it. Thus, for example, the telephone services are permitted to intercept your incoming phone calls at your request for the purpose of tracking down the maker of obscene calls.
- Where the interceptor is acting under a warrant issued by a Secretary of State (who would usually be the Home Secretary in England). Such warrants may only be issued 'in the interests of national security', 'for the purpose of preventing or detecting *serious* crime', or 'for the purpose of safeguarding the economic well-being of the United Kingdom'. 'Serious' crime is defined as crime for which a person over twenty-one with no previous convictions could expect to get more than three years' imprisonment, or which involves the use of violence or the making of 'substantial' financial gain, or which involves 'a large number of persons in pursuit of a common purpose'.

The Interception of Communications Act does not specifically cover bugs or other surveillance devices; only the 'interception' of communications in the course of transmission. This is a difficult area. If a bug is placed in a telephone and catches both sides of a conversation, this seems to be caught by the Act. But what of a bug placed elsewhere in a room which is sensitive enough to pick up one side of a telephone conversation? A bug which picks up only one side of a conversation by listening to the talker seems not to be caught by the Act, but one which avails itself in some way of the telephone system to hear the other side of the conversation would be caught.

The Act does not protect conversations between doctor and patient or lawyer and client. One warrant can cover a whole organization and so threaten the privacy of hundreds of people.

The Act provides a partial mechanism for complaining, where it is suspected that communications are being improperly intercepted: a tribunal is established to investigate whether a warrant has been issued and, if so, whether it was properly issued. Where it is found that a warrant has been improperly issued, the tribunal has power to order compensation, and the destruction of the intercepted material. It will be noted, however, that if the interception took place *without* a warrant, the tribunal has no powers.

To prosecute someone for the commission of an offence under this Act, the consent of the Director of Public Prosecutions is needed.

3.3   Bugging and surveillance

Except where the Interception of Communications Act applies, there is no general law against bugs and surveillance devices. Nor is there any law to protect you against being followed (unless a breach of the peace is threatened, which is unlikely if the follower is sufficiently skilful).

Where a bug is actually placed on your property, there may be a question of trespass, if you can find out who planted it. But there are plenty of bugging and surveillance techniques available today which do not involve any intrusion on to another's property, and there is no general law preventing or regulating such activities.

If it can be demonstrated that the police were responsible, it would be as well to complain to the appropriate Chief Constable: the police are now subject to Home Office guidelines which go further than the general law. In particular, they are forbidden to use bugs or surveillance devices to get round the controls on telephone-tapping.

The law of confidential information could also be useful in cases where conversations have been bugged. But one must bear in mind the limitation referred to above, that in certain circumstances you may be taken to have abandoned your right of confidence. If, for example, your conversation in a pub was being surveilled, it could be said that you take the risk of being overheard if you choose to discuss matters in such public places. Nor could the law of confidential information prevent a private detective from following you.

The Security Service Bill, now before Parliament, legalizes bugging, burglary and telephone-tapping by the security service. The tribunal established to receive complaints is unlikely to be an effective remedy, although it is intended to have powers to order the security service to stop investigations, to destroy documents and to pay compensation.

3.4   Intrusion or harassment by neighbours and others

In the absence of a general law to protect privacy, there is little you can do about neighbours who shout abuse, watch you from their garden and so on. If your neighbour harasses you particularly severely, you may be able to bring a civil action for nuisance. Peeping Toms can be bound over to keep the peace by the magistrates' court, so it may be worth complaining to the police. (See 1.3, p. 26 for more about binding-over.)

If a landlord harasses you by shouting abuse, banging on walls or doors, entering your room without permission, or going through your belongings, you may well be able to take legal action. Where you have an exclusive right of occupation (in other words, you are a tenant, rather than a lodger or hotel guest), you will be able to sue the landlord in the county court for trespass. If you succeed, you will be able to get damages and an injunction preventing the landlord from repeating the behaviour.

You should also report a landlord who harasses you to the local authority, who have the power to prosecute in the criminal courts (Protection from Eviction Act 1977).

People who come to your door to sell goods, ask you to give to charity, persuade you to support a particular religion or political party or ask questions for a market research or other survey, have no right to enter your home. You can refuse to talk to them, and they must leave when you ask them to.

If you are bothered by unwanted telephone calls, and know who the caller is, you can report the caller to the police. It is a criminal offence to telephone grossly offensive messages, or make indecent, obscene or menacing telephone calls, or calls which cause annoyance, inconvenience or needless anxiety (Post Office Act 1969). In the last resort, you can ask British Telecom, through the operator, to intercept your calls. Alternatively, you can change your number or go ex-directory.

3.5   Unsolicited mail

Unscrupulous traders sometimes send or deliver unasked-for goods, and subsequently demand payment for them. The Unsolicited Goods and Services Act 1971 now makes this a risky thing to do.

If such goods are delivered to you, you should keep the goods in a reasonably safe place, and *either* send a notice in writing to the sender, stating that you had not asked for the goods and requiring him to remove them from a specified place within thirty days, *or* hang on to the goods for six months. Assuming the goods are not collected within the thirty days or six months, as the case may be, they may be treated by you as if they were a gift to you. (No thank-you letter is needed.)

The Act also makes it an offence to send obscene or indecent material through the post, or to send unsolicited books, magazines, leaflets or advertising material describing or illustrating human sexual techniques. If you receive such material and object to it, you should complain to the police. (See 2.3, p. 36 for more on obscenity.)

3.6   Power of officials to enter your home

A house on fire, or infested with rats, or with a gas leak, or where building works have been carried out in a dangerous manner, is something which concerns the whole community. To cope with problems such as these, many officials are given the right to enter your home whether you like it or not.

There are, in fact, tens of thousands of officials in the UK who have the power, in certain circumstances, to enter private premises, but most of them only have the power to enter business premises and are not dealt with here. This section describes the most important powers of entry which may involve officials entering your home. (The powers of the police to enter and search private premises are dealt with in chapter 6.)

Each type of official is subject to different rules of procedure, because each is governed by a different Act of Parliament, and there is no general code which covers their conduct. Quite commonly, however, the procedure is that the official must produce evidence of his authority before entering, and he may not insist on entering without first giving you at least twenty-four hours' notice of his desire to enter your home. If, after such notice, you refuse to let him in, he may get an order from the magistrates' court authorizing him to enter without your consent, by force if necessary.

In general, if someone asks to come into your home, claiming to be an official, you should:

- ask to see the caller's identity card;
- ask the caller what authority he or she has to enter your home;
- if in doubt, refuse entry and contact the office from which the official claims to come in order to check his or her credentials.

If you have a complaint to make about the way an official behaves, you should approach the appropriate authority. For example, in the case of a local authority official, you should complain to your local councillor; in the case of a gas or electricity official, the gas or electricity board; in the case of a VAT inspector, the collector in charge of VAT at the local office; or in the case of a tax inspector, the Commissioners for the Inland Revenue.

FIRE BRIGADE

A member of a local authority fire brigade who is on duty or a constable may enter any premises where a fire has broken out, or where there is reason to believe a fire has broken out. Other premises may also be entered if this is necessary for fire-fighting purposes. The fireman can force entry, if necessary. The permission of the owner or occupier does not have to be obtained. It is an offence to obstruct or interfere with any member of a fire brigade who is involved in fighting a fire; the maximum penalty is a fine of £400 (Fire Services Act 1947).

GAS AND ELECTRICITY BOARDS

An officer of the gas or electricity board may enter your home if:

- you agree to let the officer enter; *or*
- a magistrate has given the officer a warrant, authorizing the officer to enter; *or*
- there is an emergency and the officer has reason to believe that there is a danger to life or property.

A gas or electricity board official is entitled to ask to enter your home, or to apply to a magistrate for a warrant, in order to:

- inspect the meter or any other fittings;
- disconnect the supply in certain circumstances.

In order to obtain a warrant, the official must show that:

- you have been given at least twenty-four hours' notice; *and*
- he has asked to be admitted and you have refused; *or*
- the premises are unoccupied.

Entry must be at a 'reasonable' time, and the official must leave the house as secure against trespassers as it was when he or she arrived, and make good any damage caused.

It is a criminal offence to obstruct a gas or electricity board official who has a warrant or who asks to be admitted in an emergency; the maximum penalty is a fine of £400. It is *not* an offence to refuse to let the official enter if there is no emergency and the official does not have a warrant. (Rights of Entry [Gas and Electricity Boards] Act 1954).

WATER AUTHORITIES

An authorized official of a water authority may enter any premises at a 'reasonable' hour in order to:

- inspect water meters;
- ascertain whether there has been any contravention of the law relating to water supplies;
- detect waste or misuse of water.

In the first two cases, twenty-four hours' notice must be given. In the third case, the official may enter between 7 a.m. and one hour after sunset. It is an offence to obstruct an official.

HOUSING

An official authorized by the local authority may enter any house in the area at any 'reasonable' time in order to:

- make a valuation or survey, where a compulsory purchase order is being considered or has been issued;
- examine the premises and make a survey where a notice

requiring repairs, a demolition order, a closing order or a clearance order has been issued;

- measure the rooms etc. to determine whether there has been overcrowding;
- ascertain whether there has been a contravention of the Housing Act regulations.

The official must have a written document of authority and must give at least twenty-four hours' notice. It is an offence to obstruct the official, providing the official is authorized and has given notice; the maximum penalty is a fine of £100 (Housing Act 1985).

PLANNING

An authorized local authority official may enter premises at any 'reasonable' time for various planning purposes including:

- preparing or approving development plans;
- dealing with applications for planning permission;
- making a valuation in connection with compensation;
- making a survey in connection with a compulsory purchase order.

The official must give twenty-four hours' notice. The local authority must also pay compensation for any damage caused. It is an offence to obstruct the official, provided that proper notice has been given; the maximum penalty is a fine of £100 (Town and Country Planning Act 1971).

RATING

A rating valuation officer, or any official authorized by the rating valuation officer, may enter any property in the area at any 'reasonable' time, in order to carry out a survey or make a valuation for the purposes of drawing up rating valuation lists. The official must give twenty-four hours' notice. It is an offence to obstruct the official, provided that proper notice has been given; the maximum penalty is a fine of £50 (General Rate Act 1967).

SOCIAL SECURITY

A National Insurance inspector may enter business premises at any 'reasonable' time in order to interview employers, employees and self-employed people about their contributions record. It is an offence not to produce National Insurance certificates or other relevant documents. It is also an offence to refuse to answer the inspector's questions, except that you are not obliged to give information which would incriminate you or your spouse (Social Security Act 1986). The maximum penalty for either offence is a fine of £400 and a fine of £40 for each day that the offence continues.

A supplementary benefits investigator (e.g., an official trying to find out if a woman is cohabiting) does *not* have a right to enter your home. If the official forces entry, or refuses to leave after you ask him to, he is committing a trespass and you may be able to take legal action.

TAX

A tax inspector can obtain a warrant from a High Court judge if he reasonably suspects that a tax offence has been committed. The warrant authorizes the inspector to enter and search private premises, and remove documents. Any application for a warrant must be made with the approval of a Commissioner for the Inland Revenue (Finance Act 1976).

VAT

A VAT official may enter any premises, at a 'reasonable' time, for any purposes connected with administering value added tax. The official may enter without a warrant, and may also inspect goods which are liable to tax. If the official has reasonable grounds for suspecting you of an offence related to VAT, he may apply to a magistrate for a warrant authorizing him to:

- enter, by force if necessary, at any reasonable time within fourteen days of the warrant being issued;
- seize any documents relating to the investigation;

- search any people on the premises (but a woman can only be searched by another woman).

Obstructing a VAT official could amount to an assault for which you could be prosecuted.

MENTAL HEALTH

Magistrates have the power to issue a warrant authorizing a constable to enter premises (by force, if necessary) if they have reasonable cause to suppose that a mentally disordered person is being ill-treated there, or is unable to look after himself. The constable must be accompanied by a social worker and a doctor.

INFECTIOUS DISEASES AND ILLNESS

In the case of 'notifiable diseases' (e.g., plague and cholera) a magistrate may make an order for the compulsory medical examination of suspected sufferers and carriers and for the removal to and detention in hospital of anyone suffering from such a disease where it appears that proper precautions are not being taken to prevent the spread of the disease. (Public Health (Control of Disease) Act 1984). AIDS is dealt with similarly to notifiable diseases, but slightly less stringently: there is no provision for compulsory examination provided the suspected sufferer or carrier is already receiving treatment from a doctor. Public Health (Infectious Diseases) Regulations 1985).

Magistrates have the power to issue a warrant authorizing an officer of a local authority to enter premises to remove to hospital persons who are so chronically ill or old as to be unable to look after themselves, and who are not being properly looked after by others. Seven days' notice of such an application must be given (National Assistance Act 1948).

On a certificate from the appointed local authority officer, the local authority may serve notice on the occupier to disinfect or destroy articles likely to retain infection within a fixed period, if doing so would tend to prevent the spread of any infectious disease. The occupier has twenty-four hours to inform the local authority that he will comply, failing which, the local authority has the right to enter and do the necessary work. The occupier can be forced to reimburse the local authority, and the provision for compensation for articles destroyed is not very satisfactory. Where an infectious disease occurs in a house, the local authority may also, at their own cost, remove persons from the premises, acting with a magistrates' warrant if there is no consent. This is not limited to the 'notifiable' diseases mentioned earlier.

PESTS AND VERMIN

The occupier of land is under an obligation to notify the local authority if rats or mice in substantial numbers live on or resort to the land.

The local authority may serve notice on the owner or occupier (or both) of land (including buildings) requiring them to take specified steps within a specified time to keep the land free of mice or rats.

Where premises are so filthy or unwholesome as to be prejudicial to health, or are verminous, the local authority may require corrective measures, including, for example, disinfection or the removal of wallpaper. If necessary, the notice may require the occupiers of infested premises (and neighbouring premises which might be affected) to vacate the premises while gas is employed to destroy vermin. In such a case, the local authority must provide temporary alternative accommodation at its own expense.

It is an offence to disobey the notice (maximum penalty £50, or £400 in the case of a mice or rat notice). In the event of disobedience, the local authority also has the power to enter the land to do the work itself (Public Health Act 1936, Prevention of Damage by Pests Act 1949).

FOSTER HOMES

A local authority can authorize someone (e.g., a social worker) to inspect any home where a child is being fostered. The inspector must produce an official document, proving that he or she has the right to enter. It is an offence to refuse to allow the inspector to enter; the maximum penalty is a fine of £2,000 or imprisonment for up to six months, or both (Foster Children Act 1980).

THE ANTON PILLER ORDER

Over the past ten years, the courts have developed a form of civil search-warrant, called an 'Anton Piller' order. This is usually issued in cases involving 'pirate' goods, such as unauthorized video copies of popular films, but it can be issued in any case where the court is persuaded that the defendant is the sort of person who might destroy relevant evidence in his possession if the order is not made. Strictly speaking, an Anton Piller order is not a search-warrant, because it does not directly empower the holder to enter or search premises. What the order does is to instruct the person in charge of the premises to let the holder in. But since it is a contempt of court to refuse to let him in, the order has much the same effect as a search-warrant.

The order must be served by a solicitor, but it will usually allow him to be accompanied by others. If you are served with an Anton Piller order, the person serving it will give you an opportunity to take legal advice. In view of the seriousness of the matter, it would be sensible to do so. It would, however, be a very rare case in which your lawyer could advise you not to comply with the order. Nearly all Anton Piller orders contain a provision forbidding you to tip off others (apart from your lawyer) about their existence. In fact, the plaintiff often has means of telling whether others have been tipped off; he may have persons watching for such activity, and, if you were caught arranging for others to dispose of inconvenient evidence, you would risk prison for contempt of court.

The solicitor serving the order is under a strict duty to behave responsibly, and in one case where it was held that he acted oppressively, he was ordered to pay substantial compensation.

3.7   More information

USEFUL ORGANIZATIONS
      Law Centres
      Citizens' Advice Bureaux

Consult your local telephone directory for addresses and telephone numbers.

4   The right to know

This chapter deals with:

Since writing was invented, governments have kept records relating to their subjects' affairs. The advent of the computer has made it possible for governments and businesses to collect and store far more information than ever before, and to cross-reference it more easily with information kept elsewhere.

In the United States, the Freedom of Information Act has established the general principle that government files are open to public inspection (subject to some closely defined exceptions). In the United Kingdom, the general rule is the opposite: there is no right to inspect any files maintained about you, and the Official Secrets Act in its present form makes it unlawful to reveal nearly all governmental information. In the following sections, we discuss various classes of records and some very important recent exceptions to the general rule.

4.1   The Data Protection Act 1984

The Data Protection Act contains important provisions to control the keeping of computer data about 'identifiable living individuals'.

So far as the businessman is concerned, the main effect of the Act is that, in many cases, he is required to register with the Registrar of Data Protection, who will then exercise considerable control over the use made of the data.

As to the ordinary citizen, and so far as this book is concerned, the importance of the Act is that it gives you various rights:

- A right of inspection of data relating to you;
- A right of correction of such data;
- A right to compensation if data about you is misused.

There are numerous exceptions and qualifications to the various provisions of the Act, and in the next paragraphs it is examined in more detail.

DATA COVERED BY THE ACT

The basic principle of the Act is that it only covers data relating to identifiable living persons. Thus, pure statistics which cannot be related to any individuals are not covered. But data is covered by the Act if it can be related to an individual by the use of other information, such as an index, to which the data-user has access.

Not all collections of personal data are covered: the Act only covers collections of data which are stored in such a way that they can be processed mechanically. In other words, a simple old-fashioned filing cabinet of personal records is *not* covered by the Act, but the Act will apply as soon as the data in the files is put into a computer. As time goes on, this limitation will probably become less significant, but at present it is a serious defect in the scope of the Act.

Other important exceptions to the scope of the Act are:

- It does not cover collections of data held by an individual for the 'management of his personal, family or household affairs'.
- It does not cover collections of data held by individuals for 'recreational purposes'.
- It does not cover payroll, pension and accounting records used solely for the purpose of ensuring that people are paid (or pay) the correct amount at the correct time. This exemption is lost if the data is used for most other purposes without the subject's consent.
- It does not cover membership records of a club, provided that

the records only relate to members of the club *and* that the members have individually been asked whether they object to the data being held, and have not objected. It follows therefore, that a club which intends to computerize its records must inform the membership and ask if they have any objections. This exemption is lost if the club misuses the information. (The most likely misuse would be to disclose the information to any third party without the consent of the member in question.)

● It does not cover certain mailing-lists, namely those where the persons concerned have been asked whether they object to the data being held, and have not objected. This exemption is also lost if the user of the list misuses it.

REGISTRATION OF DATA AND THE DATA PROTECTION PRINCIPLES

Applicants for registration must specify what kind of data they are going to collect, how they are going to collect it, and what they propose to do with it.

The duty of the Registrar is to examine applications for registration to ensure that the manner in which the data is collected, and the uses made of it, comply with the eight Data Protection Principles:

1. The information to be contained in personal data shall be obtained, and personal data shall be processed, fairly and lawfully.
2. Personal data shall be held only for one or more specified and lawful purposes.
3. Personal data held for any purpose or purposes shall not be used or disclosed in any manner incompatible with that purpose or those purposes.
4. Personal data held for any purpose or purposes shall be adequate, relevant and not excessive in relation to that purpose or those purposes.
5. Personal data shall be accurate and, where necessary, kept up to date.

6. Personal data held for any purpose or purposes shall not be kept for longer than is necessary for that purpose or those purposes.
7. An individual shall be entitled:
   (a) at reasonable intervals and without undue delay or expense
       (i) to be informed by any data user whether he holds personal data of which that individual is the subject; and
       (ii) to access to any such data held by a data user; and
   (b) where appropriate, to have such data corrected or erased.
8. Appropriate security measures shall be taken against unauthorized access to, or alteration, disclosure or destruction of, personal data and against accidental loss or destruction of personal data.

Non-disclosure of data

One of the most fundamental requirements of the Act is that personal data is not to be disclosed to persons not entitled to receive it. The *only* persons entitled to receive the data are those provided for in the registration, and the person who is the subject of the data.

The Register

Details relating to all registered collections of data are available for inspection free of charge, at main public libraries throughout the country, and copies of entries in the Register may be obtained at a cost of £2 each.

The details on the Register will include the identity of the data user, where he is collecting the data from, and who he is permitted to disclose it to.

Complaints

If you have good reason to complain about the latitude given to a data user in a particular registration, or if you know of a misuse of data outside the scope of a registration, you may complain to the Registrar, at:

Office of the Data Protection Registrar
Springfield House
Water Lane
Wilmslow SK9 5AX (0625 535777)

It is up to him to decide whether he will take any action, but he does have wide powers to force data users to change their behaviour, or even to strike them from the Register.

Compensation for wrongful disclosure

If you suffer damage as a result of the disclosure of personal information about you to someone not entitled to receive it, you are entitled to damages, and also to compensation for any 'distress' suffered. It seems that you cannot claim compensation for distress alone, unless you have suffered actual damage as well.

Clearly, before taking any such action it is vital to inspect the Register at your library to check that the person to whom the information was communicated was not a person entitled to receive it.

Inspecting the data

Any individual has the right to be informed whether a data user is keeping any data relating to him, and to inspect the data in question. But any such request must be in writing, accompanied by a fee (maximum currently £10).

There are several important exceptions to this right of access. In all the following cases, not only are you not entitled to inspect your file, but you are not even entitled to find out if one exists:

- Purely manual records. As explained above, the Act does not cover files which are kept manually.
- All data 'necessary for the purpose of safeguarding national security'. The certificate of a Cabinet Minister, the Attorney-General or (in Scotland) the Lord Advocate is conclusive as to whether the data is necessary for such a purpose.
- All data held for the purposes of the 'prevention or detection of crime', the 'apprehension or prosecution of offenders' or the

'assessment or collection of any tax or duty'. This applies not only, for example, to information in the hands of the police, but also where the same information has been passed on to persons 'discharging statutory functions'. Thus it would seem, for example, that police information passed over to social services departments remains exempt from disclosure, although, of course, the police must be careful when passing it on that they do not contravene any of the data protection principles.

Regulations made under the Act have excluded, from the subject access provisions, all records and reports relating to adoption applications and also statements of children's special educational needs. Special exceptions have also been made for social work files and medical records (see below).

Correcting data and compensation for inaccuracy

The Act gives jurisdiction to the High Court or a county court (or, in Scotland, the Court of Session or the Sheriff) to order a data user to correct or obliterate data which the court is satisfied is inaccurate. The court may also order the correction or obliteration of an opinion on the file which appears to have been based on inaccurate data. Where the information in question was supplied to the data-user by third parties, the court may, instead of obliterating it, order that a corrective statement be added to the file.

Where damage has been suffered as a result of the inaccuracy, compensation can be ordered. Compensation may also be awarded for distress, but (as in the case of wrongful disclosure) only if actual damage has been suffered as well.

4.2   Police records and the security services

The police and security services maintain numerous computer records, as can be seen by inspecting the Data Protection Register at your local library. As mentioned above, many of these records are exempt from the subject access provisions, though the Act as a whole still applies. Thus, if the police were officially to pass information about you to third parties, contrary to the terms of their registration, the compensation provisions of the Data Protection Act would apply.

More commonly, however, information from the Police National Computer is passed on unofficially, as a favour to a friend. Where information is passed on in a manner not unauthorized by the police, the person doing so is probably committing a disciplinary offence, and a complaint may be made to the Police Authority concerned.   In a recent case some police officers and private detectives were successfully prosecuted for breach of the Official Secrets Acts. But even if such offenders are identified, it may be difficult to get compensation: the legal situation is complicated, and advice should be sought.

4.3   Education records

Apart from the Data Protection Act, which only applies to computer files (as to which, see above), there is no general right to inspect records held by an Education Authority. Some authorities do, however, have a policy of allowing access for parents and children to at least some records, and, in the absence of more general legislation, it is necessary to make inquiries of your own authority to see what their policy is. The issue is a sensitive one, because parents and children may have conflicting interests – as anyone who destroyed his school report on the way home knows.

4.4   Medical records

Apart from such rights as exist under the Data Protection Act, there is no right to inspect your, or your children's, medical records. Under the Data Protection Act, the right to inspect does not cover manual records, and even the right to inspect computer records is now subject to a special procedure: you are entitled to know whether a file about you exists, but before you can be given a copy of it, a 'health professional' (usually a doctor) has to decide whether your inspection of them could cause serious physical or mental harm to you or another. If so, you will not be allowed a copy.

4.5   Housing and social work records

It is hoped that the Access to Personal Files Act 1987 will soon make local authority housing and social work files available to the subjects of such files. The Act does not take effect until the government makes regulations about the manner in which such right of access is to be exercised, and there may be limitations contained in such regulations.

In principle, if you are a tenant of a local authority (or a member of a tenant's family) or you have had dealings with a Social Services Department you will be entitled to inspect any information kept about you in any file kept about you for those purposes. This includes expressions of the local authority's opinions about you. Two important exceptions spelled out in the Act are:

- you are not entitled to inspect information collected before the new law comes into force (unless such information is essential for an understanding of later information); *and*
- you are not allowed to see any information which consists of an indication of the local authority's intentions towards you.

4.6   Employment records

There is little you can do if a prospective employer asks you extremely detailed questions about your personal life. If you refuse to answer them, you may be refused employment and, in some cases, if you give false answers which are later discovered, you may be dismissed. (In certain circumstances you need not tell the truth about old previous convictions. See 7.7, p. 170.)

If your employer keeps personnel records on employees, which the employees are not allowed to see, you should ask your trade union to take up the issue. But you have no general legal right to insist on seeing your personnel records. If they are on a computer, the Data Protection Act may assist (see above). If you are dismissed and bring a tribunal complaint, you may be able to get access to the records on yourself during the case.

If an employer or employment agency refuses to give you a reference, there is nothing you can do. Similarly, there is very little you can do if a previous employer gives you a reference which is misleading or inaccurate. You have no legal right to see the reference. If you do manage to obtain a copy of the reference and consider that it is defamatory, you may want to get legal advice. In theory, it is possible to sue an employer who gives you a defamatory reference, but there are two problems: firstly, a reference is covered by 'qualified privilege', which means that you would have to prove that the employer was malicious in saying what he did about you; secondly, since there is no legal aid for libel actions, you would have to pay your own legal costs, and the other side's if you lost. NCCL is pressing for reform of the law in this area.

The Department of Education and Science maintains a blacklist, List 99, of people who are not allowed to be employed in schools, colleges or within the youth service. Someone may be placed on the list following a criminal conviction, or after suspension as a teacher, if the Secretary of State decides that he or she is unfit for employment with children and young people. The person has a right to make representations, either in writing or at a hearing, against being placed on the list. The list, which is updated regularly, is circulated to principals of schools (including independent schools), colleges of further education and so on.

Until the Access to Personal Files Act is brought into force, the Data Protection Act gives some right to inspect the contents of social work computer files relating to you, but this is subject to two special exceptions:

- you are not entitled to inspect the file if serious harm (physical, mental or emotional) would be likely to arise to you or some other person from your inspection of the file;
- you are not entitled to inspect the files if they would disclose (or enable you to deduce) the identity of an informant or another data subject.

These special exceptions apply not only to local authorities' social work files, but also to similar files in the possession of the National Society for the Prevention of Cruelty to Children (NSPCC) or the Royal Scottish Society for the Prevention of Cruelty to Children (RSSPCC).

4.7   More information

Law centres
Citizens' Advice Bureaux
Campaign for Freedom of Information, 3 Endsleigh Street,
London WC1H 0DD (01-278 9686)

Consult your local telephone directory for addresses and telephone
numbers.

5 The right to complain

This chapter deals with:

5.1   The Ombudsman

This section deals with the Ombudsman services for central government departments:

> The Parliamentary Commissioner for Administration (the Parliamentary Ombudsman)
> Church House
> Great Smith Street
> London SW1P 3BW (01-276 2130)

In Northern Ireland:

> Office of the Northern Ireland Parliamentary Commissioner
> 33 Wellington Place
> Belfast BT1 6HN (0232 233821)

and for local authorities:

> Commission for Local Administration in England
> 21 Queen Anne's Gate
> London SW1H 9BU (01-222 5622)

There are different addresses for local Ombudsmen for Scotland and Wales and there are different Ombudsmen for different areas of England.

There is also a Health Service Ombudsman:

> Church House
> Great Smith Street
> London SW1P 3BW (01-276 2035)

and again there are different Ombudsmen for the Health Service in Scotland and Wales.

THE PARLIAMENTARY OMBUDSMAN

The Parliamentary Ombudsman investigates complaints about the way people have been treated by government departments, so long as it concerns the administration of a department rather than government policy or the law itself. Since July 1987 he can also investigate certain non-departmental public bodies, such as the Arts Council, the Equal Opportunities Commission and many others. A full list of these bodies can be obtained from the Ombudsman's office.

If you have a complaint, you should first complain directly to the department itself (and exercise any right of appeal you may have). The Ombudsman will not usually investigate complaints which could be brought to a tribunal or court, for example for wrongful dismissal.

How to complain

You must complain to the Ombudsman via an MP (though not necessarily your own MP) and should write to the MP setting out details of your complaint. Copies of all correspondence with the department concerned should be enclosed with your letter. You must ask the MP to refer the matter to the Ombudsman. You can ask someone else to assist you to make the complaint if you are not sure how to do so.

There is no fee for taking a complaint to the Ombudsman and any expenses you incur during the investigation will be reimbursed.

Usually, the Ombudsman will not see you personally but will inspect the government files and papers and may summon anyone to give evidence if necessary.

When the investigating officer has collected the facts, the Ombudsman decides whether to uphold the complaint and, if so, will recommend a suitable remedy to the government department concerned. Usually the department will follow the recommendation, although it cannot be forced to do so. There is no appeal against the Ombudsman's findings.

THE LOCAL OMBUDSMAN

There are different local Ombudsmen for different parts of the country, with their own staff. Their role is to investigate complaints about councils, such as unreasonable delay or neglect, failure to follow proper procedure or policy, or malice or bias.

Again, they will not investigate matters subject to court or tribunal proceedings and are mainly concerned with allegations of maladministration.

How to complain

Your complaint should be made via a local councillor, in writing, giving details of your complaint and requesting that he send it on to the local Ombudsman. If the councillor refuses to do so, or fails to do so in a reasonable time, you can send it direct to the local Ombudsman yourself.

The Ombudsman will decide if it is an appropriate matter to deal with – and will give you the reasons if it is not accepted for investigation. He will then ask the council for their comments on your complaint and can examine their files and interview the people involved. A formal report may take some months. You will be sent a copy, which will not mention names but will say whether injustice has been caused by maladministration.

The council must consider the report and any recommendations, and inform the Ombudsman what action it proposes to take. Again, it cannot be forced to follow the Ombudsman's recommendations, although usually it will. The council must give notice of the report in the press and make it available to the public for at least three weeks. You can also try to get publicity for the report yourself.

THE HEALTH SERVICE OMBUDSMAN

This service was set up to consider and investigate complaints concerning a failure in the service provided by a health authority or maladministration in the NHS.

It cannot investigate complaints of:

- clinical judgment of hospital, medical or dental staff (see 5.4, p. 93);
- negligence or other complaints where the appropriate remedy is by court action; *or*
- personnel or contractual matters.

As with the other Ombudsman services, you must yourself have suffered the complaint and must raise it within a reasonable time.

How to complain

You should first complain direct to the local health authority or the Family Practitioners Committee. Your local Community Health Council can help with such a complaint.

If still dissatisfied, you should write to the Health Service Ombudsman setting out your name, address and that of the health authority concerned and details of where the complaint arose, together with details of it – and copies of any correspondence with the health authority. The Ombudsman decides if the complaint can be investigated (and will give reasons if it will not be investigated). As with the other Ombudsman services, the investigation is carried out in private. You will be sent a written report on the findings, and the remedy the authority has agreed to provide, if the complaint is upheld.

5.2   Public services/authorities

This section deals with complaints about the provision of energy, water, communications and transport services, whether by public or private authorities.

ENERGY

Gas

The Gas Consumers' Council is an independent body, with regional offices throughout Britain, which can take up complaints covering gas supply or the installation or servicing of appliances.

You should first make your complaint to British Gas (or any other gas company) direct. If still dissatisfied, you can complain to the Gas Consumers' Council for your area (the address will be in the phone book under 'Gas'). This will investigate and may take up the complaint with the gas region or the board – which does not, however, have to follow the council's recommendation.

Electricity

There are twelve regional Area Electricity Consultative Councils, whose addresses can be obtained from:

> Electricity Consumers' Council
> Brook House
> 2–16 Torrington Place
> London WC1E 7LL (01-636 5703)

These councils are independent of the Area Electricity Boards. They are financed by the Department of Trade and Industry, each having a small paid staff who will deal with consumers' complaints.

After first raising the complaint with the area board, you should contact the local Electricity Consultative Council. If they cannot resolve a particular issue they may refer it to the Electricity Consumers' Council if an issue of national importance is raised. This is also a body independent of the electricity supply industry, concerned with a wide range of issues affecting consumers of electricity.

At the time of going to press, plans to alter the structure of the electricity industry were before Parliament. You should therefore check the current position with a local advice centre.

Water

There are nine regional water authorities supplying water, sewers and sewerage services (at the time of publication). In some areas, a Water Company is authorized to supply water for that region. For the address of the local water authority, look under 'water' in the phone book.

Initially, you should complain to the appropriate water authority or company. You can then take it further by contacting:

> Water Authorities' Association
> 1 Queen Anne's Gate
> London SW1H 9BT (01-222 8111)

or:

> Water Companies' Association
> 14 Great College Street
> London SW1P 3RX (01-222 0644)

You can then raise the problem with the local Consumer Consultative Committee (whose address can be obtained from the water authority). If the complaint concerns maladministration, you may also be able to complain to a local councillor, and ask for a referral to the local Ombudsman (see above), and some complaints can also be raised with your local MP. At the time of going to press, plans to alter the structure of the water industry were before Parliament. You should therefore check the current position with a local advice centre.

COMMUNICATIONS

Post Office

The Post Office has a code of practice, setting out the standards of service it aims to achieve, levels of compensation and methods of dealing with disputes and complaints. A copy of the code is available from Post Offices.

Initially, contact your local Head/District Postmaster detailing your complaint (the address will be in the phone book). If you are still dissatisfied, you can pursue the complaint with the Regional Director, or refer it to:

Post Office Users' National Council
Waterloo Bridge House
Waterloo Road
London SE1 8UA (01-928 9458)

There are separate Councils for Scotland, Wales and Northern Ireland.

The council monitors specified services (e.g., letters, including recorded delivery/registered post, counter services, deliveries and others) and is an independent body.

British Telecom

First, make your complaint direct to the local Area Office, then to Regional Headquarters. It can then be pursued via:

Office of Telecommunications (OFTEL)
Atlantic House
Holborn Viaduct
London EC1N 2HQ (01-822 1650)

OFTEL can advise or negotiate the settlement of disputes and will provide copies of the code with which operators should comply. There may also be a local Posts and Telecommunications Advisory Committee in the area (whose address will be in the phone book) who may assist.

TRANSPORT

British Rail

There are a number of Transport Users' Consultative Committees throughout England, Wales and Scotland, concerned mainly with British Rail. They have two main functions:

- to consider complaints on the quality of service and make appropriate recommendations; *and*
- to report any hardship likely to result from the proposed closure of a passenger-line service or station.

Roads

Complaints should be made to the transport operator concerned. If there is an unresolved complaint about a service, it can be raised with the transport authority concerned. You should contact your local authority to find out the appropriate body to complain to about failures of a service.

London Transport

Complaints about bus services should be raised first with the District General Manager of the bus district. Further complaint can be made to:

> London Buses Public Relations
> 55 Broadway
> London SW1H 0BD (01-222 5600)

and complaints about the Underground to **London Underground Ltd** at the same address. Complaints can also be sent to:

> London Regional Passengers' Committee
> Golden Cross House
> 8 Duncannon Street
> London WC2 8JF (01-839 1898)

Airlines

You should complain first of all to your travel agent, tour operator, airport manager or the customer relations department of the airline concerned, as appropriate. If it cannot be resolved, you should raise the matter with:

> Association of British Travel Agents (ABTA)
> 55–7 Newman Street
> London W1P 4AH (01-637 2444)

or:

> Air Transport Users' Committee
> 129 Kingsway
> London WC2B 6NN (01-242 3882)

5.3   The police

If you have a genuine grievance against the police you can make an official police complaint. In a particularly bad case, you can bring a civil action against the police in order to obtain compensation.

The Police and Criminal Evidence Act 1984 set up the Police Complaints Authority (PCA), an independent body, and the current procedure for dealing with complaints against the police.

MAKING A COMPLAINT

If you want to make a complaint about the way the police have behaved, you should first of all try to note:

- the identity of the officers concerned (their number, or that of the police vehicle concerned);
- the date, time and place of the incident;
- any witnesses who saw what happened (and get their names and addresses);
- your own record of what happened as soon as possible afterwards, while your memory is clear;
- if any injury occurred, obtain a medical examination as soon as possible, and photographs if the injury is visible.

You may also wish to obtain legal advice on whether you have grounds for bringing a court action against the police as a result of the incident (see p. 92).

If you decide to make a complaint against a particular police officer (or generally), you should write to the police officer's Chief Constable, or in London to the Commissioner of Police for the Metropolis. You can make the complaint yourself or let someone else do so on your behalf, although they need your written consent for this. Make sure it is as accurate as possible, as the police could sue for defamation of character if the complaint is false.

The Chief Officer must record the complaint and will decide if it needs formal investigation or is appropriate for informal resolution. If the latter, the Chief Officer will appoint an officer of at least Chief Inspector rank to seek the views of the complainant and officer involved. Only minor complaints can be resolved informally and only if the complainant agrees to this. It may be appropriate where, even if the police officer had behaved in the way complained of, no disciplinary or criminal proceedings would be justified.

If a formal investigation is needed, the Chief Officer will appoint an investigating officer to look into the complaint and report back. He will talk to you and the officer – who will see your letter of complaint.

When the investigation is over, the Chief Officer may decide:

- to refer the matter to the DPP because the officer may have committed a criminal offence;
- if he feels a possible criminal offence has been committed but does not intend to refer it to the DPP, he must notify the PCA of his views and state what disciplinary action he is considering;
- if no possible criminal offence was committed, the Chief Officer must again report to the PCA and notify them of any disciplinary charges made;
- if the Chief Officer does not intend to bring disciplinary charges, he must again notify the PCA of this.

The PCA can direct the Chief Officer to refer a matter to the DPP or bring disciplinary charges where he does not intend to do so.

Serious complaints may be referred to the PCA by the Chief Officer for supervision and some complaints must be referred (e.g., where the conduct alleged caused death or serious injury). When the PCA acts in a supervisory capacity, it will approve the appointment of an investigating officer and liaise throughout the investigation. The investigating officer will report to the PCA in serious complaints.

Complaints against senior police officers are dealt with differently and they must be made to the Police Authority for the area (or the Metropolitan Police Commissioner in London). The Police Authority must then investigate the complaint and appoint a senior officer from their own/another force to investigate. The Authority will then decide whether to bring disciplinary charges or refer the case to the DPP if they find the complaint proved.

It is often difficult to prove a complaint against a police officer because a high standard of proof is needed (beyond all reasonable doubt) and often there will be no witnesses to what happened. Most complaints against the police are unsuccessful, often because the complaint is resolved in the police officer's favour when it is your word against his. If a police officer is acquitted or convicted of a criminal offence, he cannot then be disciplined for the same issue (the double jeopardy rule). If you have no satisfaction from the local Chief Constable, apply direct to:

> Police Complaints Authority
> 10 Great George Street
> London SW1P 3AE (01-273 6450)

SUING THE POLICE

If the police assault you, wrongfully arrest you, detain you without good reason, search your premises unlawfully or bring a prosecution against you without good cause, you may sue the police for:

- *assault*, e.g., for striking you without any reason after you have been arrested or for using excessive force in the course of the arrest;
- *false imprisonment*, e.g., for keeping you at a police station following a wrongful arrest (see chapter 6) or for keeping you at the police station for an unnecessarily long time;
- *trespass*, e.g., for searching your home illegally;
- *malicious prosecution*, for bringing a prosecution against you (in which you are eventually acquitted) without any good reason.

Cases against the police are difficult to bring and difficult to prove. You should take legal advice about bringing a case, and you may be entitled to legal aid (see 5.6, p. 99).

The following points should be remembered:

- If you wish to sue the police, you must start a *civil* action in the county court or the High Court. You can bring a private *criminal* prosecution against individual police officers in the magistrates' court, but such cases rarely succeed.
- Cases should normally be commenced against the Chief Constable and not individual officers.

- Cases often take two or three years, sometimes more, to come to court.
- If you win the court will award you compensation (called 'damages'). If you lose you may be liable to pay legal costs.
- The police treat the commencement of legal proceedings as an official police complaint and will ask to interview you under the complaints procedure (see above). It may be better to refuse to be interviewed if you are suing the police; if you agree to be interviewed you will give the police all the details of your evidence which you would normally keep from the police until the case gets to court. You should take legal advice about this.
- Suing the police or making a complaint may expose the complainant to the risk of being sued for defamation (see 2.2, p. 31) by the officer complained about.

In any incident in which you have been arrested or searched by the police or where you may wish to make a complaint about police conduct, it is advisable to make and keep *full notes* as soon as possible after the events in question and to collect all evidence (see 6.6, p. 152).

5.4   The professions

MEDICAL PROFESSION

There are a number of different organizations dealing with complaints against professionals in the health services.

If you have a complaint concerning provision of a service by a GP, dentist, optician or chemist you should address your complaint to the local Family Practitioner Committee (FPC) (whose address is in the phone book) for England and Wales, or the Secretary of the Health Board in Scotland, or the Chief Administration Officer of Health and Social Services Board in Northern Ireland.

Complaints should be made promptly – there is generally a time limit of six weeks in England (eight for Scotland and Northern Ireland). A medical services committee will investigate and produce a report for the FPC or Health Board, outlining the conclusions and recommendations of the investigation. The person against whom you complained will be given a copy of your letter and you will be able to reply to their comments on it. It may be necessary to hold a formal hearing to investigate your complaint, at which you give evidence.

The FPC or Health Board may, if it upholds your complaint, limit the number of patients on a GP's list, or refer the matter to a NHS Tribunal if it seems that the GP should be stopped from practising.

Complaints of serious professional misconduct may be addressed to the professional body concerned – for doctors it is:

> General Medical Council
> 44 Hallam Street
> London W1N 6AE (01-580 7642)

The Council will investigate and may give the doctor a warning or refer the matter to the Health Committee of the GMC or the Professional Conduct Committee.

Other professional bodies dealing with complaints of misconduct are:

> UK Central Council for Nursing, Midwifery and Health Visiting
> 23 Portland Place
> London W1N 3AF (01-637 7181)

> Dental Council
> 37 Wimpole Street
> London W1M 8DQ (01-486 2171)

> Pharmaceutical Society
> 1 Lambeth High Street
> London SE1 7JN (01-735 9141)

> Association of Optometrists
> Bridge House
> 233–4 Blackfriars Road
> London SE1 8NW (01-261 9661)

As with the GMC, these bodies have disciplinary committees (although their procedure varies) which can expel or impose other disciplinary action on their members.

Community Health Councils represent the interests of the public in the health service in local areas and can advise individuals on the procedure for making a complaint, and may assist with the complaint. They are usually listed under 'Community' in the phone book.

For complaints about the administration of the health service, complaints can be made to the Health Service Ombudsman (see 5.1, p. 85), after first raising the complaint with the hospital/health authority concerned.

LEGAL PROFESSION

Solicitors

If your complaint concerns the way your solicitor has dealt with you – for example, by failing to reply to your inquiries, unreasonable delay, acting for both sides in a dispute where there are conflicting interests, or overcharging – then you make your complaint to:

> Solicitors Complaints Bureau
> Portland House
> Stag Place
> London SW1E 5BL (01-834 2288)

They will investigate the complaint and can take disciplinary action against the solicitor concerned, if he has failed to observe proper standards of behaviour when dealing with you (or other solicitors).

If your complaint alleges a serious breach of the rules of professional conduct, it may be referred to the solicitors' disciplinary tribunal. This is an independent body which can strike a solicitor off the register or suspend him from practice or impose a reprimand.

Neither the Complaints Bureau nor the disciplinary tribunal can order compensation to be paid to you.

If your complaint is one of negligence (e.g., the solicitor has failed to protect your interests in the case as he should and you have consequently suffered) then your remedy may be to sue the solicitor concerned for negligence, or refer the case under the arbitration scheme. The complaints bureau can arrange an appointment for you to see a member of the negligence panel, who is a solicitor who will see you (free) for up to an hour to advise whether you have a claim against your solicitor for negligence, and how best to take it further.

If you are dissatisfied with the way your complaint against your solicitor has been investigated, you can take it up with:

> The Lay Observer
> Royal Courts of Justice
> Strand
> London WC2A 2LL (01-936 6000)

Barristers

If you have a complaint against a barrister who has acted for you – such as that he has disregarded your instructions, or touted for business – you can complain to:

> Senate of the Inns of Court and the Bar
> 11 South Square
> Gray's Inn Road
> London WC1R 5EL (01-242 0082)

who will refer the matter to its professional conduct committee. However, you cannot sue for negligence about the way the case was conducted in court, although you can complain to the Bar Council about this.

INSURANCE AND BANKING

In addition to other remedies, there is now an insurance Ombudsman who can investigate complaints concerning the conduct of an insurance company. Complaints should be raised first with the company, then with the Association of British Insurers. If the company is not a member of the Ombudsman scheme, it may be a member of the Person Insurance Arbitration Service. If the company is a member of neither scheme, you may want to consider bringing legal action against them if your complaint concerns breach of contract or negligence.

Similarly, a complaint against your treatment by a bank should be raised first with the bank and then may be referred to:

> Banking Ombudsman
> Citadel House
> 5–11 Fetter Lane
> London EC4R 1BR (01-583 1395)

OTHER PROFESSIONS

Most professionals belong to an association which can deal with complaints against their members. In general, a complaint sent to the professional body will be investigated and may be referred to a disciplinary committee consisting of other members of the profession. If the complaint is upheld, membership of the body may be withdrawn, or the person prevented from describing himself as a member of that body. The professional body will not deal with complaints of negligence where court action is appropriate, nor will it usually order financial compensation.

5.5   The media

There is no enforceable 'right to reply' over publication of matters concerning you (see 2.10, p. 56). Other than an action for defamation (see 2.2, p. 31), for which no legal aid is available, you can only complain through the following channels:

NEWSPAPERS/MAGAZINES

The most immediate way to complain about a published article is by writing to the editor setting out the basis of the complaint and, if appropriate, asking for a correction or retraction. The letter may be published (unless you mark it 'not for publication') or the editor may take up the complaint.

If dissatisfied with this, you can complain about an item you consider unethical to:

> Press Council
> 1 Salisbury Square
> London EC4Y 8AF (01-353 1248)

The complaint should be made within three months. After the Council has investigated the complaint, its judgement should be published in the paper complained of. However, it may appear long after the item which led to the complaint being made and receive little prominence (or coverage from other papers) and the Council cannot order compensation to be paid.

RADIO AND TV

Initially, complaints can be made by ringing or writing to the producer of the programme concerned, followed up by a complaint to:

> Director-General BBC
> Broadcasting House
> Portland Place
> London W1A 1AA (01-580 4468)

or the Programme Controller of a commercial station or company. If dissatisfied with the response, you can write to:

> Broadcasting Complaints Commission
> Grosvenor Gardens House
> 35 Grosvenor Gardens
> London SW1 (01-630 1966)

This is an independent body which investigates complaints about programmes by the BBC and IBA with powers set out by law. It may also investigate complaints about satellite TV programmes. It investigates written complaints concerning, for example, unjust or unfair treatment in a programme or an unwarranted infringement of privacy. The person making a complaint must be directly affected by the treatment complained of.

The BCC cannot require a broadcaster to apologize or pay compensation, and may take a long time to investigate the complaint. It can however direct the radio/TV station to publish a summary of the complaint and findings, and specify a period in which it must do so.

If the complaint concerns a commercial station, you can complain to:

Independent Broadcasting Authority
70 Brompton Road
London SW3 1EY (01-584 7011)

This is a public body responsible for ensuring the Broadcasting Act
is observed and will consider complaints (other than those subject
to legal action). There is no formalized procedure for the outcome,
although the IBA may take action with the company concerned.
At the time of going to press, the IBA had no brief to deal with
complaints about satellite TV programmes.

5.6   The courts

You may have a complaint about the way you have been treated
which cannot be resolved through the usual complaints channels.
In these circumstances you will have to consider whether you can
take court action against the person/body concerned.

LEGAL ADVICE

Before starting any court proceedings you should get advice.
Depending on your income and savings, you may be eligible for free
legal advice under the 'green form scheme' from a solicitor. This
would cover a solicitor advising whether you had grounds for
bringing a case, and advising on the procedure. It will *not* cover legal
representation in the proceedings. However, you may be eligible for
legal aid to bring the case and the solicitor can advise on this also.

Some solicitors operate the '£5 fixed fee interview' scheme,
whereby they give a one-off interview of up to thirty minutes for
£5, in which you may be able to get advice about your complaint.

Alternatively, there may be a law centre, Citizens' Advice Bureau
or other advice agency near you which can offer advice and
sometimes assistance with bringing a case.

COURTS AND TRIBUNALS

If you are claiming a sum of money, or trying to obtain a court
order for the other party to carry out some action, the most likely
place for you to bring your claim is in the civil courts. However,

some cases – for example, where you feel you have been unfairly dismissed, discriminated against on grounds of race or sex, or refused some social security benefit – are dealt with by *tribunals*. Although you may be able to get advice from an advice agency or solicitor about your case, you cannot get legal aid to be represented at the tribunal hearing.

Magistrates' courts usually deal only with criminal cases, which are normally brought as a result of the police charging or summonsing someone. A private individual can bring a private prosecution if he thinks a criminal offence has been committed, but no legal aid is available for this.

A *county court* (or High Court in some cases, for example, if you are claiming financial compensation of over £5,000) will deal with claims that someone is in breach of their contract or agreement with you, or if you are claiming that someone has broken a legal or professional duty towards you. Many claims involve allegations of negligence causing injury, for example, resulting from a road accident or accident at work, where you claim that a person or body is at fault.

HOW TO BRING A CASE IN THE COUNTY COURT

It is possible to take a case to court without being legally represented, and in county court cases where you are claiming compensation of under £500 (this figure may be increased) your case will be dealt with under the small claims court procedure. This means that neither side will usually be represented, as neither will be able to recover the costs of legal representation even if they win the case, and legal aid is not normally granted in such cases.

You can find the address of your local court in the phone book (under 'Courts'). They produce booklets to help people to act for themselves in small claims, enforcing money judgments and in undefended divorces. They will also give advice on court procedure, though not whether you have a good case.

Before starting the case, you need to know the name and address of the person/body against whom you are claiming. If it is a limited company you need to know the registered office address. The case will usually have to be brought in the county court in the area where the other side lives or carries on business, although it may be brought in the area where the cause of the action arose.

You will need to complete court forms, giving the name and address of the other party and brief details of your claim. You will also have to pay a court fee (which varies according to the sort of case it is – the court will advise on the amount). You will recover the fee if you win your case.

The court will serve the proceedings and inform you of the date of service. This is important, for if your claim is simply for money, you can apply for judgment to be given to you if no defence to the claim is entered within fourteen days from the date of service. Otherwise, the court will have to make an order as to the steps which both sides have to take before a hearing date can be given. This is to make sure that, for example, all relevant documents have been shown to each side before the hearing. You do not, however, have to tell the other side what evidence you will be calling at the hearing – for example, what witnesses you will call or what they will say.

Before the hearing you must make sure that you have copies of all the papers and letters you want to show the court and you must ask all your witnesses who can help you to come to the hearing.

If you win, the other party will usually be ordered to pay your costs (although not legal representation costs if the sum claimed is under £500). Equally, if you lose, then you may be ordered to pay the other side's costs – which can be very expensive if you are not legally aided. It is therefore as well to get advice, however strong you think your claim is, and to find out if you are eligible for legal aid before starting proceedings. You can obtain names, addresses and telephone numbers for local solicitors from local libraries, the Yellow Pages of a local phone book or from a local advice centre and should inquire about your entitlement to legal aid from the solicitor when you first contact the firm.

5.7 The European Commission and Court of Human Rights

The United Kingdom is bound by many international treaties which oblige it to respect human rights. One of the most important of these is the European Convention for the Protection of Human

Rights and Fundamental Freedoms. This treaty offers the possibility of redress where a person's civil liberties are being infringed and no remedy can be obtained from the British courts or government.

The Convention was drawn up under the auspices of the Council of Europe, an organization of West European countries which is based in Strasbourg, France, and is quite separate from the European Community. It was adopted on 4 November 1950 and came into force on 3 September 1953. Its provisions guarantee most, but not all, civil liberties, including the right to life, freedom from torture, freedom from arbitrary arrest, the right to a fair trial, the right to privacy, freedom of religion, freedom of expression, and freedom of assembly and association. The rights guaranteed by the Convention have been expanded on several occasions by the adoption of 'protocols' (i.e., additions) but the UK has yet to accept the fourth, sixth and seventh protocols. The Convention's principal shortcoming remains, however, the absence of any general prohibition of discrimination; at present it only prohibits discrimination affecting the enjoyment of the rights and freedoms set out in the Convention and protocols. The text of those rights and freedoms is set out on pp. 109–119.

The enforcement of the Convention is entrusted to the European Commission and Court of Human Rights, together with the Committee of Ministers of the Council of Europe. The Commission and Court each consist of one person nominated by each of the countries belonging to the Council of Europe. These persons act in their individual capacity and cannot be government officials. The Committee of Ministers consists of the foreign ministers (or their deputies) of the member states of the Council of Europe.

There are two ways in which alleged breaches of the Convention's provisions by the UK can be brought to the attention of these bodies. The first is through a complaint made by any of the other countries which are also bound by the Convention – Austria, Belgium, Cyprus, Denmark, France, Greece, Iceland, Ireland, Italy, Liechtenstein, Luxembourg, Malta, Netherlands, Norway, Portugal, Spain, Sweden, Switzerland, Turkey and West Germany. It was as a result of a complaint by Ireland that certain interrogation practices used in Northern Ireland were held to amount to inhuman and degrading treatment. Countries are, however, reluctant to bring cases against each other and will only do so in the most extreme cases or where their own interests are affected.

The second method of complaint – by the person whose rights have been infringed – is used much more frequently and with greater effect. Any person, non-governmental organization or group of individuals (whatever their nationality) can complain about a country bound by the Convention where it has declared that it is prepared to accept such complaints. The UK has allowed complaints by individuals since 1966 and the current declaration is in force until 13 January 1991.

The complaints can be about the law, acts of governmental bodies or the decisions of courts. They will be dealt with first by the European Commission of Human Rights and may go later to either the European Court of Human Rights or the Committee of Ministers.

During 'war or other public emergency threatening the life of the nation' governments can derogate from their obligations under the Convention. This enables them to restrict the exercise of some of the rights and freedoms, but only in so far as that is necessary to deal with the emergency. The UK has, in the past, made such a derogation with respect to Northern Ireland but none is currently in force. No derogation is ever possible in respect of the right to life (other than in respect of deaths resulting from lawful acts of war), freedom from torture and slavery and the prohibition of retrospective penalties.

USING THE CONVENTION

The procedure for making a complaint where you believe that any of your rights under the Convention has been violated is relatively straightforward. It is not, however, a speedy process (a case can take five years to be resolved) and the delays are undoubtedly exacerbated by the many complaints that do not fall within the ambit of the Convention or do not comply with its requirements. It is important, therefore, to check whether the subject-matter of your complaint has previously been considered and to ensure that you have complied with the admissibility requirements set out below. It is not essential to be represented by a lawyer but it is better to get advice from a solicitor, NCCL, or one of the organizations listed on

p. 122. Although the UK's legal aid scheme does not cover comp'aints under the Convention, limited legal aid may be provided by the Commission (but only towards the end of the examination of a complaint's admissibility and not before it is lodged) and legal costs are recoverable where a complaint is successful. There are no fees payable to the Commission and Court and there is no liability to meet the costs of the government in any event.

MAKING A COMPLAINT

A complaint does not have to be started on a special application form although you will eventually be asked to complete one. Complaints should be directed to:

> Secretary of the Commission of Human Rights
> Council of Europe
> BP 431 R6
> 67006 Strasbourg Cedex
> France

The following information will be required and should, therefore, be provided in your letter to the Commission:

- your name, age, address and occupation;
- the name, address and occupation of anyone acting as your representative (e.g., your lawyer);
- the country against whom you are complaining (e.g., the UK);
- a clear and concise statement of the facts you are complaining about – it is important to describe the events in the order in which they occurred, the way in which the legislation or decision complained about has affected you and to give exact dates;
- the provisions of the Convention on which you are relying and an explanation as to why you consider that the facts involve a violation of them;
- the object of your application (e.g., the repeal or amendment of certain legislation or the reversal of a decision);
- the details of all the remedies (including any appeal) which you have pursued within the country concerned and, where appropriate, an explanation as to why you have not pursued any available remedies;

the judgments, decisions and any other documents relating to your complaint.

Admissibility

The Commission then has to decide whether your application is admissible (i.e., falls within its terms of reference). The application will be referred to one of the Commission's members – the *rapporteur* – who may ask for further information from you or the government before reporting on the case to the Commission. It may then itself decide to ask for further information or invite the government to make observations on whether or not the application should be admitted. You will be sent a copy of the government's observations and can in turn make observations yourself. The Commission may hold an oral hearing in Strasbourg at this stage. All the proceedings before the Commission are confidential and you should not divulge information about them to the press or anyone else.

The following factors will lead to a ruling that your complaint is inadmissible:

- it was anonymous;
- it was not made within six months of the final decision relating to the alleged violation of the Convention;
- it concerned a matter already dealt with by the Commission or some other international process;
- it was incompatible with the Convention (i.e., it concerned a country, period in time or territory to which the Convention does not apply, or a right not guaranteed by it);
- the domestic remedies were not exhausted (i.e., any judicial or administrative procedure within the country concerned which could have resolved your complaint – it has to be a procedure that can lead to a binding decision and so would not include any discretionary or political remedies, such as a complaint to the Ombudsman);
- it was 'manifestly ill-founded' (i.e., the facts did not disclose any prima facie violation of the Convention);
- it was an abuse of the right of petition (e.g., the primary aim

was political, the Commission was misled, the confidentiality of the proceedings was disregarded, insulting or threatening language was used before the Commission or the government).

The overwhelming majority (95 per cent) of applications are found to be inadmissible by the Commission. This underlines the importance of a thorough evaluation of your case before you write to the Commission. There is no appeal against its decision. Moreover, a case that has been admitted can, on further examination by the Commission (or even the Court), be rejected as inadmissible.

It is likely to take at least a year before the Commission decides on the admissibility of a case but it will give priority to urgent cases (i.e., those where a person's life or well-being is immediately threatened by the action being complained about). In such cases the Commission should be contacted by telephone (010-33 88 61 49 61) or telex (Strasbourg 870 943). The Commission may then ask the government to refrain from acting until the application has been considered. Although not bound to do so, the government is likely to accede to such a request.

The later stages

If the Commission decides that your application is admissible, it will then examine the substance of your case. You and the government will be asked to present *written observations* as to whether there has been a breach of the Convention, and the Commission will usually hold a hearing in Strasbourg. When it has reached a provisional opinion on the merits of the case – which will not be published – the Commission will try to reach a 'friendly settlement' (i.e., a negotiated agreement) between you and the government.

The settlement may simply involve the payment of compensation or the making of a decision (e.g., the revocation of a deportation order) but it may also require a change in the law or administrative practice which gave rise to the complaint. The Commission has to be satisfied that any settlement takes account of the general interest (e.g., where a complaint arose out of the application of the rules restricting access by prisoners to legal advice, the settlement would require the reform of those rules as well as the payment of compensation). If a friendly settlement is agreed and approved, the Commission will prepare a brief statement of the facts and the solution reached. This is all that will be published about the case.

Where no friendly settlement is achieved, the Commission draws up a report on the case which will state whether in its opinion there has been a breach of the Convention. The report will include any dissenting views from individual members of the Commission. There is then a period of three months during which the decision whether to refer the case to the Court of Human Rights must be made. Such a decision can only be taken where the respondent state has accepted the jurisdiction of the Court (the UK has) and can only be made by the Commission or any government of a Council of Europe country involved (or whose citizen is involved) in the case; the individual applicant has no part to play in this decision. Cases tend to be referred to the Court where they involve difficult problems of interpretation or the Commission is divided. A reference is unlikely where the Court has already resolved the issue in an earlier case brought against the same government.

The proceedings before the Court amount to a fresh examination of your complaint, except on the question of admissibility. It is likely to involve written and oral submissions by the Commission, the government and yourself. You may be represented by a lawyer for this purpose. It is also possible for the Court to allow any person, organization or government to make submissions relevant to the case (e.g., the Post Office Engineering Union provided information about 'metering' in a case concerned with telephone tapping in the UK, and the International Press Institute submitted evidence on the extent to which comment on public figures was restricted in a number of countries when the Court was considering a case which had raised that issue). The case will be heard either by a chamber of seven judges or (where it raises serious questions affecting the interpretation of the Convention) the full court of twenty-one judges. The Court will issue a judgment stating whether or not the Convention has been violated. Where it considers that there was a violation, it may also (in the same or a later judgment) award you 'just satisfaction' (i.e., damages and reimbursement of your legal costs). The Court's judgment is binding on the government but it does not have any legal effect within the UK (i.e., it will not automatically overturn the legislation or decision against which you have been complaining). The government must, therefore, take the necessary steps to implement the judgment, and the Committee of Ministers is responsible for ensuring that this is done.

If the case is not referred to the Court, it will be dealt with by the Committee of Ministers. It is unlikely to require any submissions (written or oral) in addition to those already made to the Commission. The Committee can only decide that there has been a violation of the Convention by a vote of at least two-thirds of its members; in a few instances this has not been possible and the case must be left unresolved. Where it decides that the Convention has been breached, the Committee can also decide what measures the government concerned should take and may ask the Commission to make proposals regarding an award of 'just satisfaction'.

THE VALUE OF THE CONVENTION

It is often assumed by people whose civil liberties are being infringed that 'going to Strasbourg' will provide a ready solution. In fact there are many hurdles to be overcome before a case can even be considered, the procedure is slow (it may take five years from application to judgment, and a further two before its implementation by the government) and the Convention does not provide a guarantee against all infringements of civil liberties. None the less cases brought against the UK under the Convention have led to the setting aside of repressive measures and have secured important reforms in the following areas: freedom of expression; immigration; inhuman and degrading treatment; mental patients' rights; parental rights; prisoners' rights; privacy; workers' rights.

The fact that the UK is the country with the most complaints made against it under the Convention may mean either that it is one of the most repressive countries in Europe or that it is making the best use of the system. Whichever view is adopted, it is clear that without the Convention (and the right of individuals to complain) the UK would lack a valuable safeguard for its civil liberties.

The rights and freedoms protected by the Convention are set out in Articles 2 to 18 and Protocols 1, 4, 6 and 7 (the last three are not yet binding on the UK). These articles and protocols are reproduced below. The remaining articles and protocols concern the procedure for enforcing the Convention and are not included (the full text of the Convention and Protocols, together with the rules of procedure of the Commission, Court and Committee of Ministers can be found in Council of Europe – *Collected Texts* (1987)).

ARTICLE 2

1. Everyone's right to life shall be protected by law. No one shall be deprived of his life intentionally save in the execution of a sentence of a court following his conviction of a crime for which this penalty is provided by law.
2. Deprivation of life shall not be regarded as inflicted in contravention of this article when it results from the use of force which is no more than absolutely necessary:
   a. in defence of any person from unlawful violence;
   b. in order to effect a lawful arrest or to prevent the escape of a person lawfully detained;
   c. in action lawfully taken for the purpose of quelling a riot or insurrection.

ARTICLE 3

No one shall be subjected to torture or to inhuman or degrading treatment or punishment.

ARTICLE 4

1. No one shall be held in slavery or servitude.
2. No one shall be required to perform forced or compulsory labour.
3. For the purpose of this article the term 'forced or compulsory labour' shall not include:
   a. any work required to be done in the ordinary course of

detention imposed according to the provisions of Article 5 of this Convention or during conditional release from such detention;

b. any service of a military character or, in case of conscientious objectors in countries where they are recognized, service exacted instead of compulsory military service;

c. any service exacted in case of an emergency or calamity threatening the life or well-being of the community;

d. any work or service which forms part of normal civic obligations.

ARTICLE 5

1. Everyone has the right to liberty and security of person. No one shall be deprived of his liberty save in the following cases and in accordance with a procedure prescribed by law:

   a. the lawful detention of a person after conviction by a competent court;

   b. the lawful arrest or detention of a person for non-compliance with the lawful order of a court or in order to secure the fulfilment of any obligation prescribed by law;

   c. the lawful arrest or detention of a person effected for the purpose of bringing him before the competent legal authority on reasonable suspicion of having committed an offence or when it is reasonably considered necessary to prevent his committing an offence or fleeing after having done so;

   d. the detention of a minor by lawful order for the purpose of educational supervision or his lawful detention for the purpose of bringing him before the competent legal authority;

   e. the lawful detention of persons for the prevention of the spreading of infectious diseases, of persons of unsound mind, alcoholics or drug addicts or vagrants;

   f. the lawful arrest or detention of a person to prevent his effecting an unauthorized entry into the country or of a person against whom action is being taken with a view to deportation or extradition.

2. Everyone who is arrested shall be informed promptly, in a language which he understands, of the reasons for his arrest and of any charge against him.

3. Everyone arrested or detained in accordance with the provisions of paragraph 1. *c.* of this article shall be brought promptly before a judge or other officer authorized by law to exercise judicial power and shall be entitled to trial within a reasonable time or to release pending trial. Release may be conditioned by guarantees to appear for trial.

4. Everyone who is deprived of his liberty by arrest or detention shall be entitled to take proceedings by which the lawfulness of his detention shall be decided speedily by a court and his release ordered if the detention is not lawful.

5. Everyone who has been the victim of arrest or detention in contravention of the provisions of this article shall have an enforceable right to compensation.

ARTICLE 6

1. In the determination of his civil rights and obligations or of any criminal charge against him, everyone is entitled to a fair and public hearing within a reasonable time by an independent and impartial tribunal established by law. Judgment shall be pronounced publicly but the press and public may be excluded from all or part of the trial in the interests of morals, public order or national security in a democratic society, where the interests of juveniles or the protection of the private life of the parties so require, or to the extent strictly necessary in the opinion of the court in special circumstances where publicity would prejudice the interests of justice.

2. Everyone charged with a criminal offence shall be presumed innocent until proved guilty according to law.

3. Everyone charged with a criminal offence has the following minimum rights:
   a. to be informed promptly, in a language which he understands and in detail, of the nature and cause of the accusation against him;
   b. to have adequate time and facilities for the preparation of his defence;
   c. to defend himself in person or through legal assistance of his own choosing or, if he has not sufficient means to pay for

legal assistance, to be given it free when the interests of justice so require;

d. to examine or have examined witnesses against him and to obtain the attendance and examination of witnesses on his behalf under the same conditions as witnesses against him;

e. to have the free assistance of an interpreter if he cannot understand or speak the language used in court.

ARTICLE 7

1. No one shall be held guilty of any criminal offence on account of any act or omission which did not constitute a criminal offence under national or international law at the time when it was committed. Nor shall a heavier penalty be imposed than the one that was applicable at the time the criminal offence was committed.

2. This article shall not prejudice the trial and punishment of any person for any act or omission which, at the time when it was committed, was criminal according to the general principles of law recognized by civilized nations.

ARTICLE 8

1. Everyone has the right to respect for his private and family life, his home and his correspondence.

2. There shall be no interference by a public authority with the exercise of this right except such as is in accordance with the law and is necessary in a democratic society in the interests of national security, public safety or the economic well-being of the country, for the prevention of disorder or crime, for the protection of health or morals, or for the protection of the rights and freedoms of others.

ARTICLE 9

1. Everyone has the right to freedom of thought, conscience and religion; this right includes freedom to change his religion or belief and freedom, either alone or in community with others

and in public or private, to manifest his religion or belief, in worship, teaching, practice and observance.

2. Freedom to manifest one's religion or beliefs shall be subject only to such limitations as are prescribed by law and are necessary in a democratic society in the interests of public safety, for the protection of public order, health or morals, or for the protection of the rights and freedoms of others.

ARTICLE 10

1. Everyone has the right to freedom of expression. This right shall include freedom to hold opinions and to receive and impart information and ideas without interference by public authority and regardless of frontiers. This article shall not prevent States from requiring the licensing of broadcasting, television or cinema enterprises.

2. The exercise of these freedoms, since it carries with it duties and responsibilities, may be subject to such formalities, conditions, restrictions or penalties as are prescribed by law and are necessary in a democratic society, in the interests of national security, territorial integrity or public safety, for the prevention of disorder or crime, for the protection of health or morals, for the protection of the reputation or rights of others, for preventing the disclosure of information received in confidence, or for maintaining the authority and impartiality of the judiciary.

ARTICLE 11

1. Everyone has the right to freedom of peaceful assembly and to freedom of association with others, including the right to form and to join trade unions for the protection of his interests.

2. No restrictions shall be placed on the exercise of these rights other than such as are prescribed by law and are necessary in a democratic society in the interests of national security or public safety, for the prevention of disorder or crime, for the protection of health or morals or for the protection of the rights and

freedoms of others. This article shall not prevent the imposition of lawful restrictions on the exercise of these rights by members of the armed forces, of the police or of the administration of the State.

ARTICLE 12

Men and women of marriageable age have the right to marry and to found a family, according to the national laws governing the exercise of this right.

ARTICLE 13

Everyone whose rights and freedoms as set forth in this Convention are violated shall have an effective remedy before a national authority notwithstanding that the violation has been committed by persons acting in an official capacity.

ARTICLE 14

The enjoyment of the rights and freedoms set forth in this Convention shall be secured without discrimination on any ground such as sex, race, colour, language, religion, political or other opinion, national or social origin, association with a national minority, property, birth or other status.

ARTICLE 15

1. In time of war or other public emergency threatening the life of the nation, any High Contracting Party may take measures derogating from its obligations under this Convention to the extent strictly required by the exigencies of the situation, provided that such measures are not inconsistent with its other obligations under international law.
2. No derogation from Article 2, except in respect of deaths resulting from lawful acts of war, or from Articles 3, 4 (paragraph 1) and 7 shall be made under this provision.

3. Any High Contracting Party availing itself of this right of derogation shall keep the Secretary General of the Council of Europe fully informed of the measures which it has taken and the reasons therefor. It shall also inform the Secretary General of the Council of Europe when such measures have ceased to operate and the provisions of the Convention are again being fully executed.

ARTICLE 16

Nothing in Articles 10, 11 and 14 shall be regarded as preventing the High Contracting Parties from imposing restrictions on the political activity of aliens.

ARTICLE 17

Nothing in this Convention may be interpreted as implying for any State, group or person any right to engage in any activity or perform any act aimed at the destruction of any of the rights and freedoms set forth herein or at their limitation to a greater extent than is provided for in the Convention.

ARTICLE 18

The restrictions permitted under this Convention to the said rights and freedoms shall not be applied for any purpose other than those for which they have been prescribed.

PROTOCOL 1

Article 1

Every natural or legal person is entitled to the peaceful enjoyment of his possessions. No one shall be deprived of his possessions except in the public interest and subject to the conditions provided for by law and by the general principles of international law.

The preceding provisions shall not, however, in any way impair the right of a State to enforce such laws as it deems necessary to control the use of property in accordance with the general interest or to secure the payment of taxes or other contributions or penalties.

Article 2

No person shall be denied the right to education. In the exercise of any functions which it assumes in relation to education and to teaching, the State shall respect the right of parents to ensure such education and teaching in conformity with their own religious and philosophical convictions.

Article 3

The High Contracting Parties undertake to hold free elections at reasonable intervals by secret ballot, under conditions which will ensure the free expression of the opinion of the people in the choice of the legislature.

PROTOCOL 4

Article 1

No one shall be deprived of his liberty merely on the ground of inability to fulfil a contractual obligation.

Article 2

1. Everyone lawfully within the territory of a State shall, within that territory, have the right to liberty of movement and freedom to choose his residence.
2. Everyone shall be free to leave any country, including his own.
3. No restrictions shall be placed on the exercise of these rights other than such as are in accordance with law and are necessary in a democratic society in the interests of national security or public safety, for the maintenance of *ordre public*, for

the prevention of crime, for the protection of health or morals, or for the protection of the rights and freedoms of others.

4. The rights set forth in paragraph 1 may also be subject, in particular areas, to restrictions imposed in accordance with law and justified by the public interest in a democratic society.

Article 3

1. No one shall be expelled, by means either of an individual or of a collective measure, from the territory of the State of which he is a national.

2. No one shall be deprived of the right to enter the territory of the State of which he is a national.

Article 4

Collective expulsion of aliens is prohibited.

PROTOCOL 6

Article 1

The death penalty shall be abolished. No one shall be condemned to such penalty or executed.

Article 2

A State may make provision in its law for the death penalty in respect of acts committed in time of war or of imminent threat of war; such penalty shall be applied only in the instances laid down in the law and in accordance with its provisions. The State shall communicate to the Secretary General of the Council of Europe the relevant provisions of that law.

Article 3

No derogation from the provisions of this Protocol shall be made under Article 15 of the Convention.

PROTOCOL 7

Article 1

1. An alien lawfully resident in the territory of a State shall not be expelled therefrom except in pursuance of a decision reached in accordance with law and shall be allowed:
   a. to submit reasons against his expulsion;
   b. to have his case reviewed; and
   c. to be represented for these purposes before the competent authority or a person or persons designated by that authority.
2. An alien may be expelled before the exercise of his rights under paragraph 1(a), (b) and (c) of this Article, when such expulsion is necessary in the interests of public order or is grounded on reasons of national security.

Article 2

1. Everyone convicted of a criminal offence by a tribunal shall have the right to have conviction or sentence reviewed by a higher tribunal. The exercise of this right, including the grounds on which it may be exercised, shall be governed by law.
2. This right may be subject to exceptions in regard to offences of a minor character, as prescribed by law, or in cases in which the person concerned was tried in the first instance by the highest tribunal or was convicted following an appeal against acquittal.

Article 3

When a person has by a final decision been convicted of a criminal offence and when subsequently his conviction has been reversed, or he has been pardoned, on the ground that a new or newly discovered fact shows conclusively that there has been a miscarriage of justice, the person who has suffered punishment as a result of such conviction shall be compensated according to the law or the practice of the State concerned, unless it is proved that the non-disclosure of the unknown fact in time is wholly or partly attributable to him.

Article 4

1. No one shall be liable to be tried or punished again in criminal proceedings under the jurisdiction of the same State for an offence for which he has already been finally acquitted or convicted in accordance with the law and penal procedure of that State.
2. The provisions of the preceding paragraph shall not prevent the re-opening of the case in accordance with the law and penal procedure of the State concerned, if there is evidence of new or newly discovered facts, or if there has been a fundamental defect in the previous proceedings, which could affect the outcome of the case.
3. No derogation from this Article shall be made under Article 15 of the Convention.

Article 5

1. Spouses shall enjoy equality of rights and responsibilities of a private law character between them, and in their relations with their children, as to marriage, during marriage and in the event of its dissolution. This Article shall not prevent States from taking such measures as are necessary in the interests of the children.

For further details about the Convention, see 5.9, p.122.

5.8   Compensation for victims of crime

Anyone who has been injured or whose property has been damaged or stolen can sue the person responsible in the civil courts. An offender can be ordered by the criminal court to pay compensation to the victim and there is a state-financed scheme to provide compensation for victims of violent crime.

CRIMINAL COMPENSATION ORDER

If damage or injury is caused by an offender the court may make a *compensation order* in favour of the victim. Compensation may be awarded instead of, or in addition to, any penalty for the offence. It may be up to £2,000 (or £3,500 for bereavement). The court must give its reasons for not making a compensation order.

CRIMINAL INJURIES COMPENSATION BOARD

The Criminal Injuries Compensation Board (CICB) administers the scheme which provides compensation to people injured as a result of violent crime. It consists of thirteen legally qualified members appointed by the Home Secretary and the Secretary of State for Scotland.

You can claim compensation only for personal injury (not for damage to goods or property) if the injury was received in Great Britain as a result of:

a. a crime of violence (including arson and poisoning); *or*
b. the arrest or attempted arrest of a suspected offender (even though the suspect was not involved in a violent crime); *or*
c. the prevention of an offence (whether a violent offence or not); *or*
d. helping a police officer to do either (b) or (c) above.

A dependant of someone who died because of injuries received in any of these circumstances can also claim compensation from the CICB.

MAKING THE CLAIM

If you wish to claim compensation, you should obtain the application form from

> CICB
> 10–12 Russell Square
> London WC1E 7LG (01-636 2812 or 01-636 4201)

The form should be completed and returned as soon as possible; no fee is payable. You can complete it yourself or a solicitor can help you using the green-form scheme (see 5.6, p. 99). You will have to include on the form details of the injury and how it happened. The

Board's staff will then collect together police reports, details of your loss of earnings, medical reports and details of any social security payments.

The papers are then considered by a member of the CICB and an offer will be made to you. If you are dissatisfied with the offer, you can appeal to three other members of the Board who will hold a hearing at which you can be represented and you can submit further evidence, such as medical reports, and call witnesses. As with completing the application form, your legal expenses may be covered by the green-form scheme, but if you receive compensation from the Board, the money will have to be used to repay to the Law Society the cost of the legal advice.

The amount of compensation awarded should be approximately the same as would be obtained by suing the offender for damages in the civil courts, but, in practice, tends to be rather lower. The award will cover loss of earnings, expenses and compensation for pain and suffering. The value of any social security and national insurance benefits will be deducted and so will a sum for any pension received as a result of the injury.

CASES OUTSIDE THE SCHEME

The CICB will not pay compensation if:

- the injury is worth less than £550;
- the offence was not reported to the police without delay;
- the claim is for damage to, or loss of, property;
- you have not given the CICB every reasonable help, such as making medical reports available;
- the injuries were caused by a traffic offender, unless there was a deliberate attempt to run you down. You can claim from the driver's insurance company. If the driver was uninsured, or is unknown, you can claim from:

  Motor Insurers' Bureau
  New Garden House
  Hatton Garden
  London EC1N 8JZ (01-242 0033)

- the claim is not made within three years;
- the CICB decides that you provoked the incident or were misbehaving in some other way, such as taking part in a gang fight;
- you have a criminal record or associate with criminals. In these cases, the CICB has a discretion to refuse or reduce compensation.

FAMILY VICTIMS

There are additional rules if the victim is living with the offender as a member of the same family. The CICB will pay compensation only if:

- the offender has been prosecuted, even if not convicted; *and*
- the offender will not benefit from the award; *and*
- when the victim is a child, it is in the child's best interests that an award should be made.

5.9   More information

USEFUL ORGANIZATIONS

There are two organizations which may be able to help in taking cases under the Convention:

Interights, 46 Kingsway, London WC2B 6EN (01-242 5581)

Justice, 95a Chancery Lane, London WC2A 1DT (01-405 6019)

BIBLIOGRAPHY

The following books provide analysis and explanation of the Convention's case law and procedure:

R. Beddard, *Human Rights and Europe*, 2nd edn, Sweet and Maxwell, 1980.

J. E. S. Fawcett, *The Application of the European Convention on Human Rights*, 2nd edn, Oxford University Press, 1987.

H. Petzold, *The European Convention on Human Rights and Fundamental Freedoms – Cases and Materials*, 4th edn, N. P. Engel (Kehl, W. Germany), 1984.

P. Van Dyk and G. J. H. Van Hoof, *Theory and Practice of the European Convention on Human Rights*, Kluwer, 1984.

6 The rights of suspects

This chapter deals with the rights of suspects up to the point when they are either released by the police without charge, bailed by the police, or brought before a court. In particular this chapter deals with:

- Police powers to stop and search persons and vehicles (without arrest) 124
- Police powers to search premises 129
- Police powers of arrest 135
- Police detention 141
- The rights of suspects in the police station 145
- The right to make notes 152
- Special powers under the Prevention of Terrorism Act 153
- More information 161

Most of the police powers and corresponding rights for suspects are to be found in the Police and Criminal Evidence Act 1984, which is known as PACE, and in the Codes of Conduct issued by the Home Secretary under PACE and approved by Parliament. PACE was the product of years of discussion about police powers. It was based on the recommendations in the Report of the Royal Commission on Criminal Procedure (published in 1981 – HMSO, Cmnd 8092), a body which had been directed in its terms of reference to strike a balance between the interests of the community on the one hand and the rights and liberties of the individual suspect on the other.

If any of these police powers are abused:

- the abuse may make evidence obtained inadmissible in court;
- you may make an official police complaint (see 5.3, p. 90);
- in a particularly serious case you may be able to sue the police (see 5.3, p. 92).

6.1   Police powers to stop and search persons and vehicles (without arrest)

Part I of the Police and Criminal Evidence Act (PACE) empowers any constable acting with reasonable grounds for suspicion to stop, detain and search you or your vehicle, or anything in or on your vehicle for certain items, which may be seized. The provisions of the Act are supplemented by a Code of Practice on stop and search. The contents of the Code must be observed by the police, although the remedy for failure to observe it is usually to make a police complaint (or if prosecuted to raise an objection in court) rather than to take legal proceedings against the police (see 5.3, p. 90).

PACE creates a new power of stop and search, and also provides some safeguards for other police powers of search. These relate to drugs (on reasonable suspicion of being in unlawful possession), evidence of liability to arrest under the Prevention of Terrorism legislation, suspected possession of firearms, animal conservation and evidence of offences under the Sporting Events (Control of Alcohol etc.) Act 1985. For search powers on arrest, see 6.3, p. 140.

STOLEN OR PROHIBITED ARTICLES OR KNIVES

The new power enables a constable to search for stolen or prohibited articles or knives (except shortbladed penknives see 1.3, p. 24). PACE defines two categories of prohibited article:

- an offensive weapon; *and*
- an article made or adapted for use in connection with one of a list of offences including burglary, theft, taking a conveyance without authority (or being carried in one) and obtaining property by deception. Virtually any article could come within this definition but there would have to be some evidence of the use of the article or the intention of the person making, adapting or carrying it, otherwise a constable would not have reasonable grounds to search.

WHERE THE SEARCH MAY TAKE PLACE

This new power of stop and search may be used by the police in most public and some private places. In law the power is limited to one of the following types of place:

- a place to which, at the time of the proposed stop and search, the public (or any section of the public) has access as a matter of legal right or because there is permission; *and*
- any place (other than a dwelling) to which people have ready access at the time of the proposed stop and search.

These categories are obviously very wide and can include much private property, including front gardens and car parks. Whether you have ready access might depend on whether a gate or door is locked, or whether a plot of land is fenced.

However, a constable may not search you or your vehicle if you are on land which is used for the purpose of a dwelling, without having reasonable grounds for believing that you do not reside in the dwelling and are not in the place with the express or implied permission of a person who does reside in the dwelling.

There is clearly a heavy duty on the constable in such cases, since the reasonable grounds must be justified objectively. These provisions should protect people behaving normally: window cleaners, post and milk deliverers and casual visitors.

REASONABLE GROUNDS FOR SUSPICION

The power of stop and search under PACE can only be exercised if the constable has reasonable grounds for suspecting that stolen or prohibited articles will be found. The Code of Practice elaborates this requirement. There must be some concrete basis for the officer's belief, related to you personally, which can be considered and evaluated by an objective third person. Mere suspicion based on hunch or instinct might justify observation but cannot justify a search.

Reasonable grounds for suspicion cannot be based on attitudes or prejudices towards certain types of people, such as membership of a group within which offenders of a certain kind are relatively common (e.g., young football fans). Nor can it be based on your skin colour, hairstyle, mode of dress, or previous convictions.

STOPPING AND DETAINING

Any police officer, whether or not in uniform, may search you personally, but usually only a constable in uniform may stop a vehicle. A police officer may detain you or your vehicle for a search, but not in order to find grounds to justify a search. The reasonable grounds must already exist.

The detention may only last for so long as it is reasonably required to permit a search to be carried out at the place of detention or nearby. The Code provides that it is an unusual search that cannot be completed within a minute or so. You cannot be compelled to remain with your vehicle while the vehicle is searched, but you may wish to do so.

The Road Traffic Act 1972, gives power to a police officer to stop a vehicle, for example to check whether it is roadworthy or stolen, but not to search it.

SEARCHING

In carrying out a search the police may not force you (but may request you) to remove any clothing in public (even if the street is empty) other than an outer coat, jacket or gloves. A more thorough search, involving the removal, e.g., of a hat or shoes, or a strip search (but not an intimate search: see below) may take place other than in public, but only at the place of arrest or nearby. Thus it could take place, for example, in a police van. The Code lays down rules for searching in the absence of members of the opposite sex and for minimizing any embarrassment.

The power to search a vehicle includes a power to search anything in or on it. If an unattended vehicle is searched, a notice to this effect must be left behind (inside the vehicle if reasonably practicable) stating the police station to which the constable is attached, that any claims for compensation should be made to that police station, and that you are entitled to a copy of the search record if requested within twelve months of the search.

A constable may use reasonable force, if necessary, in the

detention and conduct of the search, but force can only be necessary if you are first given the opportunity to co-operate and refuse.

A constable who discovers an article reasonably suspected to be stolen or prohibited may seize it. It should be noted that the safeguards in PACE and in the Code of Practice do not apply to the routine searching of those entering sports grounds etc., with their consent or as a condition of entry or under some other legal power.

INFORMATION TO BE GIVEN

A constable contemplating a search under any power to search (before or without arrest) must take reasonable steps to bring to your attention:

- if the constable is not in uniform, proof that he or she is a constable, which the Code says must be by showing a warrant card;
- the constable's name and police station;
- the object of the proposed search;
- the constable's grounds for proposing to search; *and*
- the availability of a search record (see below) if it is practicable to make one.

The search may not be commenced until the constable gives you such information, and the information *must* be given even if not requested, although it is unclear how much detail must be given.

SEARCH RECORDS

A constable who has carried out a search under any power to search (without or before making an arrest) must make a written record on the spot, or later if impracticable on the spot, unless it is totally impracticable to make a record at all. The Code suggests that it will not be practicable to make a record if a considerable number of searches are quickly required such as during public disorder or searches of football crowds.

The Code requires the search record to include a note of whether you are 'White, Afro-Caribbean or Asian'. The record must identify the person making it and state the object of the search, the grounds for making it, the date, time and place, whether anything, and if so what, was found, and whether any, and if so what, injury or damage resulted from the search.

You are entitled to get a copy of any record made, on request, within twelve months of the date of the search.

ROAD BLOCKS

The provisions in PACE dealing with road blocks (referred to in PACE as road-checks) have been widely misreported and mis-understood. PACE does not create any new power to set up road blocks. The power to do so derives from the Road Traffic Act 1972, and from common law breach of peace powers (see 1.3, p. 25).

'STATUTORY UNDERTAKERS' – OTHER POLICE FORCES

'Statutory undertakers' include bodies authorized by statute to carry on a railway, transport, dock or harbour undertaking, the larger of which employ their own police forces (e.g., the British Transport Police) whose members have the powers of constables within a geographically limited area. Members of these forces have many of the same powers as members of regular police forces, subject to certain limitations. These are not the same as private security organizations which enjoy no special 'policing' powers.

A constable employed by a statutory undertaker may stop, detain and search any vehicle (but not a person) before it leaves a goods area on the premises of the statutory body.

Such stops are carried out routinely and need not be justified by any suspicion nor recorded. There is no statutory limitation on what may be searched for and the Code of Practice does not apply.

6.2   Police powers to search premises

The police have power to enter and search your premises for many reasons. Some of these powers are set out in the Police and Criminal Evidence Act 1984 (PACE) but the police also have power to enter and search under other statutes, for instance the Theft Act 1968. It should be noted that the police do not always need to have a search warrant, although they must always have a reason for the search. There is a Code of Practice stating how the police should conduct searches. (For what you should do if the police do not follow the Code see p. 123).

SEARCH WITH YOUR CONSENT

The police may search your premises if you consent. However, the Code of Practice on searching premises provides that before seeking your consent the officer in charge should state the purpose of the proposed search and inform you that you are not obliged to consent. For the search to be lawful you must consent *in writing*. If you live in rented accommodation the police should not search the premises solely on the basis of your landlord's consent unless you are unavailable and the matter is urgent.

SEARCH OF PREMISES UNDER A MAGISTRATE'S WARRANT

Magistrates have the power to issue search warrants under many Acts of Parliament, for example to search for stolen goods under the Theft Act 1968, Misuse of Drugs Act 1971 and for racially inflammatory material under the Public Order Act 1986. In addition they have a power under the Police and Criminal Evidence Act to issue a warrant authorizing the police to enter and search premises for evidence of a *serious arrestable offence* (see 6.3, p. 137). They were given this power in order to fill in gaps in the earlier law. For example, magistrates did not have any power to issue a warrant to enable the police to search for a murder weapon.

Magistrates should only issue warrants under this section if there are reasonable grounds for believing that the police will not be able to obtain access to the evidence without a warrant, for example, if consent will not be forthcoming. In addition magistrates should be satisfied that there are reasonable grounds for believing:

- the material is likely to be of substantial value (whether by itself or together with other material) to the investigation of the offence; *and*
- that it is likely to be 'relevant evidence', that is, anything which would be admissible as evidence at a trial; *and*
- that it does not consist of or include items subject to legal privilege, 'excluded material' or 'special procedure material' (see below).

This new power clearly extends search warrants to premises owned or occupied by someone who is not implicated in the alleged offence.

MATERIAL WHICH HAS SPECIAL SAFEGUARDS

PACE gives special protection from search (but not necessarily from seizure) to some types of material felt to be sensitive. These categories are 'excluded material', 'special procedure material' and legally privileged material.

Excluded material

There are three kinds of 'excluded material':

- personal records – examples of material which should normally be excluded are medical and psychiatric records, records kept by priests, the Samaritans, possibly school and college records, records of advice given by law centres, Citizens' Advice Bureaux, the National Council for Civil Liberties;
- human tissue or tissue fluid;
- 'journalistic' material – i.e., material acquired or created for the purposes of journalism. There is no need for the holder of such material to be a professional journalist.

In order to qualify as 'excluded material' the items must have been held in confidence. This is a concept which can be legally complex.

The police cannot easily obtain a warrant to search for this material. They must follow a set procedure which will normally involve a hearing before a judge who will decide, amongst other things, whether it would be in the public interest to allow the police access to the material. Only the person in possession of the material, who will not necessarily be the suspect, and the police may make representations at the hearing. If the judge considers it appropriate he will make an order compelling production of the material to the police.

If the person in possession fails to produce the material he may be in contempt of court (see 2.6, p. 41) and the judge may be able to issue a warrant to the police to search his premises. However, in some circumstances, if the police can convince the judge that the situation is urgent they may be able to obtain a warrant from the judge without the party in possession of the material knowing.

Special procedure material

There are two categories of special procedure material:

- material which is not excluded material but is held in confidence by certain persons; *and*
- journalistic material which is not excluded material, either because it is not held in confidence or does not consist of documents.

Examples of special procedure material are company accounts or stock records held on behalf of a client by a bank, solicitor or accountant. The procedure enabling the police to obtain this material is broadly the same as for 'excluded material' (see above).

Legally privileged material

The definition of items subject to legal privilege is crucial, since these items are exempt from most powers of search. The police have no power at all to seize material which they have reasonable grounds for believing to be legally privileged.

There are three categories of legally privileged material:

- communications to do with giving legal advice;
- communications to do with legal proceedings;
- items connected with either of the above communications.

In each category the definition hinges on the term 'professional legal adviser', which clearly includes barristers, solicitors and solicitors' clerks. There is no requirement that the adviser should work for a firm of solicitors and, therefore, the adviser may come from a law or advice centre. Although the advice of an unqualified person will not be privileged unless acting as agent for a solicitor or barrister, it will in most cases be 'excluded material'. This would not protect it from seizure, however (see below).

Items held with the intention of furthering a *criminal purpose* are not legally privileged, but clearly a letter from a solicitor advising a client of potential criminal liability if a particular course of conduct were pursued would be privileged.

ENTRY AND SEARCH WITHOUT A SEARCH-WARRANT

The police are given powers to enter premises without a warrant by many Acts of Parliament, for example, under the Gaming Act 1968 they have power to enter licensed premises to carry out inspections. Other powers include searches for drugs under the Misuse of Drugs Act 1971, for articles under the Obscene Publications Act 1959, for illegal immigrants under the Immigration Act 1971, and for firearms under the Firearms Act 1968. In addition, they may have the right to enter premises without a warrant to deal with or prevent a breach of the peace (see 1.3, p. 25). The Police and Criminal Evidence Act provides them with several other powers:

- to execute a warrant of arrest or commitment;
- to arrest someone for an arrestable offence;
- to arrest someone for various offences under the Public Order Acts 1936 and 1986 (such as riot, violent disorder, affray, threatening behaviour and disorderly conduct) and the Criminal Law Act 1977 (offences relating to trespass);
- to recapture a person who has escaped from lawful custody.

The police officer need not be in uniform unless entering in connection with the Public Order Acts or the Criminal Law Act. He has a power to search the premises but this is only to the extent that is *reasonably* required for the purpose of entry. Any further search may be unlawful and may be the subject of a complaint or civil action (see 5.3, p. 90).

SEARCH OF PREMISES ON ARREST

The Police and Criminal Evidence Act 1984 (PACE) provides the police with clear authority to enter and search premises after arrest. If you have been arrested for an 'arrestable offence' (see above) the police may search premises occupied or controlled by you for evidence of that offence or of some other arrestable offence connected with or similar to that offence. The police officer conducting this search should normally have written authorization for the search by an officer of at least the rank of inspector, with him, or her.

If you have been arrested for any offence (not just an 'arrestable offence') the police may enter and search any premises you were in at the time of arrest or immediately before it for evidence of the offence for which you were arrested. Again, in both cases the police are only permitted to search to the extent reasonably required to find the evidence sought and if the search is excessive you may have the remedy of a police complaint or a civil action against the police.

CONDUCT OF SEARCHES OF PREMISES

The conduct of searches is governed by the Police and Criminal Evidence Act 1984 (PACE) and the Code of Practice (see 6.1, p. 124). A search warrant may authorize anyone to accompany the constable who is executing it. Entry and search must be within one month from the date of the warrant's issue. You have a right to see the warrant and to be supplied with a copy. You are also entitled to see the police officer's warrant card as a means of identification if he is not in uniform. If you are not present but someone else who appears to the police to be in charge of the premises is available then they have the same rights as you. A warrant authorizes entry on one occasion only.

The police have a right to use force if necessary to effect an entry or search, but only such force as is reasonable. All searches should take place at a reasonable hour, unless the constable conducting the search believes that the purpose of the search would be frustrated by waiting until such time. You are entitled to have a friend or neighbour to witness a search (although you do not have a right to delay a search unreasonably in your search for a witness), unless the officer in charge has *reasonable* grounds for feeling this would seriously hinder the investigation.

The warrant must be endorsed afterwards by the police to show the following:

- whether articles specified in the warrant were found;
- whether any other articles were seized;
- the date and time of its execution;
- the names of the officers who executed it; *and*
- whether a copy was handed to the occupier or left at the premises.

The occupier of the premises which have been searched has a right to inspect the search warrant (which should have been returned to the magistrates' court), within twelve months.

SEIZURE OF PROPERTY

When the police are lawfully on any premises (which includes being there with your consent) they have wide powers to seize *anything* on the premises if they have reasonable grounds for believing that:

- it has been obtained in consequence of the commission of an offence; *or*
- it is evidence in relation to *any* offence; *and*
- it is necessary to seize it in order to prevent it being seized, lost or damaged, altered or destroyed.

'Anything' includes fingerprints. The police may require computerized information which comes within these categories to be produced in a form in which they can remove it. 'Excluded material' and 'special procedure material' (see above) are not protected from seizure once the police are lawfully on the premises. No power of seizure, however, authorizes the seizure of material reasonably believed by a constable to be legally privileged.

If you request it, the police must provide a record of seized items within a reasonable time. Seized articles may be retained so long as is necessary, for example, for production in court, but the articles cannot be kept for use as evidence in a trial or for forensic examination if a photograph or copy would suffice.

6.3   Police powers of arrest

You may be summonsed in writing to appear before a criminal court (as with most motoring offences), or you may be brought before the court after an arrest.

The police may arrest with or without a warrant. There are many powers of *arrest under a warrant* issued by a Justice of the Peace or Judge and the rules governing each of them is set out in the statute creating the power. This section deals with police powers of *arrest without warrant.*

The powers of arrest without warrant are governed by the Police and Criminal Evidence Act 1984 (PACE) and can be grouped into the following categories:

● arrest at common law for breach of the peace;
● summary arrest for an 'arrestable offence';
● arrest subject to conditions;
● arrest under specific powers; *and*
● arrest for the purpose of fingerprinting.

ARREST FOR BREACH OF THE PEACE

A breach of the peace is not in itself a criminal offence (as it is in Scotland – see 15.2, p. 327), but it may give rise to a power of arrest. For full details see 1.3, p. 25.

SUMMARY ARREST FOR 'ARRESTABLE OFFENCES'

PACE uses the phrase 'summary arrest' to mean arrest without warrant and lists the arrestable offences for which the police can arrest without warrant.

The following are arrestable offences:

- offences for which the sentence is fixed by law (including murder – life imprisonment);
- offences carrying a maximum sentence of imprisonment for five years or more (these include serious offences of violence and dishonesty, but also some relatively minor offences such as shoplifting and minor criminal damage);
- various statutory offences including offences under the Customs and Excise Management Act 1979, under the Official Secrets Acts 1911 and 1920, under the Sexual Offences Act 1956, and under the Theft Act 1968 (including taking a motor vehicle without the consent of the owner, and going equipped for theft).

This power of arrest may be carried out by either a *police officer* or *any other person* (a 'citizen's arrest') in the following circumstances:

Any person may arrest:

- anyone actually committing or whom he reasonably suspects to be committing an arrestable offence; *or*
- (where an arrestable offence has been committed) anyone who is guilty or whom he reasonably suspects to be guilty of the offence.

A police officer may arrest:

- in the same circumstances as any person (above); *and also*
- anyone who is or whom he reasonably suspects to be about to commit an arrestable offence; *or*
- (where he reasonably suspects an arrestable offence has been committed) anyone whom he reasonably suspects to be guilty of the offence.

'Serious arrestable offences'

There is a further concept in PACE described as the 'serious arrestable offence'. The definition of a 'serious arrestable offence' does not affect the powers of arrest, but the more draconian police powers under PACE relating to the detention of a subject can be invoked where the offence is a 'serious arrestable offence', such as detention without charge for up to ninety-six hours, denial of access to a solicitor and delaying notification of detention to a friend for up to thirty-six hours, the authorization of road-checks etc.

The following are serious arrestable offences:

- treason, murder, manslaughter, rape, kidnapping, incest or intercourse with a girl under thirteen, buggery with a boy under sixteen or a person who has not consented, indecent assault constituting gross indecency, causing an explosion likely to endanger life or property, certain offences under the Firearms Act 1968, causing death by dangerous driving, hostage-taking and aeroplane hijacking;
- any other arrestable offence if its commission has led or is intended or is likely or is threatened to lead to any of the following consequences: serious harm to the security of the state or to public order, serious interference with the administration of justice or with the investigation of offences, the death or serious injury (including disease and impairment) of any person, or a substantial financial gain or serious financial loss to any person;
- (for the purposes of denial of access to a solicitor and notification of detention) certain offences under the prevention of terrorism and drug trafficking legislation.

ARREST SUBJECT TO CONDITIONS

Often, in a minor case, an arrest should be unnecessary. The alleged offender can be summonsed by post to attend court on a particular date, and there is no need to go to a police station at all.

However, PACE also gives the police a power of arrest for all offences, no matter how trivial, petty or minor, which do not carry a power of arrest under the previously discussed powers. This power of arrest can only be used where:

- a constable has reasonable grounds for suspecting that you have committed or attempted, or are committing or attempting to commit an offence (but not where it is suspected that an offence *will* be committed in the future); *and*
- it appears to the constable that *service of a summons is impracticable or inappropriate* because any of the general arrest conditions (see below) is satisfied.

Thus, the assumption is that the police should proceed by way of *summons* for minor offences, and the power of arrest ought to be used only if this is impracticable or inappropriate. The impracticability or inappropriateness of the summons must arise from one of the *general arrest conditions*:

Name and address

- if your name is unknown to, and cannot be readily ascertained by, the police (you cannot be made to wait while your name is ascertained or confirmed, but might agree to do so to avoid being arrested);
- if the police have reasonable grounds for doubting that you have given your real name;
- if you have failed to furnish a satisfactory address for the service of a summons (i.e., one at which it appears to the constable that you will be for a sufficiently long period to be served or at which some other specified persons will accept service of a summons);
- if the police have reasonable grounds for doubting whether an address furnished is satisfactory.

Prevention

- if the police have reasonable grounds for believing that an arrest is necessary to prevent you causing physical injury to yourself or to somebody else, or suffering physical injury, or causing loss of or damage to property (including your own), or committing an offence against public decency, or causing an unlawful obstruction of the highway (see 1.2, p. 16).

Protection

- if the police have reasonable grounds for believing that arrest is necessary to protect a child or other vulnerable person (undefined) from you.

If you have been arrested under this power, and are on the way to the police station, you must be released if a constable is satisfied that there are no longer any grounds for keeping you under arrest – for example, if you suddenly find some kind of identification or if there is no longer any risk of damage or injury.

ARREST UNDER SPECIFIC POWERS

The specific statutory powers are listed in PACE and some subsequent legislation, and relate mainly to the armed forces, animals, absconders, children, and offences under legislation concerning immigration, emergency powers, public order, trespass and the prevention of terrorism. They are not subject to the general arrest conditions (set out above), but many of them carry other conditions (for example, that the arresting constable must be in uniform). These powers of arrest include, for example, powers under the Road Traffic Act 1972 to arrest motorists for drink driving offences.

ARREST FOR FINGERPRINTING

This power of arrest is designed to apply to somebody who appears at court after receiving a summons and who has not been taken to a police station under arrest. A constable may make an arrest without a warrant in order to have fingerprints taken at a police station. The following conditions must apply:

- you must have been convicted of a recordable offence;

- you must not have been fingerprinted in the course of the police investigation (or in connection with any matter since conviction); *and*
- you must have failed to comply, within seven days, with a requirement made within one month of the date of conviction to attend a police station for fingerprinting.

INFORMATION TO BE GIVEN ON ARREST

An arrest is unlawful unless you are told that you are under arrest and the grounds for the arrest at the time. This information must be given at the time of the arrest or as soon as practicable afterwards. The information need not be given if it was not *reasonably practicable* to do so because of your escape from arrest before it could be given. If you attend voluntarily at a police station (or any other place with a constable) without having been arrested you are entitled to leave at will unless placed under arrest.

ARREST OTHER THAN AT A POLICE STATION

After arrest, a constable must take you to a police station as soon as practicable (subject to certain exceptions and the power to release you *en route*). However, a constable may delay taking you to a police station if your presence elsewhere is necessary in order to carry out such investigations as it is reasonable to carry out immediately, such as a search of premises.

SEARCH OF A PERSON ON ARREST (OTHER THAN AT A POLICE STATION)

A police officer may search you to the extent reasonably required if there are reasonable grounds for believing that:

- you may present a danger to yourself or to somebody else; *or*
- you may have concealed on you anything which might be used to assist an escape from lawful custody or which might be evidence relating to any offence.

There are similar restrictions on searching in public to those discussed above (see 6.1, p. 126).

6.4   Police detention

The circumstances in which an arrested person may be kept in police detention are set out in the Police and Criminal Evidence Act 1984 (PACE). The detention is not lawful unless the provisions of PACE are complied with. A key figure in the scheme is the 'custody officer', a police officer of at least the rank of sergeant.

Normally, the period of detention without charge should not exceed twenty-four hours, although in some cases the maximum period, with extensions, is as long as ninety-six hours. There are a number of stages at which continuation of custody must be authorized, in the early stages by police officers and in the later stages by magistrates. Provision is made for the appointment of custody officers and the performance by them (and any other constable in charge of the prisoner) of important duties. In particular, if the custody officer becomes aware (perhaps after representations from a solicitor) at any time that the grounds for the detention have ceased to apply and that there are no other grounds for continued detention, it is the duty of the custody officer to order your immediate release from custody. Conversely, you may not be released except on the authority of a custody officer at the police station where detention was last authorized.

ON ARRIVAL AT, OR AFTER ARREST AT, THE POLICE STATION

The custody officer must, as soon as practicable after your arrival at the police station (or after arrest at the police station), determine whether there is sufficient evidence to charge you with the offence for which the arrest was made. He may detain you for as long as is necessary to make such a determination. If the custody officer decides that there is sufficient evidence to charge you, then you should be charged and must be released unless one of the post-charge detention conditions applies (see p. 145).

DETENTION WITHOUT CHARGE

If the custody officer decides that there is insufficient evidence to charge you, then you must be released, unless he has reasonable grounds for believing that detention without charge is necessary to secure or preserve evidence relating to an offence for which you are under arrest, or to obtain such evidence by questioning you. In such a case he may order further police detention, but the grounds for the detention must be recorded in writing on the custody record. You must be given these reasons.

Detention without charge cannot be authorized in your own interest, or to prevent the repetition or continuation of an offence, or to authorize police 'fishing trips' (since the evidence must relate to an offence for which you are under arrest). If the custody officer has reasonable grounds to believe that you will not answer questions (for example, because your solicitor has said so), detention cannot be necessary to obtain evidence by questioning, and detention for questioning in such circumstances may well be unlawful.

There are special rules relating to children and the rules set out here only apply to those aged fourteen or over, or to younger children arrested for homicide. Other children are dealt with under the Children and Young Persons Act 1969.

The code of practice on detention, treatment and questioning prohibits the placing of any juvenile in police cells, unless no other secure accommodation or practicable supervision is available. In any event, the juvenile may not be placed in a cell with an adult. There are also rules as to the identifying of and giving information to those responsible for the juvenile's welfare.

A juvenile who is not released after being charged should, if practicable, be transferred to the care of a local authority.

Review of detention

Periodic reviews of detention must be carried out for all persons in police custody pending the investigation of an offence. If you have been charged, the review is carried out by the custody officer. If you have not been charged, it is carried out by an officer of at least the rank of inspector who has not at any stage been directly involved with the investigation.

The general rule is that *the first review* must be *not later than six hours* after the detention was first authorized, and *subsequent reviews* must take place at *intervals of not more than nine hours*.

Before deciding whether to authorize your detention, the review officer must give you (unless asleep) and your solicitor (or the duty solicitor) an opportunity to make oral or written representations. Representations by a solicitor may be made over the telephone. A non-solicitor (e.g., a solicitor's employee or an unqualified law centre worker) does not have the same statutory right to make representations – but there is provision in the code to hear representations from such persons unless a senior officer considers that such a visit will hinder the investigation of the crime. The representations might relate, for example, to the amount of evidence already obtained, or to your refusal to answer questions, these matters being connected with the grounds on which continued detention can be authorized.

The detention clock

PACE limits the length of time for which you can remain in police detention. Such limitations are based on the passage of time from a particular point.

The general rule is that the time starts on your arrival at the first police station to which you are taken after arrest. If arrest takes place at the police station the time starts when you are arrested. There may be some delay between arrest and arrival caused by necessary investigation, but there is a general provision that an arrested person must be taken to a police station as soon as practicable after arrest.

There are special rules if the arrest takes place outside England and Wales or in a different Police Area from the one in which you are arrested. Questioning in transit is prohibited by the Code.

Detention limits and police extensions

The general rule is that you may not be kept in police detention for more than *twenty-four hours* without being charged. This period can be extended by a maximum of *twelve hours* on the authority of an officer of the rank of superintendent or above after giving opportunity for representations to be made.

The extension can only be authorized where:

- the officer has reasonable grounds for believing that the offence is a serious arrestable offence (see 6.3, p. 137);

- the investigation is being conducted diligently and expeditiously; *and*
- detention without charge is necessary to secure or preserve evidence of an offence for which you are under arrest or to obtain evidence by questioning.

The authorization cannot last beyond *thirty-six hours* from when the detention clock began.

Detention limits and magistrates' extensions

You must be released by the end of *thirty-six hours* from the starting point, unless an application is made to a magistrates' court sitting in private.

The application is made on oath by a police officer and supported by a written 'information', which must state the nature of the offence, the general nature of the evidence for the arrest, what inquiries have been made and are proposed, and the reason for believing the continued detention to be necessary.

You are entitled to a copy of the information and to be legally represented (you can have an adjournment to obtain legal representation). The police officer will be at court to be cross-examined and representations may be made to the magistrate(s). These might be directed, for example, towards any delay in the investigation or in making the application, whether there is a serious arrestable offence involved, whether detention is necessary, and whether there is sufficient evidence for you to be charged.

The court may only authorize further detention if:

- the offence is a serious arrestable offence;
- the investigation is being conducted diligently and expeditiously; *and*
- further detention is necessary to secure or preserve evidence relating to the offence or to obtain such evidence by questioning you.

The court may authorize further detention for up to *thirty-six hours* from the time that the application is granted.

A further extension of up to *thirty-six hours* may be granted if the same procedure is followed. The total maximum period of detention is *ninety-six hours* from the original starting point (except under the Prevention of Terrorism Act where the maximum is seven days – see 6.7, p. 156).

DETENTION AFTER CHARGE

After you have been charged, the custody officer must order your release unless one of the *post-charge detention conditions* applies:

- your name or address is unknown or doubted;
- detention is necessary to prevent physical injury or damage to property, your non-appearance at court, or interference with the investigation or the administration of justice; *or*
- a juvenile needs to be detained in his or her own interest.

A person who has been detained after charge must normally be taken to court on the day after the day of charge (unless that following day is Sunday, Christmas Day or Good Friday).

6.5   The rights of suspects in the police station

The rights of suspects after arrest are contained principally in the Police and Criminal Evidence Act 1984 (PACE) and in the Code of Practice on the Detention, Treatment and Questioning of persons and the Code of Practice on Identification of Persons by the police.

It is in this area that the provisions of the Codes are most important. Any breaches by the police may result in disciplinary action against them and, if the breaches are sufficiently serious, any confession you make may not be admitted as evidence in a trial (see p. 123). The Codes contain detailed provisions governing the conditions of detention, for instance on the right to legal advice and the right not to be held incommunicado, as well as on searches, exercise and medical treatment. The Codes also provide that if you are classed as a vulnerable person, for instance if you are mentally handicapped or a juvenile, an appropriate adult (not a police officer) should be present to look after your interests.

PERSONAL SEARCHES AT THE POLICE STATION

The custody officer (see 6.4, p. 141) is under a duty to list all the property you have with you on your custody record. You may be searched, using reasonable force if necessary (if you refuse to co-operate), by a police officer of the same sex, and you should be told the reasons for the search. You are allowed to check the list of property and you should only sign it if it is correct.

Clothes and personal effects (not including cash) may only be seized if the custody officer believes you may use them to cause physical injury to yourself or to somebody else, to damage property, to interfere with evidence, to assist an escape, or if he has reasonable grounds for believing that they may be evidence relating to an offence.

Strip searches

A *strip search* may take place if the custody officer considers it necessary, but he has no power to authorize an *intimate body search* (see below). The courts have recognized that strip searches may be deeply humiliating and that the removal of a brassiere, for instance, would require considerable justification. No person of the opposite sex who is not a medical practitioner or nurse may be present at such a search, nor anyone whose presence is unnecessary. Reasons for a strip search and the results of the search must be recorded.

Intimate body searches

An intimate body search consists of the physical examination of any one or more of a person's bodily orifices, including the anus, vagina, mouth, ear and nose. The police can only carry out an intimate body search in limited circumstances. They can search you *if you consent*, or if a police officer of at least the rank of superintendent has reasonable grounds for believing that:

- you may have concealed on you either something which you could use to cause physical injury to yourself or to others, and that you might so use it while you are in police detention or in the custody of a court; *or*
- you have concealed Class A drugs (heroin and cocaine, but not cannabis or amphetamines) on yourself and that you are in

possession of the drugs either with intent to supply them to somebody else or with a view to committing a customs offence.

A search for drugs (Class A drugs only) may only be carried out by a registered medical practitioner or a registered nurse. It should only be carried out at a hospital, at a registered medical practitioner's surgery or at some other place used for medical purposes. An intimate search for potentially harmful items should also be carried out by a doctor or nurse, but may be conducted by a police officer if an officer of at least the rank of superintendent believes that it is not practicable for it to be carried out by a doctor or nurse. The search may be carried out at a police station.

THE RIGHT TO DECENT CONDITIONS

The Code says that there should only be one person in each cell, but only 'so far as is practicable'. Police cells must be adequately heated, cleaned, ventilated and lit. Bedding should be clean. Access to toilet and washing facilities must be provided.

The police should check on persons in cells once an hour, or every half hour on those who are drunk.

At least two light meals and one main meal shall be offered in any period of twenty-four hours. Brief outdoor exercise shall be offered daily 'if practicable'.

THE RIGHT TO MEDICAL TREATMENT

A detained person is entitled to a medical examination by a police surgeon on request (but not for minor ailments). He may also be examined by a GP of his own choice at his own expense. He is entitled to have medication where appropriate.

The custody officer must also call the police surgeon if a detained person is injured, or appears to be suffering from physical or mental illness, or otherwise appears to need medical attention.

All of this must be recorded on the custody record and when a doctor is called he must also make a record.

THE RIGHT TO LEGAL ADVICE

If you are arrested and held at a police station or other premises you have a statutory right to consult a solicitor (if you wish), in private and free of charge at any time. A duty solicitor scheme should be in operation at every police station in England and Wales, so that free telephone advice or a free visit from a solicitor is available. You should be informed by the custody officer, orally and in writing, of this right, the right to have someone informed of the arrest (see below) and your right to consult the Codes of Practice on detention at a police station.

Access to legal advice may be delayed by the police, however, if you are detained for a 'serious arrestable offence' (see 6.3, p. 137), a drug trafficking offence or certain other specified offences where the police are attempting to recover property, and you have not yet been charged with an offence for up to thirty-six hours from the relevant time, or for up to forty-eight hours in the case of a person detained under the Prevention of Terrorism legislation (see 6.7, p. 153). Delay may be authorized only by an officer of at least the rank of superintendent if he has reasonable grounds (which must be recorded in writing) for believing that the exercise of the right to legal advice would lead to:

- interference with evidence of a 'serious arrestable offence';
- harm to others;
- the alerting of accomplices; or
- hindering the recovery of property.

(There are further grounds where a person is detained under the Prevention of Terrorism legislation.) Once the reason for authorizing delay ceases to exist there may be no further delay in permitting access.

The Code provides that if you ask for legal advice you should not be interviewed until you have received it, unless delay is authorized (as above), or an officer of at least the rank of superintendent reasonably believes that delay caused by waiting for a solicitor involves risk or harm to persons or property or would unreasonably delay the investigation, or if you consent in writing or on tape to the interview going ahead.

THE RIGHT NOT TO BE KEPT INCOMMUNICADO

If you are detained in a police station or other premises you are entitled to have one friend or relative or person who is known to you or likely to take an interest in your welfare, notified, at public expense, of your whereabouts. This right is subject to the same delay as consultation with a solicitor (see above). You may exercise this right each time you are transferred to another police station.

With juveniles, the police have an additional duty to inform a parent or guardian as soon as practicable and to request their attendance at the police station. There are no provisions permitting delay.

THE CONDUCT OF INTERVIEWS

The conduct of interviews is covered by the Code of Practice. The overriding principle is that all persons in custody must be dealt with expeditiously, and released as soon as the need for detention has ceased to apply. An accurate written record should be made of each interview (whether or not it takes place at a police station) unless the interview is tape recorded. You have a right to see the interview record, and you should only sign it if it records *exactly* what you have said.

Interviews should normally be in 'contemporaneous note' form, that is, questions and answers should be written down at the time. But less formal interviews which are subsequently written up by police officers in their note books are still quite common and you usually have no chance to check the accuracy of their notes. The use of prolonged or oppressive questioning, or the denial of access to a solicitor, or other breaches of the Codes or the Act (so long as they are not merely technical) may render confessions inadmissible in evidence at court.

Questioning should cease as soon as the interrogating officer believes that there is sufficient evidence for a prosecution to be brought successfully. You should then be taken before the custody officer and charged or informed that you may be prosecuted.

THE RIGHT OF SILENCE

It is a fundamental principle of English law that you need not answer any questions or provide any information which might tend to incriminate you. You should be cautioned on arrest, on arrival at the station and before questioning, to remind you of this right. The caution should be in the following or similar terms: 'You do not have to say anything unless you wish to do so, but what you say may be given in evidence.' No adverse inference may be drawn from this silence at any trial that takes place, but in practice both juries and magistrates may draw their own conclusions.

In 1988 the government restricted the right of silence in Northern Ireland by permitting the prosecution and the judge to invite the jury's attention to the defendant's silence at the police station or in court (if the defendant declines to give evidence) and to invite them to draw adverse inferences from that silence. Similar restrictions are expected to be introduced in England and Wales in later 1989 or early 1990.

FINGERPRINTS

Fingerprints (the term includes palmprints) may be taken from anyone over the age of ten *without consent* and without a court order in any of the following circumstances:

- if an officer of the rank of superintendent or above believes that fingerprints will confirm or disprove involvement in an offence and authorizes the fingerprinting; *or*
- if you have been convicted of a recordable offence; *or*
- if you are charged with a recordable offence or informed that you will be reported for such an offence, and fingerprints have not already been taken in the course of the investigation.

Recordable offences are specified in regulations.

Where fingerprints are taken without your consent reasons must be given before they are taken and those reasons must be recorded. Reasonable force may be used.

If the police obtain your *consent* to fingerprinting it must be in writing if given at a police station. Consent in the case of a child (aged ten to fourteen) is the consent of his parents alone and in the case of a young person (aged fourteen to seventeen) of his parents and himself.

PHOTOGRAPHS

Your photograph may not be taken without your consent unless you have been convicted of a recordable offence (see above) and your photograph is not already on record. The police may not use force to take a photograph.

INTIMATE AND NON-INTIMATE SAMPLES

An *intimate sample* is a sample of blood, semen or any other tissue fluid, urine, saliva or pubic hair or a swab taken from a bodily orifice. In Northern Ireland, however, a mouth swab is classed as a non-intimate sample. An intimate sample (other than urine or saliva) may only be taken by a medical practitioner, and only if an officer of at least the rank of superintendent authorizes it and you consent in writing (consent for juveniles is the same as for fingerprinting). The authorization may only be given if the officer has reasonable grounds for believing the sample will confirm or disprove involvement in a serious arrestable offence. If you refuse to consent 'without reasonable cause' the court or jury may (in committal proceedings or at a trial) draw such inferences from the refusal as appear proper, and the refusal may be treated as corroboration of any evidence against you to which the refusal is material. This provision was inserted with rape suspects in mind. The provisions for breath tests and blood or urine samples in cases of drunk drivers are quite separate.

A *non-intimate sample* is a sample of hair other than pubic hair, a sample taken from a nail or from under a nail, a swab taken from any part of a person's body other than an orifice, and a footprint or a similar impression of any part of a person's body other than a part of his hand.

Non-intimate samples may be taken with your written consent (consent for juveniles is the same as for fingerprinting) or without consent where you are in police detention or being held in custody on the authority of a court and an officer of at least the rank of superintendent authorizes it. He may do this if he has reasonable grounds for believing the sample will confirm or disprove your involvement in a serious arrestable offence. Reasons for taking the sample must be provided to you and recorded.

DESTRUCTION OF FINGERPRINTS, PHOTOGRAPHS AND SAMPLES

If you are prosecuted for an offence and acquitted, or if you are not prosecuted, all samples, fingerprints, photographs, copies and negatives must be destroyed as soon as practicable. You are entitled to be present to witness the destruction of your photographs and fingerprints.

Fingerprints and samples taken under the Immigration Act or the Prevention of Terrorism legislation may, however, be retained.

IDENTIFICATION BY WITNESSES

Procedures for identification parades or other group identifications, confrontation by witnesses and the showing of photographs to witnesses are set out in detail in a Code of Practice.

If identification is in dispute an *identification parade* must be held if you want one and if it is practicable to hold one. You are entitled to have a solicitor or friend present. An identification parade should have at least eight persons (in addition to the suspect) who, so far as possible, resemble the suspect in age, height, general appearance and position in life. Two suspects should not be on the same parade unless they are of roughly similar appearance.

If you refuse to go on a parade or if it is impracticable to have one then there may be a *group identification*. Again, you may have a solicitor or friend present. Only if it is impossible to conduct either of the above, either because you will not consent, or through impracticability, should you be *confronted* directly by a witness. You have no right of veto over this last method, but the confrontation must take place in the presence of your solicitor, interpreter or friend, unless this would cause unreasonable delay.

6.6   The right to make notes

If you have been involved in any incident with the police or you have witnessed an incident, it is advisable to make and keep *full notes* as soon as possible after the events in question.

The police are allowed to refer to notes in court. This happens not because police officers have some special status as witnesses (they do not), but because the notes are *contemporaneous notes*, that is, notes which are made at the time or as soon as reasonably practicable thereafter. Contemporaneous notes are not in themselves evidence, but they can be used to refresh the witness's memory.

You have the same right to use notes. A delay in writing the notes of several hours or even a day or so may not prevent you from using the notes. Even if you cannot use them at court they will be a helpful record of the events.

If you are detained at a police station the codes of conduct provide that you should be supplied on request with writing materials.

When making a note:

- write out a full and legible note of everything that happened in the correct sequence of events;
- write down everything that was said, word for word if possible, particularly any conversation you had with police officers;
- record the name and number, if you know them, of the police officers involved;
- sign the notes at the bottom, and put the time and date;
- if you see a solicitor, hand over the notes and make sure you get a copy to keep for yourself;
- if you are going to court take the notes with you.

If there are *witnesses* to the incident take the names and addresses of the witnesses if possible and ask them to make notes.

If you have been injured (for example, by the use of excessive force by the police during your arrest), you must:

- have *photographs* taken if there are any visible injuries;
- see a *doctor* so that your injuries are recorded.

The photographs and medical evidence may be of great value to you if you are charged with a criminal offence or if you wish to make a police complaint or sue the police (see 5.3, p. 90).

6.7   Special powers under the Prevention of Terrorism Act

The Prevention of Terrorism (Temporary Provisions) Act 1989 (PTA) covers the whole of the UK. It is based on three earlier Acts, the first of which was rushed through Parliament after the Birmingham pub-bombings in November 1974. The 1974 and 1976 Acts mainly

covered activities associated with affairs in Northern Ireland. The
1984 Act, however, extended the power of arrest for questioning to
cover anyone suspected of being involved in 'international terrorism',
for example, anyone suspected of being associated with or knowing
about political violence in the Middle East, India or any other part
of the world. The 1989 Act creates new offences and court powers
of restraint and forfeiture relating to terrorist funds. It also creates
new powers of investigation into terrorist activities.

The PTA does not deal directly with acts of violence usually
associated with the word 'terrorism', such as bombings and killings.
These are crimes under ordinary criminal law. It is essentially a law
that increases the power of the police to detain and interrogate
anyone who may have information about 'terrorism', whether or
not they are personally involved. Terrorism is defined as 'the use of
violence for political ends'. It includes 'any use of violence for the purpose of putting the public or any section of the public in fear'. The PTA
is also intended to discourage support for certain Irish organizations.

It has been largely forgotten that this Act was first introduced as
a temporary measure for six months and, while it must be renewed by
Parliament each year, it has effectively become an integral part of our
criminal law. This section covers the provisions of the Act as they
apply to acts of political violence related to Irish or international
affairs. Great Britain includes England, Scotland and Wales. The
United Kingdom includes Great Britain and Northern Ireland.

ARREST AND QUESTIONING

Under the PTA, a police officer can arrest you without a warrant if
he has 'reasonable grounds' to suspect that:

- you are involved in the 'commission, preparation or instigation
  of acts of terrorism' connected with Northern Ireland or any
  foreign country. Any act connected solely with the UK or any
  part of the UK unconnected with Northern Ireland is not
  covered by the PTA; or
- you belong to or support any section of the Provisional or Official
  IRA, or the INLA (see banned organizations 15.1, p. 317); or
- you have solicited, lent, given or received money or other
  property for use in connection with acts of terrorism, or you

have been involved with the movement of terrorist funds; *or*
- you wear, carry or display anything in public which gives rise to reasonable fear that you are a member or supporter of a banned organization; *or*
- you are subject to an exclusion order and enter a territory forbidden to you, or you have helped or given accommodation to any excluded person while they were in a territory forbidden to them (see exclusion orders p. 157).

If you are unsure that you are being arrested under the PTA ask the police officer making the arrest which power is being used. Once arrested, the police can detain you for up to forty-eight hours, and then for up to a further five days with the consent of the Secretary of State (see 5.7, p. 103). During this time, they do not have to charge you or take you before a court.

During your detention, the police (or prison officer) can take any 'reasonably necessary' steps to identify you, including photographing, fingerprinting and measuring you without your consent or a court order and with reasonable force if you refuse.

It is a *criminal offence* not to give the police, or the Army if in Northern Ireland, specific information you may have about people or events concerned with acts of political violence connected with Irish affairs. You should always be careful not to pass on anything based on rumour, and you are not obliged to pass on any information at all if you have a reasonable excuse, for example, if the information incriminates you personally or if you would have reason to fear for the safety of either yourself or your family. You can be fined and/or imprisoned if convicted. Although very few have actually been charged or convicted of this offence, people have been threatened with this during interrogation. This offences does not apply to information relating to acts of international terrorism. Other than the offence of 'withholding information', the general principle of the 'right to silence' applies during detention under the PTA and you are therefore not obliged to answer any other type of question (except about your identity). For restrictions on the right of silence, see 6.5, p. 150.

Your rights under the PTA are, in certain other respects, more limited than those of other suspects. For example, in England and Wales, the 'safeguards' provided in the Police and Criminal Evidence

Act (see 6.5, p. 150) do not apply to limit the circumstances in which you can have your fingerprints taken or provide circumstances under which they will be destroyed. Under the related Code of Practice you do not have an absolute right to legal advice until after forty-eight hours and then, under certain circumstances, a senior officer can decide that you can only consult your solicitor in the sight and hearing of a police officer unconnected with your case. You do not have an absolute right to have someone informed of your detention, even after forty-eight hours. The related Code of Practice does not, however, restrict the physical conditions of your detention, and your heating, meals, lighting etc., should therefore be the same as for other suspects, as should those concerning medical treatment. Nevertheless, the police do not have to keep a custody record of your detention unless you are formally arrested (for further details about PACE and the Code of Practice, as they generally apply, see 6.5, p. 145).

An arrest under the PTA does not necessarily mean that you have been suspected of a specific offence; the vast majority of people are released without being charged.

EXAMINATION OR DETENTION AT PORTS OR AIRPORTS

Under the PTA, you can be stopped, questioned and detained by an *examining officer* while entering or leaving Great Britain or Northern Ireland to find out whether you have any connection with, or information about, the use of violence in relation to Irish or international affairs, or whether you have breached an exclusion order or assisted someone else to do so.

Examining officers can be police, immigration or certain customs and excise officers and, in Northern Ireland, soldiers. They can require you to fill in a Landing or Embarkation Card, which asks for your name and the details of your address, occupation, name of your employer, address where you will be staying and the purpose of your trip. They can also require you to produce a passport or other papers establishing nationality and identity, or produce any other documents considered relevant. They can search any baggage and keep anything which they consider could be relevant in a court case or in considering an exclusion order. You can be asked any reasonable question.

If you are examined for more than an hour you should receive a

Notice of Prisoner's Rights. You can be detained for up to twelve hours in the absence of any suspicion; after this the officer must have 'reasonable suspicion' to continue your detention and you should receive a Notification of Further Examination. As with PTA arrests elsewhere, you cannot be held beyond forty-eight hours without the authority of the Secretary of State and, with the appropriate authority, you can be held for up to a total of seven days (see 5.7, p.103).

It is an *offence* to refuse to comply with directions from an examining officer and you can be fined and/or imprisoned if convicted.

SEARCH OF PERSONS OR PREMISES

Under the PTA you can be stopped and searched without a warrant if the police suspect you of being involved in terrorism and need to establish if you are carrying anything which makes you liable for arrest. You can also be stopped and searched if you are suspected of supporting a banned organization or of breaking an exclusion order.

The police can apply to a magistrate for a warrant to search premises in the usual way (see 6.2, p. 129). However, they can also carry out a search with a note signed by a superintendent (or officer of higher rank) if he considers the case is one of great public emergency.

Using these powers of search the police can seize anything considered to be evidence of an offence relating to a proscribed organization or an exclusion order, or which would justify the Secretary of State exercising powers of proscription or exclusion.

EXCLUSION ORDERS

Under the PTA, an exclusion order can be used to expel you from either Great Britain or Northern Ireland, or from the whole of the UK. This process does not happen through the courts. Instead, the Secretary of State – usually the Home Secretary or Secretary of State for Northern Ireland – signs an order when satisfied that:

- it appears expedient, in order to prevent acts of terrorism intended to influence government policy or public opinion with respect to Northern Ireland affairs;

- you are or have been concerned in the 'commission, preparation or instigation of acts of terrorism'; *or*
- you are attempting to enter Great Britain or Northern Ireland with a view to being concerned in the 'commission, preparation or instigation of acts of terrorism'.

Terrorism is defined as the use of violence designed to influence public opinion or government policy with respect to *affairs in Northern Ireland.* This includes any use of violence intended to put the public or any section of the public in fear. You cannot, therefore, be excluded if you are believed to be only *involved* in international terrorism. It is possible, however, that you could be deported under the Immigration Act (see 10.3, p. 237). 'Commission, preparation or instigation' covers any type of involvement.

Restrictions on exclusion

The type of exclusion order depends on whether or not you are a UK citizen.

If you are a UK citizen you cannot be completely excluded from the UK. You can, however, be forbidden to enter (or be in) either Great Britain or Northern Ireland unless you are already excluded from one of these areas or you have been living in the area from which you are to be excluded for the previous three years (not including time spent in prison in the UK, Channel Islands or Isle of Man). If you are excluded you will be removed to the part of the UK you are allowed to be in.

If you are not a UK citizen, you can be forbidden to enter or be in the UK or any part of it. Before excluding you the Secretary of State should consider whether you have connections which would make it appropriate to send you to another country. You can be excluded irrespective of the length of time you have been living in the UK.

Challenging exclusion

If you are excluded, you should be given a written order that says this and tells you about your *right to object* as soon as possible. If you want to object, you must write to the Secretary of State within seven days and try to prove your case. If you ask, you also have the *right to a private interview* with a government adviser appointed by the Secretary of State. You can have a solicitor with you at this interview if the adviser agrees. You will remain in custody while the Secretary of State considers your arguments against exclusion. If you do not make representations within seven days you will be removed whether you agree to this or not. If you agree to being removed before making representations you must write making your case against exclusion and asking for an interview, if you want one, within fourteen days of your removal. By making representations after you are removed you lose your absolute right to an interview, since you can only have one if the Secretary of State considers it 'practicable'.

If you follow this procedure the Secretary of State must consider whether or not to cancel the order, taking into account the report of any interview with the adviser, the adviser's opinion and anything else considered relevant. You can ask people to write supporting your case. However, you cannot call a witness or appeal to a court. The procedure also denies you your right to know what evidence has satisfied the Secretary of State that you should be excluded or the reasons why your representations against the order are successful or not. In a test case taken by NCCL, the government's arguments for this, based principally on grounds of national security, were accepted by the court. You cannot, there-fore, be confident of being able to provide the evidence necessary to challenge adequately the decision. It is, nevertheless, worth mak-ing representations since a number of orders are cancelled as a result.

If your exclusion is not cancelled after you make representations it will last for *three years*. The Secretary of State can then make a new order excluding you for another three years after considering a review of your case. This is done by the Home Office which writes to you at your last known address asking you to fill in a form or write if you want to take part in that review. You may also be offered an interview with the police and you can ask to take a solicitor to this. If you do not hear from the Home Office you can write asking if you are still excluded and, if necessary, asking for a review. If you are excluded for another three years you can write making representations against this within fourteen days.

Related criminal offences

You can be arrested and charged if you have received an exclusion order and do not obey it or if you help anyone who you know has broken their exclusion order. You can be fined and/or imprisoned if convicted. The consent of the Attorney General is necessary before you can be prosecuted.

BANNED ORGANIZATIONS

Any organization in Britain can be banned ('proscribed') under the PTA if it *appears* to the Secretary of State to be involved in terrorism in the UK that is connected to affairs in Northern Ireland, or appears to be promoting or encouraging it. Organizations in Northern Ireland are banned under the Emergency Provisions Act (see 15.1, p. 317). Organizations which appear to be connected with international terrorism cannot be banned. An organization is defined as any association or combination of people. The Provisional and Official IRA were proscribed in 1974, and the INLA in 1979.

Related criminal offences

It is a criminal offence:

- to belong or to say you belong to a proscribed organization, except where you prove that you were a member before the organization was banned and that you have not been a member since;
- to raise or receive money or goods on behalf of a banned organization or to encourage any other form of support for it, except where you can prove that you did not know the money or goods were for this purpose;
- to help organize a public or private meeting of more than three people in support of a banned organization, or where a speaker belongs or says he belongs to one of these organizations, except where you prove that you did not know this was the case;
- to display, carry or wear in public anything which gives rise

to a reasonable fear that you are a member or supporter of a banned organization, even if you are not.

Apart from the IRA and INLA, it is not illegal to belong to any other group or party in Great Britain and, provided you do not call for support for a banned organization or for political violence, you can express any views you like about the situation in Northern Ireland. The IRA and INLA are also illegal in Northern Ireland under the Emergency Provisions Act, as are certain other organizations and groups (see 15.1, p. 317).

What to do if arrested, excluded or charged

If you are arrested, questioned, excluded or charged under the PTA you should contact NCCL who can give you advice and, if necessary, arrange for you to see a solicitor with experience of the PTA. It is also important to let NCCL know about your case and help in the efforts being made to monitor the way this Act is being used. NCCL is the only organization which has monitored the Prevention of Terrorism Acts in detail, and we hope that by bringing together information not easily available elsewhere to alert all those concerned with civil liberties to the dangers inherent in the continued existence of this law.

6.8   More information

BIBLIOGRAPHY

D. Feldman, *The Law Relating to Entry, Search and Seizure*, Butterworth, 1986.

F. Hargreaves and H. Levenson, *A Practitioner's Guide to the Police and Criminal Evidence Act 1984*, Legal Action Group, 1985.

J. Harrison, *Police Misconduct: Legal Remedies*, Legal Action Group, 1987.

Home Office, *Police and Criminal Evidence Act 1984: Codes of Practice*, HMSO, 1985.

Information Sheets on the Prevention of Terrorism Act, NCCL, 1985.

L. H. Leigh, *Police Powers in England and Wales*, 2nd edn, Butterworth, 1985.

C. Scorer *et al.*, *The New Prevention of Terrorism Act: The Case for Repeal*, NCCL, 1985.

7 The rights of defendants

This chapter deals with:

7.1   Advice and representation

If the police suspect that you have committed a crime, they can either arrest you, if they have lawful authority to do so (see 6.3, p. 135), or ask a magistrate to issue a summons. They must, with a few exceptions, do this within six months of the offence. If the magistrate agrees to issue a summons (which they usually do), it will be served on you by the police, probably by post, and will tell you what offence you are accused of and where and when you have to go to court. Although this procedure is used for less serious offences, if you do not turn up in court a warrant may be issued for your arrest. Some other bodies like the DHSS and the Customs and Excise can also bring criminal proceedings.

Whoever brings the proceedings and whether they use a summons or arrest you, it is advisable to have advice from a lawyer as soon as possible. You may think your innocence will be obvious to the court, but you cannot be sure you will be believed. Court procedure can be confusing and the rules of evidence which govern what you can and cannot say are complicated. If you are found guilty, a lawyer can tell the court about any special circumstances which might help to reduce the penalty you receive.

LEGAL ADVICE

If you receive a summons, you can go to a solicitor or a law centre for advice on whether to plead guilty or not guilty and what penalty you are likely to receive if found guilty. If you are charged by the police, instead of being summonsed, you may be released on bail (see 7.6, p. 167) and will be able to go to a solicitor or law centre. This advice may be free if you are within the financial limits of the legal advice scheme.

If the police keep you in custody, you will be entitled to receive advice from a duty solicitor chosen from a rota for that area. The duty solicitor can also apply to the court for you to be given bail and he can help you make an application for a legal aid order.

7.2   Legal advice and legal aid

To receive legal aid you must complete an application form which you can get from a solicitor or a magistrates' court. It must be completed and sent to the magistrates' court where you have to appear. The application must be granted if you cannot pay for your own defence and if it is in the interests of justice that you should be defended. Refusals of legal aid are rare, except on financial grounds, if the offence is a serious one or there are complicating factors in the case. If the application is granted the legal aid order is sent to your solicitor, if you have one, or to a solicitor you can choose from a list kept at the court. The legal aid order may say you have to contribute towards the cost of defending the charge. It will cover any proceedings in the Crown Court as well as the magistrates' court.

USING A MCKENZIE ADVISER

If you are refused legal aid and cannot afford to pay a lawyer privately, or you prefer to defend yourself, you are entitled to have a friend with you in court. This friend cannot speak openly to the court but he can sit beside you, take notes and give you advice. The friend is known as a McKenzie adviser because of the case which confirmed this right.

As soon as possible after the case begins you should say to the court: 'I would like to have a friend as a McKenzie adviser to sit beside me to help me in representing myself.' If this application is refused, you should ask for an adjournment to obtain legal advice because the High Court can compel magistrates to accept the presence of a McKenzie adviser and you can get civil legal aid for your application to the High Court.

If you are representing yourself in committal proceedings (see 7.4, p. 165), the prosecution cannot hand to the court copies of the statements made by their witnesses. They must call the witnesses to give evidence.

If you have been refused bail and are remanded in custody, you must be brought to the court every eight days. It is only if you are legally represented that longer periods are permitted.

7.3   The right to trial by jury

All criminal cases start in the magistrates' courts and approximately ninety-six per cent of them are finally dealt with there. The rest go to higher courts called Crown Courts, where the case is heard by a judge and jury. The type of offence decides which court will deal with the case.

- If the offence can be dealt with only in the magistrates' court it is called a 'summary offence';
- If it can be dealt with only in the Crown Court it is called an 'indictable offence';
- If it can be dealt with by either court it is called an 'offence triable either way'.

Whether to choose trial by jury of 'an offence triable either way' is a difficult decision requiring legal advice and also, because of the possible consequences, discussion with your family. Amongst the things to bear in mind in making a decision are:

- the case is likely to be heard sooner in a magistrates' court than a Crown Court;
- the chances of acquittal by a jury are greater than by magistrates;
- penalties are generally lighter in a magistrates' court but they can send a defendant to the Crown Court for sentencing if they think it is appropriate.

7.4 Committal proceedings

If you are charged with an indictable offence, or an offence triable either way which is being treated as an indictable offence, the magistrates must decide if there is enough evidence to send you for trial to the Crown Court. This can be done by accepting the written statements of the prosecution's witnesses, or by the defence insisting that they be called to give evidence in court. Usually, the statements are accepted but sometimes there are advantages in not doing so and you should get careful legal advice on which course to choose.

Remember that the magistrates are not deciding if you are guilty or not; they have only to decide if the prosecution's evidence shows there is a case for you to answer.

7.5 The right to appeal

APPEALS FROM THE MAGISTRATES' COURT

If you are convicted in a magistrates' court of a summary offence or an 'either-way' offence you may appeal to the Crown Court against the conviction and the sentence, unless you pleaded guilty. You can appeal against the sentence even if you pleaded guilty, except for certain orders, such as a probation order, an order for payment of costs or an order which the court is compelled to make, for example, an order for the endorsement of a driving licence.

An appeal must be made within twenty-one days of the sentence, unless the Crown Court extends this time limit in exceptional circumstances. You can obtain the appeal forms from the magistrates' court or the Crown Court. The forms must be completed and returned to the magistrates' court and a copy sent to the prosecutor. You should also apply to the magistrates' court for legal aid and, if you are in custody, for bail to be granted until the appeal is heard. If bail is refused you can apply to the Crown Court.

The hearing of the appeal against conviction does not involve a jury even though there is a complete re-hearing of the case. The Crown Court may confirm, reverse or change the decision of the magistrates' court. The hearing of the appeal against sentence is usually on the basis of the facts given to the magistrates, and no evidence need be called. In both cases, the Crown Court can impose any sentence which the magistrates' court could have given, whether greater or less than the one they actually gave.

APPEALS ON A POINT OF LAW

If you think the magistrates made a mistake in law, you can appeal to the Divisional Court of the Queen's Bench Division of the High Court. The application can be made by a letter to the clerk to the magistrates and must be made within twenty-one days of the decision. You must say in your letter why you think they were wrong in law and ask them to state a case for the opinion of the High Court. They may ask you to guarantee the costs up to a certain sum (e.g., £500) before they agree to state a case, or they might refuse to state a case on the ground that the application is frivolous. If they refuse, they must give you a certificate of refusal if you want one and you can then go to the High Court for an order compelling them to state a case.

Because this procedure is complicated, you should obtain legal advice under the green-form scheme and legal aid under the civil legal aid scheme. Your lawyer will also consider applying for emergency legal aid and for you to be granted bail if you are in custody.

APPEALS FROM THE CROWN COURT

An appeal against conviction or sentence after a trial on indictment is to the Court of Appeal (Criminal Division). The necessary forms

can be obtained from the Crown Court or the Registrar of Criminal
Appeals. You should ask your lawyer to help you to complete them.
If leave to appeal is necessary, the application is considered by a
single judge. If he refuses, you can have the application heard by
the full court of three judges. You cannot appeal against a sentence
which is fixed by law, such as life imprisonment for murder.

APPEALS TO THE HOUSE OF LORDS

An appeal from the Court of Appeal to the House of Lords is only
possible if it is on a point of law which is of 'general public
importance'. Permission must be given either by the Court of
Appeal or the House of Lords itself. Very few criminal appeals reach
the House of Lords; the procedure is complicated and expensive and
legal advice is essential.

7.6   The right to bail

'Bail' means that you are released from custody either by the police
or by a court, but you have a duty to appear either at a police station
or a magistrates' court at a specified time. Failure to appear without
a reasonable excuse is an offence in itself. Bail can be granted by a
court subject to conditions, but the police cannot impose any
conditions. The most common conditions are to report to a police
station at specified times, to reside at a particular address, to stay
indoors between certain hours, not to interfere with witnesses, to
surrender your passport and to provide one or more sureties.

SURETIES

A surety is someone who undertakes to forfeit a sum of money if
you do not appear in court for your trial. The exact sum is fixed by
the court when granting bail and the court decides if someone is a
suitable surety by considering:

- the person's financial position;
- the person's character; *and*
- how effective the person is likely to be in influencing you to
  attend court.

BAIL AT A POLICE STATION

For your rights before you are charged see chapter 6. After you
have been charged, you must be given bail unless:

- your name and address are unknown or doubted on reasonable
  grounds;
- the custody officer reasonably believes detention is necessary
  for your own protection or the protection of others or their
  property;
- the custody officer reasonably believes you will fail to appear
  at court or that detention is necessary to avoid interference
  with the investigation or the administration of justice.

BAIL AT THE MAGISTRATES' COURT

An accused person is entitled to bail unless certain exceptions
apply. Because you are allowed only one full application for bail,
unless there is a change of circumstances, you should make sure
you have as much information as possible to support your
application. If the offence *does not* carry a prison sentence, bail must
be granted unless:

- you have previously been given bail and failed to come to
  court;
- the court believes you should be kept in custody for your own
  protection;
- you have been granted bail in connection with the present
  charge and have broken the conditions of your bail or been
  arrested for absconding.

If the offence *does* carry a prison sentence, bail must be granted
unless the court believes:

- any of the above conditions apply;
- you would probably not turn up for your trial;
- you would probably commit an offence while on bail;
- you would probably interfere with witnesses or in some other
  way obstruct the course of justice.

In deciding whether or not to give you bail, the court must consider:

- your character, background, associations and community ties;
- your record in turning up for trial after receiving bail;
- the strength of the evidence against you;
- anything else which the court thinks relevant.

If the police object to your being given bail, you or your lawyer can question the police officer on any point on which you think he or she is wrong. You can then make a statement to the magistrates explaining why you think you should be given bail.

BAIL AT THE CROWN COURT

You can apply to a Crown Court judge for bail if:

- the magistrates refuse bail and certify that they have heard a full application;
- you are sent to the Crown Court for sentence;
- you are sent to the Crown Court for jury trial.

If you have legal aid for your case it will cover an application for bail.

BAIL BY A HIGH COURT JUDGE

You can apply to a High Court judge in chambers when:

- you are refused bail; *or*
- the magistrates have imposed conditions you do not accept.

This appeal is heard in private and you can apply either through your own lawyer or through the Official Solicitor who is an official of the High Court. Applications made by your own lawyer are more likely to be successful but legal aid is not available to do this, so it will be necessary for you or your family to find the money. If you want to use the Official Solicitor, the prison should be able to provide the necessary form.

REASONS FOR BAIL DECISIONS

Normally, a court has to give reasons if it *refuses* to grant bail but, under the Criminal Justice Act 1988, a court must give the reasons why it *grants* bail in murder, manslaughter and rape cases, if it is contrary to the view of the prosecution.

7.7   Spent convictions and the rehabilitation of offenders

The Rehabilitation of Offenders Act 1974 was an attempt to counter, at least in part, the effects of the belief that 'a leopard never changes its spots'. It was felt to be unfair that people who had at some time in the past acquired a conviction, should have to carry it around their necks for the rest of their lives. The Act, therefore, provides an opportunity for offenders to wipe the slate clean.

HOW A SENTENCE BECOMES SPENT

The Act applies to all types of sentences whether prison, a fine, probation, absolute or conditional discharges, findings in a juvenile court that an offence has been committed, and convictions of certain offences in service disciplinary proceedings.

The rehabilitation period depends on the sentence and runs from the date of conviction. When the period has expired, the sentence becomes 'spent' and need not be revealed in the future, e.g., when applying for a job, completing an insurance proposal form, applying for credit facilities or for a tenancy of a property. The table opposite sets out the rehabilitation periods according to sentence.

The following sentences can never become spent:

- a sentence of imprisonment of more than 2½ years;
- a life sentence;
- detention during Her Majesty's pleasure.

If you are convicted during the rehabilitation period of an offence which can only be tried in the magistrates' court, it will carry its own rehabilitation period and will have no effect on the earlier one. If the second offence is more serious and you receive a sentence within the limits of the Act, the earlier conviction will become spent only when the later one becomes spent.

Sentence	Rehabilitation period	
Prison for more than 2½ years	never	
Prison for more than 6 months but not more than 2½ years	10 years	These periods are reduced by half if the offender was under 17 at the date of conviction
Prison for 6 months or less	7 years	
Fine	5 years	
Cashiering, discharge with ignominy or dismissal with disgrace from Her Majesty's service	10 years	
Dismissal from Her Majesty's service	7 years	
Detention in respect of conviction in service disciplinary proceedings	5 years	
Borstal	7 years	
Detention for over 6 months but not more than 2½ years	5 years	
Detention for 6 months or less	3 years	
Hospital order under Mental Health Act 1983	5 years, or 2 years after order ceases to have effect, whichever is the longer	
Absolute discharge	6 months	
Conditional discharge, probation order, binding over, care order, supervision order	1 year after conviction or the order or 1 year after the order ends, whichever is the longer	
Disqualification	The period of the disqualification	

THE EFFECT OF REHABILITATION

Once the rehabilitation period has expired, not only do you not have to reveal it, but also it cannot be revealed by anyone else without your permission.

Evidence in legal proceedings

A spent conviction cannot be used in evidence in a civil court, tribunal, arbitration or disciplinary or similar hearing. You should not be asked questions about spent convictions and, if they are asked, you need not answer them unless you wish to.

This does not apply in:

- service disciplinary proceedings;
- applications for adoption, custody, wardship, guardianship or care proceedings;

- where the court or tribunal is satisfied that justice cannot be done except by hearing the evidence involving the spent conviction;
- criminal proceedings; but the Lord Chief Justice has ruled that no one should refer in open court to a spent conviction without the authority of the judge, which authority should not be given unless the interests of justice so require.

Employment and services

If you apply for certain jobs, you must reveal any spent convictions, but only if asked. These jobs are: doctors, dentists, nurses, midwives, opticians, chemists, vets, lawyers, accountants, the police, prison officers, the armed forces, traffic wardens, probation officers, teachers, certain types of work in the health and social services (particularly if in contact with people under eighteen), in certain types of insurance and unit trust work or as a firearms dealer. This also applies if you are subject to national security vetting.

There is also a Home Office circular asking the police to report convictions of people in specific jobs if the offence:

- is punishable by a month or more imprisonment without the option of a fine. (Jobs covered: doctors, dentists, midwives, nurses);
- is such that it is believed it makes a person unsuitable to teach or care for children. (Jobs covered: teachers, youth leaders, clergymen and those employed in the care of children in various schools and homes, such as an approved school or remand home);
- involves fraud, dishonesty or moral turpitude. (Jobs covered: barristers);
- involves money or property. (Jobs covered: solicitors or solicitors' clerks);
- is relevant to fitness to drive, or to sexual or indecency offences. (Jobs covered: drivers or conductors of public-service vehicles);
- is other than a minor traffic offence. (Jobs covered: civil servants);
- for any offence. (Jobs covered: magistrates).

Revealing a spent conviction

If someone wrongly reveals that you have a spent conviction, you can:

- sue the person concerned for defamation (libel if it is written, slander if it is said), even though what has been said is true. You have to show that they acted with malice, that is, it was done deliberately to injure your reputation. This is difficult to prove and you cannot get legal aid for defamation cases.
- if officials with access to the information wrongly disclose it, they can be prosecuted. The maximum fine is £1,000.
- if anyone tries dishonestly to obtain details of a spent conviction, there is a maximum fine of £2,000 and/or six months' imprisonment.
- if the police reveal a spent conviction to an employer who is not within the categories set out in the Home Office circular, you should make a formal complaint to the Chief Constable (see 5.3, p. 90).

7.8   More information

USEFUL ORGANIZATIONS

Law Centres
Citizens' Advice Bureaux

Consult your local telephone directory for addresses and telephone numbers.

8 The rights of prisoners

This chapter deals with:

8.1   Basic rights

The rights of prisoners are in a state of change and the range of rights recognized and enforceable under English law is developing all the time. However, two basic principles apply.

Firstly, prisoners retain certain basic rights which belong to them as citizens and survive despite their imprisonment. The rights of access to the courts and of respect for one's bodily integrity (i.e., not to be assaulted or medically treated against one's will) are such fundamental rights which survive despite imprisonment. Others may be recognized as the law develops (e.g., the right to marry – or to have conjugal relations). The test in every case is whether the right is fundamental and whether there is anything in the Prison Act and Prison Rules to authorize the prison authorities to limit its enjoyment.

Secondly, the Prison Act and the Prison Rules also confer certain rights. They give prisoners certain defined rights – to adequate food, clothing and exercise, to be given information about the Prison Rules and also to a certain number of visits and amount of correspondence. They also confer the right to have notice of charges and a fair hearing before a board of visitors or governor on a disciplinary charge. A prisoner who is deprived of these rights unfairly or without any special justification can complain to the Secretary of State and the board of visitors or, in serious cases, to the courts.

The basic rights of prisoners and the procedures to be followed by the prison authorities in dealing with prisoners are mostly laid down in the Prison Act 1952, the Prison Rules, and in Standing Orders. Standing Orders are internal directives from the Home Secretary to prison governors and officers governing every aspect of prison life. Some have already been published; others will be published in the future. They are a vital source of information about prisoners' rights.

COMPLAINTS AND REMEDIES

The Home Secretary has general responsibility for prisons and has a duty to see that the Prison Rules are respected. Prisoners or their families can petition him if the Rules are broken, or if they are maltreated, and can apply to him about other matters such as transfer, restoration of remission, or permission to attend court proceedings.

Each prison has a board of visitors which is a small group of people including magistrates whose job it is to overlook the running of the prison, to deal with serious disciplinary offences, and to look into complaints and problems raised by prisoners. They must hear any complaint or request which a prisoner wishes to make to them, but their powers to remedy grievances are limited.

COMPLAINTS PROCEDURE

There is a procedure governing the making of complaints about conditions or treatment in prison which a prisoner must follow except in those situations where he decides to consult a solicitor in order to sue the prison authorities. Normally, the prisoner should first raise his complaint with the prison governor or the board of visitors. If the prisoner feels the issue has not been satisfactorily dealt with it is possible to petition the Home Secretary for a decision. Prisoners can also write to their MP to intervene on their behalf, although the prison authorities can insist that the prisoner first makes an internal complaint.

Prisoners can also try to raise a complaint with outside individuals or organizations such as NCCL but the censor can stop such letters.

It is sometimes more effective for a friend or relative to write about the matter to the Home Secretary, the appropriate MP, or to approach a solicitor to arrange a visit.

When all remedies in this country have been exhausted a prisoner with a complaint about conditions or treatment in prison can petition the European Commission for Human Rights (see 5.7, p. 104).

THE COURTS

Prisoners have the absolute right to commence proceedings in the courts either directly and in person or through a solicitor. This right includes the conduct of normal civil proceedings (e.g., for divorce or breach of contract), and cases where the prisoner is suing the prison authorities (e.g., for assault, or medical negligence) or seeking judicial review of a disciplinary decision. The prisoner no longer has to complain first to the prison authorities in such cases before going to court. The courts have reviewed a wide range of decisions by the prison authorities concerning disciplinary adjudications, parole, parole revocation, transfer, censorship, and the separation of a mother from her baby. However, the Home Secretary has a discretion to refuse a prisoner permission to be present at court for the hearing of his case.

ACCESS TO LAWYERS

Prisoners have an absolute right to see and correspond with their solicitor in connection with current criminal or civil proceedings. They also have a right to contact a solicitor about any proposed civil proceedings, even when they involve suing the prison authorities. However, the governor can regulate the actual time and place of legal visits.

RECEPTION INTO PRISON

On reception into prison the prisoner will be searched and may be photographed. Any property which the prisoner is not allowed to keep will be taken into the governor's custody. An inventory (list) of the prisoner's property will be made and the prisoner must be given an opportunity to see that it is correct before signing it. All cash must be paid into an account under the governor's control.

Prisoners must be given a written account of certain prison rules including information about earnings, privileges and the method of making complaints, and a prison official must make sure that the prisoner has read and understood this information within twenty-four hours of reception.

8.2   Unconvicted prisoners

Prisoners who are remanded in custody to await trial have certain rights which convicted prisoners do not have:

- they may wear their own clothes and arrange for clothes to be sent in by family or friends;
- they should not be forced to have their hair cut or beard shaved except for reasons of hygiene;
- they do not have to work though they may apply to work in the same way as convicted prisoners if they choose;
- they may send and receive as many letters as they like though the letters will be censored;
- they may receive as many letters as they like though in practice this is usually limited to one a day;
- they may buy or be given books, papers and writing materials which are not considered 'objectionable' by the prison authorities;
- they may have a visit from a doctor or dentist who is not attached to the prison if they are willing to pay any expenses incurred;

- they may see their legal adviser during normal working hours and as often as necessary – their meetings will be in the sight but not the hearing of a prison officer.

8.3   Convicted prisoners

CATEGORIZATION

When they first go into prison, prisoners are placed in one of four categories according to the extent to which they are regarded as a security risk. This is done by:

- the governor at the local prison who classifies first offenders serving four years or less and those with previous convictions serving under five years;
- the regional director at a regional allocation centre who makes the final decision about those serving other sentences;
- the prison department of the Home Office who make decisions about placing prisoners in Category A (the highest security risk).

There is no appeal against the categorization decision within the prison system but the position is regularly reviewed and prisoners are recategorized during their prison career. If it is felt that there are grounds for reclassification, representations should be made to the Home Office by the prisoner's relatives, solicitor, MP or NCCL. In an extreme case – for example, when a person with no record of serious crime is put in Category A – application could be made to the High Court for judicial review.

The four security categories are:

CATEGORY A: Prisoners whose escape would be highly dangerous to the public or the security of the State.

CATEGORY B: Prisoners who do not need the highest conditions of security but for whom escape must be made very difficult.

CATEGORY C: Prisoners who cannot be trusted in open conditions but who do not have the ability or resources to make a determined escape attempt.

CATEGORY D: Prisoners who can reasonably be trusted to serve their sentences in open conditions.

ALLOCATION

Allocation to a particular prison is made after assessment of the offence and sentence, category, individual history, training needs and the domestic situation of the prisoner. There is no appeal against this decision within the prison system, but the prisoner or the prisoner's family can write to the prison department of the Home Office asking for a transfer if the decision seems inappropriate. Prisoners have no right to be sent to a prison near their home.

In an extreme case, an allocation or transfer decision which was vindictive or wholly unjustified might be reviewed by the courts – particularly if it effectively deprived an unconvicted prisoner of access to his lawyers and family.

VISITS

Prisoners are entitled to one visit every four weeks although the governor may allow more visits depending on facilities and staffing in different prisons. Extra visits may be allowed by the governor or board of visitors – particularly if it is considered necessary for the welfare of the prisoner's family or for other special reasons such as to assist a prisoner with his appeal.

Visitors must first get a *visiting order* which is usually sent by post and covers up to three visitors or visits. Visitors to Category A prisoners must complete an inquiry form with a photograph and this will have to be verified by the local police.

Prisoners who have served more than two years after being transferred from a local prison and who still have at least six months left of the sentence are eligible for *accumulated visits* if it is difficult for family or friends to travel long distances to visit. Prisoners can accumulate up to a maximum of twelve visits.

A prisoner's wife, husband or next of kin who is receiving social security can claim an allowance for the cost of the fare from the DHSS. Some probation officers are prepared to help out if the visitor is not claiming social security but is having difficulty finding the fare.

Visitors may give prisoners cigarettes to smoke during visits but this is a privilege which may be withdrawn and visitors are liable to a fine or imprisonment if they give the prisoner anything else. Visitors must not take notes of the conversation nor use the information gleaned from a visit for publication.

If the authorities feel that a prisoner has or might abuse a visit they can impose certain restrictions:

- by refusing visits from certain people;
- by granting only closed visits where the prisoner meets the visitor in a small room with a prison officer present; *or*
- by granting only 'screened' visits where there is a glass partition between the prisoner and the visitor.

Prisoners may usually receive visits from relatives or friends only, although the governor or the Home Office can use their discretion to allow other visits.

Visits by voluntary prison visitors count as ordinary visits but prisoners can have extra visits from their ministers of religion.

MPs can get authority to visit a prisoner from the Secretary of State but otherwise must have a visiting order from the prisoner or a magistrate. If an MP visits a prisoner, the interview will be outside the hearing of a prison officer, unless the MP requests otherwise or there are special security considerations.

Police officers may, with permission from the governor, interview a prisoner concerning future charges, inquiries for criminal investigation, appearance as a prosecution witness, or participation in an identification parade. The prisoner is entitled to refuse to see the police officer or to answer his questions.

LETTERS

Prisoners have a right under Prison Rule 34(A) to send and receive one letter a week. Postage will be paid by the prison for this one 'statutory' letter. Prisoners are also usually allowed to send out extra letters, provided they pay for the postage themselves, but a limit may be imposed for administrative reasons. The one letter a week statutory limit is more strictly enforced for Category A prisoners.

The prison authorities may read all letters to and from prisoners except correspondence between prisoners and their legal advisers about legal proceedings – whether current or potential. The governor may stop any letters (other than letters concerned with legal proceedings) considered to be 'objectionable' or too long and letters may be censored. 'Objectionable' can be widely interpreted to include mention of other prisoners' offences, complaints about prison treatment or matters which may attract publicity. A prisoner who wishes to complain about prison treatment must first lodge a complaint internally – unless he is writing to a solicitor or directly to a court to initiate or continue legal proceedings.

The governor may refuse to allow a prisoner to write to people not known at the time of conviction. But the prisoner will usually be allowed to write to organizations such as NCCL, Justice, Release or the Howard League for Penal Reform about his case. Prisoners may write to their MP but are not allowed to complain of treatment in prison unless the complaint has already been made to the prison authorities. Once the complaint has been made, the prisoner may mention it in correspondence. The governor may stop a letter to an MP if it is considered objectionable but the prisoner's family or friends can write on the prisoner's behalf.

Prisoners are not allowed to write business letters or conduct business from prison without the permission of the Home Office. For those requiring further information, the Standing Order governing visits and correspondence is now published and can be purchased from the Home Office.

GIFTS

All gifts will be inspected and the governor may confiscate any unauthorized article found in a prisoner's possession. Gifts of money will either be paid into the prisoner's account under the governor's control or returned to the sender. Other gifts may be delivered to the prisoner, or placed with the personal property to be given back on release or returned to the sender.

All goods and money received from unknown sources are paid into an account for the benefit of discharged prisoners even when the article or money is addressed to an individual prisoner.

WORK

All convicted prisoners are required to work, usually in association with other prisoners, unless excused by the medical officer. The medical officer may excuse a prisoner either from all work or certain types of work. It is a disciplinary offence for a prisoner to refuse to work or to be idle, careless or negligent at work.

The type of work varies from prison to prison and there is no overall training plan. Conditions also vary but the average working week is twenty-six hours and the basic prison wage is £1.55 per week for flat-rate work. Prisoners do not pay National Insurance contributions.

Prisoners employed outside in special hostels or pre-release schemes get the normal weekly wage and pay insurance and tax.

Prison workshops are exempt from the Factories Act and no claim for an industrial injury can be made in the event of an accident. However, a prisoner injured at work may be able to bring a civil claim against the Home Office for negligence.

Each prison has a labour allocation board and prisoners can apply for a change of job.

There is no absolute right to work guaranteed by the Prison Rules.

EXERCISE

Prisoners have a right to daily exercise for at least an hour (if weather permits) unless they are already engaged in outdoor work. The Home Secretary can, in special circumstances, authorize the reduction of the exercise period to half an hour. But prisoners regularly denied this minimum period of exercise could, if necessary, enforce their right through the courts.

EDUCATION

The prison department is under a general duty to provide evening classes at every prison and to encourage prisoners to 'profit' from the educational facilities provided. But this does not mean that every prisoner has a right to the educational course of his choice, and the prison authorities have a wide discretion as to what educational facilities they provide and who is allowed to benefit from them.

Local education authorities provide a programme of evening classes in all prisons but classroom space is often limited. Facilities for daytime study and remedial teaching vary. The governor is responsible for assessing the prisoner's needs and suitability for further study. He can release individuals from work duty for study. Permission from the prison authorities can also be obtained to enable a prisoner to follow a correspondence course.

All prisons have at least one library and prisoners can take out between four and six books a week. Most books sent to prisoners are eventually given to the prison library unless the prisoner applies to retain them in his property.

READING AND WRITING MATERIALS

Prisoners are entitled to have supplied to them at their own expense and to retain 'books, newspapers, writing materials and other means of occupation' except those which appear objectionable to the board of visitors or are prohibited by the Home Secretary. Generally speaking, prisoners should only be denied books, newspapers or magazines as and when they include material that incites or involves criminal or disciplinary offences (e.g., obscene books or magazines containing incitements to violence). At present there is a limit of twelve to the number of non-library books a prisoner may retain.

8.4   Discipline, adjudication and punishment

DISCIPLINARY CHARGES

The Prison Rules create a number of disciplinary offences which can be punished by the governor or board of visitors depending on how serious they are. They range from serious offences (e.g., gross personal violence, assault, escape) which are also criminal offences, to lesser offences which only involve a breach of prison regulations (e.g., treating an officer with disrespect, repeatedly making groundless complaints, or 'in any way offending against good order and discipline').

When a prisoner is reported for an offence which also involves a criminal offence, the governor may, but does not have to, inform the police. If charges are brought by the police, the case will usually be heard in an outside court in the usual way. A prisoner cannot stop this happening. But he should not be punished internally after he has been dealt with for the same offence by a criminal court; that would place him in double jeopardy.

If the governor decides to deal with the alleged offence as a disciplinary charge (or if he is directed to do so by the Home Secretary), then the internal adjudication procedure must be followed.

Governor's adjudication

Prisoners charged with a disciplinary offence (an offence against the Prison Rules) must be notified of the charge brought against them immediately. They can be removed from association with other prisoners until the charge has been dealt with. The governor must then hold a preliminary hearing to inquire into the charge.

If the charge is relatively minor, the governor may deal with it himself. He must then hear the evidence against the prisoner, and allow the prisoner both to question the witnesses against him and to put his own defence. The governor must allow the prisoner to call any witnesses essential to his defence – though he may have a discretion to limit the numbers. If the governor finds the prisoner guilty he may sentence him to punishments which include forfeiture of remission for up to twenty-eight days for any one offence. But the prisoner can appeal by petitioning the Home Secretary or by applying to the Divisional Court of the High Court for judicial review. The High Court will only intervene and quash the conviction or sentence when the governor has made an error of law (e.g., decided that something was an offence when the rules did not prohibit it) or acted unfairly (e.g., by refusing to hear the prisoner or a crucial defence witness who is readily available).

Board of visitors' adjudication

If the offence is a grave one (e.g., escape or assault on an officer) or the governor thinks that the offence is 'serious' (or 'repeated') and that the punishments he can give are too small, then the case will be referred to the board of visitors. If the case involves an 'especially grave offence' (either 'mutiny' or 'doing gross personal violence to an officer'), the board of visitors must include two members who are magistrates.

Before the board of visitors, a prisoner has the right to sufficient time to prepare his defence and a full opportunity to present his case. He should be allowed to call any witnesses who will support his case, and to question the witnesses called against him by the reporting officer. He should also be allowed to make a speech in mitigation and to call any witness crucial to mitigation.

The board of visitors has a discretion to grant a prisoner *legal representation* for an adjudication hearing. They must consider any application for legal representation. The factors they should consider in deciding whether to grant representation include: the gravity of the charge and of the potential punishment; any legal issues that may arise; any difficulty the prisoner may have in finding and interviewing witnesses; any handicap the prisoner may have in presenting his case.

The board of visitors may award punishments of up to 180 days' loss of remission and fifty-six days' cellular confinement at any hearing.

A prisoner who wishes to challenge a board of visitors' decision is always entitled to petition the Home Secretary to restore his forfeiture remission or lost privileges. He can also apply to the High Court for judicial review when the board of visitors has either misdirected itself in law (e.g., as to what constitutes an offence of 'mutiny' or making a false and malicious allegation against an officer) or acted unfairly (e.g., by refusing him permission to call a crucial witness or to cross-examine a prosecution witness). All applications to the High Court must be made quickly: unless there is some special excuse, they should be made within three months of the adjudication.

A prisoner who has lost remission as a result of a governor's or board of visitors' adjudication can also apply for restoration of his remission to the board of visitors on grounds of subsequent good behaviour.

Cellular confinement and segregation

Prisoners can be segregated from other prisoners either as a punishment, or 'in the interests of good order and discipline', or at their own request and for their own protection.

Punishments of cellular confinement (solitary confinement with loss of privileges) can be imposed by either the governor or the board of visitors. The maximum the governor can order as a punishment for a disciplinary offence is three days; the maximum the board of visitors can order as punishment for a disciplinary offence is fifty-six days' cellular confinement. No prisoner should be punished with cellular confinement unless the medical officer has first certified him fit for such punishment, and prisoners on cellular confinement should be seen daily by the medical officer and returned to normal locations if he orders it for their health.

Prisoners can also be segregated under Rule 43 in the interests of 'good order and discipline' (GOAD). This provision is sometimes wrongly used as a way of punishing those who are suspected of some offence or subversive activity and against whom there is insufficient evidence to bring charges. A prisoner segregated under Rule 43 on grounds of GOAD can only be kept on segregation after the first twenty-four hours if a member of the board of visitors or the Home Secretary authorizes it. (In fact, it is a member of the board of visitors who almost always does this.) After that the segregation can be renewed for up to twenty-eight days at a time. Prisoners need not be told the reason for their segregation when it is on grounds of 'good order and discipline'. In an extreme case, the High Court might intervene to protect a prisoner who was wrongly or unfairly segregated.

Prisoners can also ask to be segregated under Rule 43 for their own protection. This is often done when the prisoner fears that he will be attacked by other prisoners because of his offence (e.g., a sex offence) or for some other reason. Prisoners segregated at their own request should not suffer the loss of any other privileges such as the use of a radio.

Some prisons have better facilities for 'own request' Rule 43 prisoners than others and can provide for some association between them. There are special units at Reading, Gloucester and Wakefield prisons for 'own request' Rule 43 prisoners. These units allow full association at work and in lesson time with other prisoners in a similar situation. Consequently, if a prisoner seems likely to remain on Rule 43 for a long period, the prisoner, friends or family can petition for a transfer to one of these prisons.

8.5   Women prisoners, young prisoners and prisoners' families

WOMEN PRISONERS

There are far fewer women in prison than men, and women are generally sentenced for shorter periods. The prison authorities tend to believe that women in prison are in need of treatment rather than punishment and therefore more resources are allocated to psychiatric facilities in women's prisons.

Women prisoners have the right to be kept in a prison or a part of a prison where they are 'entirely separate from male prisoners'. As a matter of practice they do not have to have their hair cut and can wear their own clothes. But all other Prison Rules apply equally to men and women.

At the discretion of the Home Secretary, mothers may be allowed to keep their *babies* with them in prison in special mother and baby units. There is provision for mothers given this permission to have their babies with them in a closed prison until they reach nine months, and in an open prison (such as Askham Grange) until the babies reach eighteen months. If the baby will reach the age of eighteen months before the mother's release, then (usually) the mother will not be allowed to keep her baby with her, and may be forced to hand the baby out at an earlier stage.

YOUNG PRISONERS

Prisoners under the age of twenty-one will generally serve their custodial sentences either in a youth custody centre or a detention centre. Special rules – which are very similar to the Prison Rules for prisoners over twenty-one – apply to youth custody and detention centres. However, there are significant differences: for example, disciplinary punishments are more limited and there is a right to a minimum period of education for those of school age. Moreover, prisoners' releases at the expiration of their sentence or on parole licence are subject to compulsory supervision from their probation officer.

PRISONERS' FAMILIES

Either spouse can start an action for divorce in the usual way even if the husband or wife is in prison. Legal aid may be available (see 5.6, p. 99).

A prisoner can get married with the permission of the prison authorities but permission will generally be refused to a lifer who has not yet been given a release date.

Prisoners' families often face grave financial hardship but there are some courses of action which may help:

- the wife or husband of a prisoner may be entitled to supplementary benefits or family income supplement;
- the DHSS will sometimes help out with rates and rent or interest on mortgage repayments;
- explain the situation to the building society and ask them to allow reduced mortgage repayments for the period of imprisonment;
- wives are not normally responsible for debts incurred in their husband's name but are responsible for debts in joint names. When bills for gas, electricity etc. have been incurred before imprisonment, write offering to pay off a nominal amount each week from prison earnings;
- if the gas or electricity is cut off, the social services must provide cooking facilities if you have children;
- the social services also have funds to use at their discretion where children are deprived because of their parents' financial situation;
- if no funds are forthcoming the parent should contact the local probation office, social worker or MP.

8.6   Release

REMISSION

Prisoners are entitled to remission of one-third or one-half of their sentence – according to the length of their sentence – unless they lose remission as a punishment after conviction for a disciplinary offence. Prisoners serving sentences of twelve months or less get remission of one-half of their sentence; prisoners serving sentences of more than twelve months get remission of one-third of their sentence. The sentence cannot be reduced to less than five days. Prisoners released with remission have served their complete sentence and cannot be recalled.

PAROLE

Prisoners are eligible to apply for parole after serving one-third of a sentence or after six months as a convicted prisoner, whichever is the longer. Category A prisoners will generally have to petition for reclassification before applying for parole.

The first stage in the process of applying for parole is the review by the local review committee. Each prison has a local review committee consisting of the governor, a probation officer, a member of the board of visitors and an independent member of the public. They will consider the prisoner's case in the first instance shortly before the prisoner becomes eligible for parole and will then usually review the case every twelve months. The procedure is as follows:

- a member of the committee will interview the prisoner and report back;
- the prisoner can also make written representations to the committee if he or she wishes;
- the committee will consider reports from the governor, probation officer and medical officer;
- the prisoner should ask friends and possible employers to write supporting the application and giving details of where the prisoner could live and whether a job would be available.

The second stage is that the local review committee will make a recommendation to the Home Secretary. If it is favourable then the Home Secretary can, if he wishes, release certain types of offender on the recommendation of the review committee alone. (Prisoners serving short sentences for non-violent offences can be so released at this second stage.)

All other prisoners depend on a third and fourth stage for release. At the third stage the Home Secretary refers the prisoner's case to the full Parole Board for review. These prisoners can only be released if the full Parole Board makes a positive recommendation. However, the Home Secretary does not have to accept a positive recommendation. He takes the final decision for or against parole himself and that is the fourth stage of the parole process.

At present, prisoners are not entitled to see the reports on them that are put before the local review committee and the Parole Board. Moreover, there is no appeal against a refusal to grant parole.

The High Court will only intervene in the most extreme cases of unfairness – and then only to order a further review.

PAROLE POLICY

Prisoners serving short sentences for non-violent offences have a very good chance of getting parole. But for certain categories of prisoner there is a presumption against parole. Prisoners serving sentences of more than five years for offences of violence or drug-trafficking will only be granted parole in 'exceptional circumstances'. But they and all fixed-term prisoners must at least be considered for parole after the completion of one-third of their sentence.

Life sentence prisoners are also eligible for release on parole, subject to certain conditions, and liable to recall for the rest of their lives. Life prisoners will be given a 'tariff' date – fixed by the Home Secretary and judges as the minimum time they must serve as punishment for their offences. Their first date for review by the local review committee will be fixed three years before the completion of their tariff. But there is no guarantee that they will be released after they have served their tariff period – and they will not be, if either the Parole Board or the Home Secretary still considers them to present an 'unacceptable' danger to the public. In some circumstances, life prisoners who are given indefensibly long tariff periods may be able to win judicial review of their tariff by the courts.

RELEASE ON LICENCE

A prisoner will only be released on licence subject to certain conditions and may be recalled to prison if these conditions are breached or a criminal offence is committed. Prisoners who are recalled by the Home Secretary (rather than being sent back by the courts) have a right to know the reasons for their recall and to appeal against their recall to the Parole Board in writing. Prisoners so recalled should insist on full reasons and may wish to consult a solicitor to assist them in making their representations.

PRE-RELEASE

Prisoners may be granted home leave some weeks or months before release to visit family and make inquiries about a job. Welfare officers or probation officers may be able to help with employment, accommodation and information about hostel schemes for ex-prisoners, though these are very limited.

Prisoners serving more than four years may be able to get a placement in a hostel or pre-release scheme where they can work outside the prison in the normal way.

DISCHARGE FACILITIES

On release, prisoners' personal clothing is returned or, if this is inadequate, suitable clothing is provided. They are also given any money they had on reception into prison and a discharge grant. The grant is £19.40 for sixteen- to seventeen-year-olds, £26.05 for eighteen- to twenty-four-year-olds, £33.40 for those over twenty-four, and £68.30 for those of no fixed abode. Those serving under fourteen days are not entitled to the discharge grant though the prison authorities may give a subsistence allowance to enable the prisoner to get to the local DHSS office.

8.7   More information

USEFUL ORGANIZATIONS

Howard League for Penal Reform, 322 Kennington Park Road, London SE11 4PP (01-735 3317)

Inquest (monitors deaths in custody), Ground Floor, Alexandra House, 330 Seven Sisters Road, London N4 2PJ (01-802 7430)

National Association for the Care and Resettlement of Offenders (NACRO), 169 Clapham Road, London SW9 (01-582 6500)

Prison Department, Home Office, Eccleston Square, London SW1H 9AT (01-273 3000)

Prison Reform Trust, 59 Caledonian Road, London N1 9BU (01-278 9815)

Prisoners' Wives and Families Society, 254 Caledonian Road, London N1 0NJ (01-278 3981)

Prisoners' Wives Service, 51 Borough High Street, London SE1 1NB (01-403 4091)

PROP (National Prisoners' Movement), c/o BM-Prop, London WC1N 3XX (01-542 3744)

Women in Prison, 25t Horsell Road, London N5 1XL (01-607 3353)

BIBLIOGRAPHY

M. Maguire, J. Jagg and R. Morgan, *Accountability and Prisons: Opening Up a Closed Wall*, Tavistock Publications, 1985.
J. Plotnikoff, *The Prison Rules: A Working Guide*, Prison Reform Trust, 1988.
Prison Department, Home Office, Information leaflets for prisoners.
Prison Department, Home Office, *Manual on the Adjudications in Prison Department Establishments*, Prison Department, Home Office, 1984.

9 The right not to be discriminated against

This chapter deals with:

9.1   Race discrimination

The Race Relations Act 1976 deals with race discrimination in employment and training; education; housing; the provision of goods, facilities and services; and advertising. It also set up the Commission for Racial Equality (CRE). The Act applies in England, Wales and Scotland, but not in Northern Ireland. Complaints by individuals who believe they have been discriminated against go to the industrial tribunal (for employment-related matters) or the county court (in Scotland, the Sheriff Courts).

The Act refers to 'racial grounds' or 'racial group' which are defined to relate to colour, race, nationality or ethnic or national origin. This definition is not repeated below, but must be read into the phrase racial grounds or group as appropriate.

WHAT IS DISCRIMINATION?

The Act defines three types of discrimination:

Direct discrimination occurs when a person treats another *less favourably on racial grounds* than he would treat, or treats, some other person. Sometimes direct discrimination is very obvious (e.g., 'no coloureds here'), but it may be more subtle. Quotas are sometimes operated by some clubs or pubs to prevent their black members or customers from exceeding a specific number or proportion. Sometimes persons are refused jobs or promotion on the grounds that customers with whom they would then come into contact would be prejudiced. Both of these situations are examples of direct discrimination. Direct discrimination is usually clearly intended, but it may occur because of unspoken prejudice. It is not necessary to prove an intention to discriminate directly.

Segregation on racial grounds is defined by the Act as direct discrimination.

Indirect discrimination occurs when a racial group is unjustifiably at a disadvantage in its ability to comply with a specific requirement or condition. A requirement for a job that the employee is clean-shaven would put Sikhs in general at a disadvantage. If the requirement is not justifiable it would be indirect discrimination. The Act, however, prohibits litigation on theoretical grounds, so only people who themselves suffer this disadvantage can bring a complaint.

This provision of the Act is greatly under-used, partly because it is complex and partly because it is more difficult for inexperienced advisers to spot. If you consider you unjustifiably suffer a disadvantage in your ability to comply with a requirement or condition you should consider seeking specialist help (see 9.4, p. 228).

Victimization occurs when one person treats another less favourably than he treats, or would treat, someone else in those particular circumstances because the person victimized has:

- brought proceedings against the discriminator or any other person under the Act; *or*
- given evidence or information in connection with proceedings brought by any person against the discriminator or any other person under the Act; *or*
- otherwise done anything under or by reference to the Act in relation to the discriminator or any other person; *or*
- alleged that the discriminator or any other person has committed an act which (whether or not the allegation so states) would amount to a contravention of the Act,

or because the discriminator knows that the person victimized intends to do any of those things, or suspects that the person victimized has done, or intends to do, any of them. But the person discriminated against must have acted in good faith.

RESPONSIBILITY FOR ACTS OF DISCRIMINATION

The Act makes unlawful certain types of discrimination which are considered below. It also makes it unlawful to instruct someone to carry out an unlawful act of discrimination or to induce or attempt to induce, directly or indirectly, such an act; but only the CRE may bring proceedings in respect of such discrimination. Employers are made responsible for the unlawful acts of their employees, save where it is shown that they took such steps as were reasonably practicable to prevent their employees from doing such unlawful acts. It is also unlawful for a person, including an employee, to aid another to do an unlawful act of discrimination.

EMPLOYMENT AND TRAINING

It is unlawful for an employer to discriminate against you on grounds of race in any of the following ways:

- refusing to hire you or consider you for a job;
- offering you a job on less favourable terms than other people;
- refusing to promote you or transfer you to another job;
- refusing to make provision for you to be trained;
- giving you less favourable fringe benefits;
- putting you on short-time work, dismissing you or making you redundant.

In order to bring a case to the industrial tribunal (see 13.8, p. 295 for more information about making a complaint of race discrimination) you would need to show that you were being treated less favourably than someone of different racial or national origins would be treated.

The Act covers both permanent and temporary jobs, whatever the size of the firm. It covers apprentices and trainees as well as other employees; partners in a firm of six or more partners (such as a solicitors' firm); the police (who are not, technically, employees); sub-contracted workers (such as the 'lump' building workers or night cleaners) and employment agencies.

It is unlawful for the government to discriminate on race grounds in appointing people to serve on public bodies. It is also unlawful for trade unions and professional associations to discriminate in any of the following ways:

- deciding who to admit to membership;
- refusing to let you join;
- only allowing you to join on less favourable terms;
- by giving you fewer benefits, facilities or services, or refusing to let you have any of these benefits (e.g., legal services, representation in a dispute);
- expelling you or subjecting you to any other disadvantage.

Similarly, it is unlawful for any licensing body (e.g., the Law Society, which licenses solicitors; the Director General of Fair Trading, who licenses credit and hire businesses; the police, who license taxi-drivers) to discriminate on race grounds in deciding who can have a licence. Furthermore, whenever one of these bodies has to consider an applicant's 'good character' before giving a licence, they will be able to take into account any evidence about previous unlawful race discrimination. So, for instance, magistrates who are renewing a publican's licence should also take account of any evidence that he or his employees had previously refused to serve black people.

Racial abuse and harassment at work

Not all racial abuse and harassment at work is covered, but provided the insult, abuse or harassment is aimed at a person so that it will (or is likely to) come to their notice and they are thereby disadvantaged at work, it will be unlawful.

A complaint about race discrimination in the field of employment must be brought to an industrial tribunal (see 13.8, p. 295) within three months.

Exceptions

Racial discrimination is still lawful in any of the following situations:

- employment in a private household;
- if an employer wants to employ someone who is not ordinarily resident in Great Britain, but who will be trained here before going to work abroad;
- employment of workers on ships who were recruited outside Great Britain;
- employment outside Great Britain;
- employment in dramatic performances, or for artists' or photographic modelling, where someone of a particular racial group is needed for reasons of 'authenticity';
- employment in restaurants, etc., with a particular setting where someone of a particular racial group is needed for reasons of authenticity (e.g., Chinese waiters in a Chinese restaurant);
- employment of someone to provide personal services to a particular racial group, where someone of the same racial group can do the job most effectively.

The last three exceptions are called genuine occupational qualification exceptions. In any of these cases, the employer must try to fill a vacancy from existing workers before discriminating on racial grounds. The CRE has published an important Code of Practice for the elimination of racial discrimination and the promotion of equality of opportunity in employment, which is obtainable from the CRE (address p. 228).

Training

It is unlawful for any of the following training organizations to discriminate on race grounds:

- industrial training boards;
- Manpower Services Commission;
- Employment Services Agency;
- Training Services Agency;
- employers' organizations which provide training;
- any other organization designated by the Secretary of State.

These organizations will, however, be allowed to practise positive discrimination where there have been no people of a particular racial group, or very few, doing a particular kind of work, either in the whole of Great Britain or in a region, in the previous twelve months. In this case they will be allowed to run training courses or provide facilities for that racial group only, or encourage people from that group to take up a particular kind of work.

Employers will also be allowed to run training courses for a particular racial group only, or to encourage them to take up a particular kind of work, where there have been no people of that racial group, or very few, doing that kind of work in the firm during the previous twelve months.

Trade unions and professional organizations are also allowed to organize special training courses to encourage people from a particular racial group to hold posts within the organization (e.g., as shop stewards or officials), where there have been very few or no people from that group holding such posts in the previous twelve months.

EDUCATION

The Race Relations Act applies to schools or colleges maintained by a local education authority (LEA), independent ('public' or fee-paying) schools or colleges, special schools and universities. The Secretary of State can also designate other establishments to be covered by the law, such as polytechnics.

It is unlawful for any educational body (including the governors of a school or college and an LEA) to discriminate on race grounds in any of the following ways:

- the terms on which they admit you;
- refusing to admit you;
- providing more facilities or better facilities for particular racial groups;
- expelling you or in any other way putting you at a disadvantage;
- acting in any other way which involves race discrimination.

If you or your child has been discriminated against, you will have to make a complaint to the Secretary of State for Education (this does not apply to complaints against independent schools or universities). The Minister will have two months in which to do something about your complaint. If the Minister rejects your complaint, or the two months run out, you can make a complaint to the county court. A county court action must be brought within six months (or eight months if the complaint has first gone to the Minister).

The Act also puts a general duty on LEAs to ensure that educational facilities are provided without race discrimination. You have no way of enforcing this general duty, although of course, you can draw the attention of local councillors and school governors to it. The only way it can be enforced is by the Secretary of State ordering the LEA to carry out its duties reasonably.

It is, however, lawful for LEAs and other bodies to provide special facilities to meet the particular needs of a racial group (e.g., for language classes).

Overseas students

There is only one exception to the education sections of the Act, and this concerns overseas students. It is lawful for any organization or individual providing education or training to discriminate on racial grounds against people who are not ordinarily resident in Great Britain and who do not intend to remain in Great Britain after their period of education or training. This means, for instance, that it is lawful for colleges or halls of residence to charge higher fees to overseas students.

HOUSING

Housing and premises, such as business premises, are covered by the Act. In general, it is unlawful for someone to discriminate on race grounds, when selling, letting or managing property, in any of the following ways:

- in the terms on which you are offered the premises;
- by refusing to let you buy or rent the premises;
- by treating you differently from other people on a list of people wanting to buy or rent the premises;

- by refusing to agree to the transfer of a lease to you;
- by refusing you access to any benefits or facilities in premises you occupy;
- by evicting you or subjecting you to any other disadvantage.

The law covers private landlords and owner-occupiers, as well as local authorities.

Exceptions

There are three main exceptions. First, owner-occupiers selling or letting their property are excluded, provided that they do not advertise or use an estate agent.

Secondly, small residential premises (e.g., small boarding-houses or shared flats) are excluded. To qualify as 'small residential premises', the owner or occupier (or a near relative) has to live permanently in the house or flat; at least part of the house or flat, other than stairs or storage space, has to be shared with other people; and there must be only two households (other than the owner's or occupier's household) or not more than six people (other than the owner's or occupier's household) in the house or flat. A boarding-house containing more than six lodgers, in addition to the landlord/lady's family, would not be allowed to discriminate, but a boarding-house with fewer lodgers would be allowed to.

Thirdly, charities and membership bodies whose main purpose is to provide benefits for a particular racial group are allowed to provide housing for that group only. But these organizations will not be allowed to discriminate on grounds of colour, only on grounds of race, nationality or national or ethnic origin.

GOODS, FACILITIES AND SERVICES

The Act covers any 'goods, facilities or services' which are offered to the public or a section of the public. This means, for instance, the services and facilities offered by hotels, boarding-houses, pubs and restaurants, banks, insurance companies, credit houses and HP firms, transport authorities and local authorities. Direct or indirect discrimination (see 9.1, p. 193) by any such organization will be unlawful.

If you have been discriminated against on race grounds by someone offering goods or services to the public, you can bring an action in the county court. An action must be brought within six months.

Any contract (e.g., to buy goods or supply services) which includes a term which discriminates on race grounds is void and can be amended by applying to the county court.

Exceptions

There are a number of situations where race discrimination remains lawful:

- Any arrangement where someone takes a child, elderly person or someone needing special care and attention, into his or her home to be looked after (e.g., fostering children).
- Goods, facilities or services provided outside Great Britain, or insurance arrangements to cover a situation outside Great Britain. (But the services of, for instance, a travel agent in this country, even though it arranges foreign travel, will still be covered.)
- Charities and voluntary organizations whose main purpose is to provide benefits for a particular racial group (but these organizations will not be allowed to discriminate on grounds of colour, only on grounds of race, nationality or national or ethnic origin).
- Special arrangements can be made for members of a particular racial group who have particular needs for education, training, welfare, etc. (e.g., language classes).
- Discrimination on grounds of nationality, place of birth or length of residence is permitted in:
  - selecting people to represent a particular place or country in a sport or game; *or*
  - deciding who is eligible to compete in any sport or game, according to the rules of the competition.

PRISONS

The provisions prohibiting unlawful discrimination in housing and in relation to goods, facilities and services have been held to prevent the unlawful discrimination by prison officers in the allocation of work to prisoners. They also probably make unlawful other discrimination occurring in the prison regime (e.g., more unfavourable withdrawal of privileges from, and more frequent strip searches of, black prisoners).

CLUBS

Under the previous race relations laws, private clubs, such as political and working-men's clubs, were allowed to discriminate on race grounds. It is now unlawful for any club or society with twenty-five or more members to discriminate on race grounds in any of the following ways:

- refusing to allow you to join;
- offering you less favourable terms of membership;
- giving you fewer benefits, facilities or services or refusing to let you use or have any of these benefits (e.g., social facilities);
- expelling you from the club, or changing the terms of your membership;
- putting you at a disadvantage in any other way.

But a club or society whose main purpose is to provide benefits for people of a particular racial group, whatever its size, will continue to be allowed to discriminate on race grounds (although not on grounds of colour).

ADVERTISEMENTS

It is unlawful to insert or publish an advertisement which indicates that an employer, a company or anyone else intends to discriminate unlawfully. Only the CRE (see p. 203) will be able to take action against discriminatory advertisements, but if you see an advertisement which you believe breaks the law you should bring it to the Commission's attention.

Where there is an exception in the law which allows someone to discriminate on race grounds, then an advertisement which specifies race will usually be lawful. But an advertisement for employment in a private household must not be racially discriminating.

COMMISSION FOR RACIAL EQUALITY

The Commission for Racial Equality (CRE) was set up by the Race Relations Act 1976 with the duties of:

- working towards the elimination of discrimination;
- promoting equality of opportunity and good relations between persons of different racial groups generally; *and*
- keeping under review the working of the Act and, when required by the Secretary of State or when it otherwise thinks it necessary, to draw up and submit to the Secretary of State proposals for amending it.

In carrying out its duties, the CRE has the following powers:

- To undertake formal investigations into discriminatory practices which are unsuitable to be dealt with on an individual basis.
- To support, including financially, individuals taking up complaints of discrimination.
- To issue Codes of Practice on employment. The first Code was approved by Parliament in 1984. It is not legally binding but can be used in evidence at an industrial tribunal.
- To examine areas of policy outside the scope of the Act.
- To issue non-discrimination notices. This happens if the CRE decides, as a result of a formal investigation, that the law has been broken.
- To fund research and other projects.
- To apply for an injunction if it believes someone has broken the law and is likely to go on doing so. In the following circumstances, it is the CRE alone which can take action, such as applying for an injunction, if discrimination has taken place: – if an advertisement demonstrates an intention to discriminate unlawfully;

- if someone instructs an employee or agent to discriminate unlawfully;
- if someone puts pressure on anyone else to discriminate unlawfully.

Investigations

The CRE can conduct 'formal investigations' into any subject it chooses – for instance, employment patterns in a region; the recruitment policies of a firm; housing-allocation policies in local authorities, and so on.

The CRE must give notice of its intention to hold a formal investigation, and draw up terms of reference. If it is investigating a particular organization or person, and states in the terms of reference that it believes they are discriminating unlawfully, then it will be able to require them to give evidence or produce information. The power to take evidence and summon witnesses will also apply in other investigations with the consent of the Secretary of State, or if the aim of the investigation is to see whether a non-discrimination notice is being obeyed (see below).

Either during or at the end of an investigation, the CRE can make recommendations for changes which would promote equality of opportunity. These recommendations will not be legally binding, but could be used to bring pressure on the organization or person, or as evidence in an individual case against them.

Non-discrimination notices

The CRE will be able to issue a non-discrimination notice if it decides, during a formal investigation, that an organization or individual has discriminated unlawfully.

The non-discrimination notice requires the organization or person named in it to stop discriminating unlawfully and, if necessary, to let the people concerned know what changes have been made in their procedures or arrangements in order to obey the non-discrimination notice. Before issuing the notice, the CRE must warn the organization or person concerned that it is thinking of doing so, and give it twenty-eight days to make representations. Once the notice is issued, the organization or person named can appeal to the industrial tribunal (in an employment case) or the county court. The appeal must be made within six weeks of when the CRE issued the notice.

If the appeal fails, or no appeal is made, the non-discrimination notice becomes final – in other words, it can be enforced. The CRE will keep a register of notices which have become final and anyone is entitled to inspect this register and take a copy of any notice in it.

Injunctions

A non-discrimination notice can only be enforced if the CRE goes to court and gets an injunction. It can do this at any time within five years of when the notice becomes final, if it thinks that the organization or person named in the notice will continue to discriminate unlawfully.

An injunction is an order by a county court or the High Court ordering someone to stop acting in a particular way. If the organization or person does not obey the injunction, they will be in contempt of court and the CRE can apply to the court to have the people involved fined or imprisoned.

The CRE may also apply to the county court for an injunction, without issuing a non-discrimination notice, in the following circumstances:

- if someone has successfully brought a complaint against an individual or organization and the CRE considers that the individual or organization will go on discriminating unlawfully;
- if the CRE considers that someone has discriminated unlawfully and is likely to go on doing so; in this case, the CRE must itself apply to the industrial tribunal or county court to get a finding that the person concerned has in fact discriminated unlawfully;
- if the CRE considers that someone has published an unlawful advertisement (see 9.1, p. 202); instructed an employee or agent to discriminate unlawfully; or put pressure on anybody else to discriminate unlawfully. Only the CRE can take action on these kinds of unlawful acts.

LOCAL AUTHORITIES AND RACE EQUALITY

The Act imposes a duty on every local authority to make appropriate arrangements with a view to seeing that their various functions are carried out with due regard to the need:

- to eliminate unlawful racial discrimination; *and*
- to promote equality of opportunity and good relations between persons of different racial groups.

This duty affects every power and duty of a local authority.

CRIMINAL ACTS TO STIR UP RACIAL HATRED

The Public Order Act 1986 prohibits certain acts intended or likely to stir up racial hatred (see 2.5, p. 40). No prosecution for these offences may be brought without the Attorney General's permission. The Act covers:

- The use of words or behaviour or displays of written material which are threatening, abusive or insulting and intended to stir up racial hatred or which, in the circumstances, are likely to stir up racial hatred. The acts do not have to be committed in public; however, such acts, if committed in a private dwelling, are outside the Act.
- Publishing or distributing to the public written material which is threatening, abusive or insulting and intended to stir up racial hatred or which, in the circumstances, is likely to stir up racial hatred. This will include racist graffiti as well as newspaper articles and other similarly offensive racist material which is threatening, abusive or insulting.
- The public performance of a play which involves the use of threatening, abusive or insulting words or behaviour intended to stir up racial hatred or which, in the circumstances, are likely to stir up racial hatred. There are defences to this offence which apply in very limited circumstances. The offence is primarily aimed at the presenter and director, but actors who alter their lines will be within the prohibition.
- Distributing, showing or playing a recording of visual images (including video recordings) or sound which is threatening,

abusive or insulting and which is intended to stir up racial hatred or in circumstances in which it is likely racial hatred will be stirred up.

● Broadcasting (including a programme in a cable programme service), which is threatening, abusive or insulting and which is intended to stir up racial hatred or in circumstances in which it is likely racial hatred will be stirred up. Note, however, that programmes transmitted by the BBC or IBA are exempt. (For further controls on broadcasting see 2.9, p. 53).

INFLAMMATORY MATERIAL

The Public Order Act 1986 also makes it an offence to have possession of written material which is threatening, abusive or insulting, or a recording of visual images or sound which is threatening, abusive or insulting with a view to use, and with the intention that racial hatred will be stirred up or in circumstances in which it is likely to be stirred up.

Powers of entry, search and forfeiture are given in respect of such material. Again, prosecutions may only be brought with the Attorney General's consent.

In the Public Order Act 1986 'racial hatred' is defined as hatred against a group of persons in Great Britain defined by reference to colour, race, nationality (including citizenship) or ethnic or national origins. This definition does not include religion. It may also exclude gypsies (see also 14.1, p. 303).

9.2   Sex discrimination

This section deals with sex discrimination in education, housing, the provision of goods, facilities and services, advertising and social security. The duties and powers of the Equal Opportunities Commission are also explained here.

Sex discrimination in pay and terms and conditions of work is dealt with in chapter 13, as is information on maternity rights for working women. Sex discrimination as it relates to immigration and nationality is dealt with in chapter 10.

WHAT DOES THE LAW COVER?

The Sex Discrimination Act 1975, as amended by the Sex Discrimination Act 1986 (SDA), covers discrimination in the following areas:

- employment;
- education;
- goods, facilities and services; *and*
- housing.

The Act covers discrimination against men and women. As far as employment and training are concerned, the Act also makes it unlawful to discriminate against married people. But this does not apply to the other areas of the Act listed above. Discrimination against single people because of their marital status remains lawful.

The SDA does not cover:

- tax;
- social security;
- immigration; *or*
- nationality.

There are other exceptions within the areas that are covered by the law. These are mentioned below, under the relevant headings.

WHAT IS DISCRIMINATION?

The Sex Discrimination Act 1975 defines discrimination in two ways: *direct* and *indirect*.

Direct discrimination is when you are or would be treated less favourably in the same circumstances than someone of the opposite sex, just because of your sex. For example, admitting only boys to a GCSE course in electronics at a mixed school would be direct discrimination. So would offering HP facilities only to men, or half-price entry to a disco only to women.

Indirect discrimination occurs when a requirement or condition is applied to both sexes in any area covered by the Act, with which, in practice, far fewer members of one sex than the other can comply. Indirect discrimination is unlawful if it cannot be shown to be justifiable irrespective of sex and if the aggrieved person can show that the discrimination is to their detriment. For example, an after-school computer club open only to pupils taking an exam course in computer science could be against the law if hardly any girls took the exam course. A housing association which excluded single parents from membership would be indirectly discriminating, because the vast majority of single parents are women.

Victimization

The Act also protects you against victimization for taking action under either the Sex Discrimination Act or the Equal Pay Act. This provision makes it unlawful to treat you less favourably than anyone else because you have:

- made a complaint under either of the Acts;
- helped someone else to make a complaint;
- given evidence in a court or tribunal in a case under either of the Acts;
- accused someone of breaking either of the Acts; *or*
- taken any other action in connection with either of the Acts.

EDUCATION

The SDA makes it unlawful to discriminate on grounds of sex, directly or indirectly, in any of the following areas:

- admissions policies;
- access to classes, courses or other benefits, facilities or services provided by the school or college;
- any other unfavourable treatment.

The Act permits the continuation of single-sex schools, but also places a general duty on local education authorities to provide education without sex discrimination. This might mean, for example, that although a single-sex girls' school may not offer a design and technology course through its own curriculum, the LEA has to ensure that if boys in the same area have the opportunity to study this subject, arrangements are made to enable girls to take it, perhaps by attending a nearby mixed school for those lessons. This is, of course, easier said than done and unfortunately very few test cases on the education sections of the Act have ever been taken to court. Individual parents and children are understandably reluctant to place themselves in the public eye by so doing.

The following bodies can be held responsible for discrimination under the SDA:

- all schools, colleges and other educational establishments maintained by LEAs. Depending on the circumstances of the case, the LEA itself and/or the governors of the institution can be held responsible. Governors can be held responsible individually or collectively.
- independent or private schools. The proprietors would be responsible.
- universities. The governing body would be responsible.
- other establishments designated by the Secretary of State. These include certain independent polytechnics and other establishments in receipt of grants from the DES or the local authority. The governing body in each case is responsible for any discrimination.

Educational trusts

The SDA allows educational trusts to change their terms, with consent from the Secretary of State, in order to apply their benefits to both sexes.

Exceptions

- Single-sex schools and colleges. A single-sex institution planning to turn co-educational can apply for permission to discriminate by admitting more members of one sex for a limited period.
- Co-educational schools which provide boarding accommodation for one sex only may continue to do so. If provided for

both sexes, accommodation must be equal though it may be separate.

- Education provided by charities set up to benefit one sex only.
- Further education courses in physical training.
- In sport, single-sex competitive sport is allowed 'where the physical strength, stamina or physique of the average woman puts her at a disadvantage to the average man'. In practice, this has often been used to exclude girls from certain sports at school, although in primary schools at least, boys and girls often do all physical education together. The Equal Opportunities Commission is seeking an amendment to the Act to exclude primary school age children from this part of the Act.

HOUSING

The SDA makes it unlawful to discriminate in renting, sub-letting or selling accommodation. Owner-occupied properties, small boarding houses and flat-sharing, however, are excluded from the Act. Single-sex housing associations are also exempt.

MORTGAGES

Building Societies, local authorities or any other body which grants mortgages are breaking the law if they treat women applicants any less favourably than they would treat a man in the same circumstances. For example, they may not apply different rules regarding earnings levels, age, dependants, and so on.

GOODS, FACILITIES AND SERVICES

This covers a wide range of public and private services, including pubs, cafés, restaurants, hotels, transport, banking, insurance, hire purchase, recreation and entertainment.

The list of exceptions to this part of the Act, however, is just about as long as the list of situations it does cover, some of them understandable, others more dubious. The exceptions are:

- Private clubs, such as working men's clubs and sports clubs.

(NB These *are* covered by the equivalent section in the Race Relations Act 1976.)

- Political parties. Women's sections and conferences are still lawful.
- Religious bodies may continue to discriminate if necessary because of their doctrine or because not to do so would offend 'a significant number' of its members.
- Hospitals, prisons, hostels, old people's homes and any other places for people needing 'special care'.
- Competitive sport, if an average woman would be at a disadvantage because of her physical capacity, compared to the average man.
- Charities and non-profit-making organizations set up to provide facilities or services for one sex only. This doesn't mean such organizations may discriminate across the board, e.g., by restricting their office workers to one sex only, but they may discriminate in the provision of services, including who is employed in actually providing those services.
- Insurance companies and similar bodies. These may discriminate if it is on the basis of 'reasonable actuarial information'. For example, women can be offered cheaper car insurance than men, because statistics show they are safer drivers.
- Facilities and services which need to be restricted to one sex only in order to preserve 'decency and privacy'. This covers toilets, saunas, changing rooms, and so on.

HOW TO COMPLAIN ABOUT SEX DISCRIMINATION

A complaint under the SDA must be taken to an industrial tribunal if it concerns employment, including cases of victimization concerned with employment. Complaints of discrimination in education, housing, provision of goods, facilities or services must be made to the county court. Complaints concerning education must first be made to the Secretary of State for Education. If the matter has not been resolved to your satisfaction within two months, you may then proceed with action in the county court. Complaints about housing, goods, facilities and services must be made within six months of the discrimination taking place.

ADVERTISEMENTS

If an advertisement for a job covered by the SDA states or implies an intention to discriminate against men or women applicants, a complaint could be made to an industrial tribunal under the employment sections of the Act, as the advertisement would count as part of the arrangements made by the employer to fill a vacancy.

Advertising in other areas, e.g., for accommodation, entertainment or services, is also covered by the SDA but complaints about discriminatory advertising may only be taken up by the Equal Opportunities Commission (EOC). If you see a discriminatory advertisement, you can report it to the EOC. (The address is at the end of this chapter.)

Sexism in advertising, through offensive images of women used to sell products for example, is not outlawed by the SDA. But complaints of sexism or anything else you consider to be illegal, indecent, dishonest or untruthful can be made to:

> Advertising Standards Authority
> 15–17 Ridgmount Street
> London WC1E 7AW (01-580 5555)

THE EQUAL OPPORTUNITIES COMMISSION (EOC)

The EOC was set up under the Sex Discrimination Act 1975 (SDA) with the duties to:

- work towards the elimination of sex discrimination;
- promote equality of opportunity between men and women generally;
- keep the SDA and the Equal Pay Act under review and propose amendments to the Secretary of State.

In carrying out its duties, the EOC has the following powers:

- To undertake formal investigations into discriminatory practices which are unsuitable to be dealt with on an individual basis.
- To support, including financially, individuals taking up complaints of discrimination.

- To issue codes of practice on employment. The first code was approved by Parliament in April 1985. It is not legally binding but can be used in evidence at an industrial tribunal.
- To examine areas of policy outside the scope of the Act, e.g., social security, taxation, maternity rights.
- To issue non-discrimination notices. This happens if the EOC decides as a result of a formal investigation that the law has been broken.
- To fund research and other projects.
- To apply for an injunction if it believes someone has broken the law and is likely to go on doing so. In the following circumstances, it is the EOC alone which can take action, such as applying for an injunction, if discrimination has taken place:
  - if an advertisement demonstrates an intention to discriminate unlawfully;
  - if someone instructs an employee or agent to discriminate unlawfully; *or*
  - if someone puts pressure on anyone else to discriminate unlawfully.

LOCAL AUTHORITIES

Unlike the Race Relations Act, the Sex Discrimination Act does *not* impose a statutory duty on every local authority to carry out its functions with regard to eliminating unlawful discrimination and to promoting equal opportunity.

SOCIAL SECURITY

An EEC directive on equal treatment in social security has led to some changes in Britain's social security benefits in recent years. For example, men and women now have equal treatment in short-term, contributory benefits, such as unemployment benefit. Women may also claim income support (formerly supplementary benefit) on behalf of their partners and dependants, although in practice this is rare. Discrimination against married women claiming the Invalid Care Allowance (ICA) has now been outlawed, following a successful test case under the European directive. Married and co-habiting women claiming ICA may also put in for back payments to December 1984, if applicable to their case.

TAX

Despite endless discussion and consultation documents and virtually continuous campaigning since the SDA was passed, the tax laws in Britain remain discriminatory on grounds of sex. A married woman's income, in law, is deemed to belong to her husband for tax purposes. And a married man is entitled to a higher personal allowance than either a married woman or a single person. The most recent government proposals for reform, however, are worrying, in that they would remove the directly discriminatory elements of the system on the one hand, whilst establishing and reinforcing discriminatory trends on the other. A system of personal allowances, as proposed, transferable between spouses, would not secure independence or privacy for married women and, worse still, could deter married women from taking paid employment in the first place. The EOC estimates that about 300,000 women would withdraw from the labour market if transferable allowances were introduced. The EOC, along with other organizations campaigning in this field of social policy (notably the Child Poverty Action Group), would prefer to see individuals given an equal, non-transferable allowance and an increase made to Child Benefit, paid for with the revenue saved by abolishing the married man's tax allowance.

9.3   Sexual orientation

Consensual sexual activity between men over twenty-one in private is legal. There are no general laws specifically restricting lesbian behaviour, but the law imposes many limitations on what gay men and lesbian women can do in practice.

There is no statutory protection against discrimination on grounds of sexual orientation, such as the Sex Discrimination and Race Relations Acts (see 9.1, p. 193 and 9.2, p. 207). This means that, broadly speaking, there is little legal sanction against such discrimination in the fields of employment, housing, immigration, the provision of services and parental rights.

CRIMINAL LAW

Women

There are no laws specially restricting lesbian behaviour, except in the armed forces, where women can be charged with committing 'disgraceful conduct of an indecent or unnatural kind'.

Technically, lesbians can be prosecuted for the following acts, but rarely are:

- insulting behaviour (see 1.3, p. 23);
- indecent assault on another woman who did not consent or who is under sixteen;
- although there is no age of consent for lesbians, the Indecency with Children Act 1960 provides that a woman committing an act of gross indecency (see 9.3, p. 208) with a girl under fourteen would be breaking the law.

Men

It is legal for two men over twenty-one to have sex together, provided they are in private and both consent (this is now the law throughout the whole of the UK). In this context, sex means any form of sexual activity, including intercourse (buggery). The following restrictions apply to sex between men:

- The age of consent of twenty-one is five years older than the age at which heterosexuals can have lawful intercourse.
- 'In private' does not include places such as public lavatories (even if no one can see), or when more than two people are present, even if they all consent. It is up to the prosecution to prove that the activity did not take place in private, and many courts have decided that particular places were 'in private', even if the public theoretically had access to them (e.g., a dark lane; behind a clump of bushes; in an enclosed yard after normal working hours, etc.).
- Meeting another man with a view to having lawful sex may itself be illegal. Because of the law of importuning or soliciting,

it may be an offence to chat up another man if done in a public place. Even just smiling at someone can be classified as importuning, and if a man 'persistently' importunes for an 'immoral purpose' that is an offence. It is up to the court to decide if lawful sexual activity amounts to an 'immoral purpose' in any particular case, but they can (and sometimes do) find men guilty of this offence even though the sexual activity would have been lawful, i.e., between two consenting men over twenty-one and in private.

- Members of all branches of the Armed Forces are still denied the right to a homosexual sex life. All forms of lesbian or gay sex are illegal and can lead to a court martial and a dishonourable discharge, plus up to two years' imprisonment.
- It is illegal for merchant seamen to engage in gay sex on board a ship on which either of them is serving, though this does not apply to deep-sea oil-rigs.
- Displays of affection in public by lesbians or gay men might be illegal on the ground of 'insulting behaviour' (see 1.3, p. 23).

OFFENCES

Cruising/picking up men

Making an approach to another man, with a view to having sex may itself be a crime, even though it was intended to have sex in circumstances which would be legal. Under the Sexual Offences Act 1956, it is an offence persistently to importune in a public place for an immoral purpose. This law was enacted originally at the end of the nineteenth century to outlaw pimping for female prostitutes in the Leicester Square music-halls. Now it is used almost exclusively to stop men approaching other men with a view to sex – known as cruising, or more commonly, picking someone up.

Usually the police arrest men for importuning (also called 'soliciting') outside or near gay pubs or clubs, or in parks, public lavatories or other places where it is likely that one man can pick up another. This law is not used primarily against men who are prostitutes, though male prostitution is covered by it.

Importuning is any kind of approach to another person: a smile is enough, and either words or gestures will do. 'Persistently' means more than once to the same person, or repeatedly to a number of persons. If a man speaks to or gestures towards another man just once it is not an offence under this section, but it may still be caught by the offence of 'attempting to procure an act of gross indecency' (see below). Whether a purpose is an 'immoral purpose' depends entirely on the view of the court, applying its own standards. Magistrates are known to convict of this offence much more frequently than juries. (It is an offence that can be tried either by magistrates or by a judge and jury.) The higher courts have made it clear that a man can be convicted of this offence even though he was chatting someone up with a view to having perfectly lawful sex – i.e., both consenting, twenty-one or older, and in private. Many juries have taken the view that picking up another man, even a stranger, for sex is not an 'immoral purpose' caught by this Act, and the majority of such cases result in acquittals if fought in the Crown Court.

Sentences vary widely from place to place. For most men convicted of this kind of offence publicity, exposure and humiliation are far greater penalties than those imposed by the courts. They often lead to loss of jobs, break-up of families and even suicide.

SEXUAL ACTIVITY

All forms of sexual activity between men are legal if done in private between consenting adults aged twenty-one or older, but any kind of sexual activity involving a man *under* twenty-one, or taking place in public, is illegal. The law uses the term 'gross indecency' to describe all sexual activity between men other than buggery (anal intercourse). By a curious anomaly, the 1967 Sexual Offences Act made buggery (in private, etc.) between men legal but it remains illegal between a man and a woman, though it is almost never enforced.

'Gross indecency' includes sexual activity short of physical contact as well as touching. For example, two men masturbating in sight of each other, although separated by a wall, have been found guilty of gross indecency even though they were in adjacent locked cubicles of a public lavatory and no one else could see them (except police officers peering down from a hole in the ceiling). It is not 'gross indecency' to engage in sexual activity merely directed towards another man unless he too is a willing participant, in the sense that he is aware of what is going on and co-operates in an 'indecent exhibition'. This offence has been used to prosecute the director of a play in which the actors simulated gay sex.

The term 'gross indecency' is not defined anywhere in the law. It is a question for the court (i.e., either the magistrates or the jury) as to whether the activity that was taking place amounts to 'gross indecency'. If either or both of the parties is under twenty-one they also can be prosecuted, though in practice this is rarely done if both are under twenty-one, and the Director of Public Prosecutions must give his consent to a prosecution for an offence involving someone under twenty-one.

Sexual activity will only be illegal in many cases because it takes place in public. It is for the prosecution to prove that an act of gross indecency took place otherwise than in private, and whether a place is public or private is a question for the court. In the case of Reakes (1974) the Court of Appeal approved the following definition of 'in private':

Look at all the surrounding circumstances, the time of night, the nature of the place including such matters as lighting and you consider further the likelihood of a third person coming upon the scene.

As with cases of importuning, a majority of juries acquit on charges of gross indecency, and there is a better chance of acquittal in the Crown Court than in the magistrates' courts.

It can also be an offence to approach another man with a view to having sex, either by 'importuning' (see p. 217), or by 'attempting to procure an act of gross indecency'. This means no more than making an approach to another man. It differs from importuning in two ways: there does not need to be any 'persistency' or repetition of the approach; but also, for it to be an offence, the prosecution must prove that the sexual activity sought would have been illegal, i.e., usually, in public.

Buggery is legal or illegal in the same circumstances as gross indecency, i.e., it depends on the ages of the parties and the place where it happens.

DISPLAYING AFFECTION IN PUBLIC

Lesbians or gay men who hold hands or kiss or fondle each other in public in the same way as heterosexuals, may be committing an offence of 'insulting behaviour', under the Public Order Act 1986. Much will depend on the particular facts of the case, and, as it is an offence which can only be tried in the magistrates' court, it will usually depend on the moral and political views of the magistrates as to whether the behaviour is regarded as insulting. The term 'insulting' is not defined by the law; it has to be given its ordinary meaning, but the higher courts have upheld a conviction under similar (though not identical) legislation where two men were fondling each other's genitals and buttocks over their clothes, in the course of saying goodnight in a public place.

POLICING AND AGENTS PROVOCATEURS

The police have a very wide discretion in the way they enforce the offences referred to above. In some areas of the country they are far more rigorous about seeking out gay offences than in others, and the attitudes of the same police force may change from time to time, depending on the views of the senior officers responsible for operational decisions.

In some instances the police themselves try to lure gay men into committing offences, especially importuning. They do this by standing around, often dressed to attract an advance, usually outside gay pubs or in public lavatories, making it obvious that they are looking for a pick-up. A man who approaches a policeman who is acting as an *agent provocateur* will not thereby automatically have a defence to a charge of importuning or attempting to procure an act of gross indecency, despite the fact that police and Home Office regulations specifically prohibit this activity. However, a jury in such a case may well be more disposed to acquit the man on other grounds as an indication of their disapproval of the police behaviour.

PENALTIES

The *maximum* penalties for the various consensual sexual offences we have considered will depend on a number of factors, namely whether the case is heard in the magistrates' or the Crown Court and, in some offences, the age of the parties involved.

CONSPIRACY TO CORRUPT PUBLIC MORALS

This is a rarely-used but powerful criminal offence, invented by the judiciary rather than passed by Parliament. It has been used in particular to prohibit gay men advertising in the 'contact' pages of magazines. Essentially, it is an offence to conspire or agree to do some act which, in the opinion of a jury, is calculated to corrupt or debauch public morals. In 1973 the House of Lords upheld, by a majority, the conviction of a magazine containing explicit gay contact ads, on the ground that encouraging homosexuality is the sort of thing a jury might properly consider to be a 'corrupt practice'.

In practice, this offence operates more by inhibition than by enforcement. Gay contact ads are permissible if they are discreetly worded rather than explicit; but the effect of the offence goes well beyond the world of magazine publishing in so far as it inhibits many worthwhile projects, especially those concerned with social provision for young lesbians and gay men. It is unlikely to be used successfully against genuine counselling and advice agencies but it remains in the background as a potential weapon.

YOUNG LESBIANS AND GAY MEN

While the criminal law prohibits any kind of gay sex life for men under twenty-one, lesbian and gay teenagers who assert their independence once they become sixteen may find themselves taken into care by the local authority on the grounds that they are in 'moral danger' (see 12.10, p. 264).

If they are under seventeen they can be detained by the police, placed under a 'place of safety' order for up to twenty-eight days in a Community Home, or even taken into care by the local authority. There are a number of cases of young lesbians and gay men who have been dealt with in this way simply because they wanted to live with other lesbians or gay men, even at an age when they were old enough to marry and live with another person of the opposite sex.

CIVIL LAW

There is no difference in the way in which the civil law affects lesbians and gay men. Both groups are treated in the same way in principle, though in practice there may be a difference if a man's civil rights are threatened as a result of a conviction for one of the consensual sexual offences referred to above, which do not affect lesbians. There are no specific statutes protecting lesbians and gay men from discrimination on the grounds of their sexual orientation.

EMPLOYMENT

Recruitment

Broadly speaking, there is no way a lesbian or gay man can challenge an employer who refuses to give her or him a job on the grounds of their sexual orientation. The Sex Discrimination Act 1975 prohibits discrimination on grounds of sex or marital status (see 9.2, p. 208), but not sexual orientation. However, in rare cases it might be possible to use this legislation when the real reason for the discrimination is sexual orientation.

An example is the Dan Air case. The company had a policy of not even considering for interview men who applied for cabin-staff posts, on the grounds that, if any of them were gay, passengers might be exposed to the risk of contracting AIDS.

The Equal Opportunities Commission investigated Dan Air's policy and found that there were no medical grounds for doing so, with the result that the company was in breach of the Sex Discrimination Act. They issued a non-discrimination notice (see 9.1, p. 204) and subsequently Dan Air changed their policy.

The case illustrates the point that the company was discriminating against *all* men in their desire to exclude gay men, and so was breaking the law.

Existing workforce

Many employees suffer discriminatory treatment at work because they are known or believed to be lesbian or gay. There are even some cases of discriminatory treatment of gay men by colleagues and employers on the grounds that they may be carrying HIV, the virus which can lead to AIDS, solely because they are gay.

The difficulty in challenging such treatment is that there is no specific law prohibiting it, and lesbian and gay workers are thrown back on general employment laws which have not proved of much use in these circumstances.

If an employer discriminates against a lesbian or gay worker, for example, by denying them promotion, or responds to hostile pressure by colleagues (e.g., by moving the worker concerned to different duties or a different location), the only way that the worker can challenge the decision in law is by resigning and claiming 'constructive dismissal' (see 13.5, p. 288), on the ground that the employer has acted in breach of contract.

Dismissal on grounds of sexual orientation

The response of the Industrial Tribunals and the Employment Appeal Tribunal (EAT) to dismissals on grounds of sexual orientation has varied from case to case and is difficult to predict, except that it is more often unfavourable to the employee than the employer. In one notorious decision in 1980, the EAT in Scotland upheld as fair the dismissal of a maintenance worker at a children's camp solely on the ground that he was gay. It was held reasonable for the employer to dismiss him on the basis of prejudice by parents whose children attended the camp, even though there was scientific evidence to show that a gay employee poses no risk in himself to children or anyone else. Most of these cases come to the Tribunals following a man's conviction for a gay offence (see 9.3, p. 217).

In another of the few sexual orientation cases to be heard by the EAT, it was held fair to dismiss a teacher following his conviction, outside working hours, for gross indecency. The EAT went to some pains to emphasize that each case must be decided on its merits, and it was neither automatically fair nor automatically unfair to dismiss in such cases.

The overall impression is that, with a few exceptions, Industrial Tribunals are more likely to uphold the dismissal of a gay employee who is convicted of a consensual offence if he works with, or in proximity to, children and young people than other kinds of employees.

Even in cases when dismissal has been found unfair, the Tribunals often make remarks to the effect that no danger is posed because the worker concerned does not have contact in their job with young people, the public etc. This fails to recognize the nature of the offences for which gay men are usually convicted – i.e., consenting acts with other adults.

Few cases involving lesbians have reached the Tribunals, partly because of the different criminal laws. However, the best known case, Boychuk (1977), demonstrated the hazard of showing one's sexual orientation openly at work. Ms Boychuk wore a badge with the words 'Lesbians Ignite' in her job as a receptionist at an insurance company's office. She was dismissed for refusing to take it off and her dismissal was upheld as fair by the EAT.

Although the decision was based on general principles of what an employer might reasonably require by way of standards of dress, it is very unlikely that the dismissal would have occurred or been upheld had the badge borne a heterosexual message.

There are a number of trade unions which have specific lesbian and gay sections or groups, which have effectively campaigned within the workplace to prevent discrimination and they can be contacted through the lists of lesbian/gay organizations in this book.

HOUSING

A lesbian or gay relationship is not treated as equivalent to a heterosexual marriage in the eyes of the law. The result in housing law is that lesbians or gay men have no right to succeed to a tenancy if their partner dies, regardless of how long-established their relationship was, even though the surviving partner in a heterosexual couple living together 'as husband and wife' would be entitled to succeed to the tenancy under the Housing Act 1985.

IMMIGRATION

The same approach has been taken by the courts to lesbian/gay relationships in immigration law as in housing law, i.e., that they cannot be compared to a heterosexual marriage. Even so, the immigration rules, like the Housing Act, contemplate heterosexual relationships that may not have been formalized as a marriage in law and make provision for them to be treated as a case of husband and wife.

It seems that the practice of successive governments has been to allow some lesbian/gay foreign nationals to enter or remain in the UK if they can demonstrate a long-standing, stable relationship, though it is impossible to predict with certainty which cases will get through. The procedure is to make representations to the Minister via a member of either House of Parliament.

TRANSVESTITES

There is nothing in the law to stop anyone dressing in clothes traditionally worn by members of the opposite sex. Sometimes, however, transvestites have been arrested for 'insulting behaviour' (see 1.3, p. 23), and in theory they could in some circumstances be convicted of this offence, but such situations are very rare.

TRANSSEXUALS

It is lawful to undergo an operation to change sex but there is no consequent right in law to be regarded as a member of the opposite sex from that into which you were born. In practice, however, transsexuals are able to obtain most official documents except a birth certificate in their new name and sexual identity. Medical cards, driving licences, income tax forms, passports, etc., will be issued by the relevant authorities in the new identity.

There is no right to be married as a member of the opposite sex and for the purposes of the law any such marriage is void.

The European Court of Human Rights has ruled that refusal of an amended birth certificate and the right to marry is not a breach of the right to a private life contained in the European Convention on Human Rights.

PARENTAL RIGHTS

Many lesbians and gay men marry, or live in heterosexual relationships before coming out, and often have children. Lesbians and gay men who seek custody of, or access to, their children following the breakup of such relationships discover that the law treats them far less favourably than heterosexuals in the same circumstances. Although there is a right to apply to the courts for an order granting custody of, or access to, their children, this right is entirely at the discretion of the judges, who have shown themselves strongly biased against lesbian or gay parents. For example, a mother is usually likely to obtain custody if it is disputed, but if the court is told that she is lesbian, her chances of being awarded custody are much less than that of the father, no matter how unsuitable he is.

BAN OF PROMOTING HOMOSEXUALITY

The most significant piece of legislation affecting homosexuals since the reforming 1967 Act is section 28 of the Local Government Act 1988, which bars the 'intentional promotion of homosexuality' by local authorities. The section prohibits the intentional promotion of homosexuality, or the publishing of material with the intention of promoting homosexuality or the promotion of teaching in any maintained school of 'the acceptability of homosexuality as a pretended family relationship'.

There is a let-out in that the section does not prohibit anything done for the purpose of treating or preventing the spread of disease. Because the section came into force only on 24 May 1988, there have been no court decisions interpreting its precise breadth and meaning at the time of printing this book.

Legal opinion generally expects that the section will be interpreted narrowly by the courts to prohibit only things done or publications

which actively advocate a homosexual lifestyle or sexual experimentation to those not otherwise so inclined. Nevertheless, many
local authorities throughout Britain have reacted to its enactment
by adopting policies of self-censorship and extreme caution, in most
cases probably unnecessarily. There have been examples of local
authorities banning:

- the publication of a list of advice agencies for young people
  because a couple of the hundreds of entries were lesbian
  and/or gay organizations;
- the performance of a play by a 'theatre in education' group
  because it contained a scene involving homosexuals;
- the publication of a cartoon in a Women's Unit newsletter
  because it was a lesbian parody of heterosexual attitudes;
- the confirmation by a gay teacher of his sexuality when asked
  about it by children in his class.

Expert legal opinion is of the view that none of those examples fell
within the terms of section 28, and all those local authorities
misinterpreted the section by imposing such bans. Those cases do,
however, illustrate the real impact of the section, which is to
inhibit, censor and undermine the legitimate functions of local
government and schools.

The ban on promoting the teaching of the 'acceptability of
homosexuality as a pretended family relationship' in maintained
schools is, in strict legal terms, greatly weakened by two factors.
First, it is school governors and not local authorities who are
legally responsible for sex education in schools. Therefore, although
there are other limitations laid down in statutes and circulars in
relation to teaching about homosexuality, school governors are not
affected by section 28. Second, it is unlikely on any interpretation
of the section that discussion of and counselling about homosexuality would be prohibited or restricted by this law. However, as
we noted, some local authorities have already acted as though they
are prevented from discussing or offering advice and counselling
about homosexuality, despite the fact that the law will not prohibit
it. Its effect is far deeper in practice than it is ever likely to be in
the eyes of the courts.

9.4   More information

RACE DISCRIMINATION

Useful organizations

Commission for Racial Equality, 10–12 Allington Street, London SW1E 5EH (01-828 7022)

Community Relations Councils exist throughout the country. You can get the address of your nearest CRC from a Citizens' Advice Bureau, the town hall or the telephone directory.

Law Centres Federation, Duchess House, 18–19 Warren Street, London W1P 5DB (01-387 8540). Contact them to find out the address of your nearest Law Centre.

Runnymede Trust, 62 Chandos Place, London WC2N 4HG (01-836 3266)

Trade Unions will often be able to help you if you suffer discrimination at work.

Bibliography

C. Palmer and K. Poulten, *Sex and Race Discrimination in Employment*. Legal Action Group, 1987.
The CRE publish a number of useful pamphlets on the workings of the Race Relations Act 1976, including a code of practice.

SEX DISCRIMINATION

Useful organizations

Citizens Rights Office, Child Poverty Action Group, 1 Bath Street, London EC1V 9PY (01-253 3406)

Equal Opportunities Commission, Overseas House, Quay Street, Manchester M3 3HN (061-833 9244)

NCCL Rights for Women Unit, 21 Tabard Street, London SE1 4LA (01-403 3888)

Rights of Women (ROW), 52–4 Featherstone Street, London EC1Y 8ET (01-251 6577)

The addresses of your local *Citizens' Advice Bureau* or *Rape Crisis Centre* can be found in the telephone directory

Bibliography

M. Benn etc., *The Rape Controversy*, NCCL Rights for Women Unit, 1986.
A. Coote and T. Gill, *Women's Rights: A Practical Guide*, Penguin Books, 1981.
R. Evans and L. Durward, *Maternity Rights at Work*, NCCL, 1986.

SEXUAL ORIENTATION

Useful organizations

Campaign for Homosexual Equality (CHE), Room 221, 38 Mount Pleasant, London WC1X 0AP (01-833 3912)

Friend (Counselling and advice Organizations for Lesbians and Gay Men), BM National Friend, 33A Seven Sisters Road, London N7 6AX (01-837 3337)

Gay Rights at Work, c/o Pikwick Court, London SE9 4SA

GLAD (*Gay and Lesbian Legal Advice*), BM/GLAD, London WC1N 3XX (01-253 2043)

LAGER (*Lesbian and Gay Employment Rights*), Room 205, Southbank House, Black Prince Road, London SE1 7SJ (01-587 1643 (Gays)/01-587 1636 (Lesbians))

London Lesbian and Gay Switchboard, BM Switchboard, London WC1X 3XX (01-837 7324)

Terrence Higgins Trust, BM/AIDS, London WC1N 3XX (01-242 1010). For advice and support on HIV and AIDS issues.

Organization for Lesbian and Gay Action, PO Box 147, London WC2H 0BB (01-833 3860)

Bibliography

C. Beer etc., *Gay Workers, Trade Unions and the Law*, NCCL, 1982.
Changing the World: A Charter for Lesbian and Gay Rights, GLC, 1986.
P. Crane, *Gays and the Law*, Pluto Press, 1982.
Gay Men at Work, LAGER (Lesbian and Gay Employment Rights), 1987.
Lesbian Custody Handbook, Rights of Women, 1987.

10 The rights of immigrants

This chapter deals with:

10.1   Immigration control

The present laws on immigration are the Immigration Acts of 1971 and 1988, which came into force on 1 January 1973 and 1 August 1988 respectively. These Acts lay down general principles about who is subject to immigration control and who is not. The details of how control is to be carried out are in the immigration rules; the main rules in force now (September 1988) are called House of Commons Paper 169 of February 1983, 503 of July 1985 and 555 of July 1988. The Home Office has promised to publish a consolidated edition later this year. The rules are changed frequently; there have been five major changes since 1973. There are also detailed instructions to immigration officers as to how they should operate the rules; these instructions are secret and have never been published. To understand immigration law, therefore, it is necessary to know about the practice of the Home Office too, and it is advisable to contact one of the organizations listed at the end of this chapter for advice before approaching the Home Office.

WHO IS SUBJECT TO CONTROL?

British citizens, Commonwealth citizens with the right of abode and Irish citizens travelling from Ireland are *not* subject to immigration control. If you fall into one of these categories, you can come and go as you like, you do not require permission from an immigration officer to enter and your passport will not be stamped when you travel in and out. Commonwealth citizens have the right of abode if *either*:

- one of their parents was born in the UK; *or*
- they are women who were married before 1983 to a man who was a British citizen or a Commonwealth citizen with the right of abode.

There are special regulations for citizens of the EEC (Belgium, Denmark, France, West Germany, Ireland, Italy, Luxembourg, the Netherlands, Greece, Spain and Portugal), who are subject to only a limited form of immigration control. As an EEC citizen you can come here to take up a job or to look for work, to do business or to become self-employed; if you find work you can then get a residence permit, usually valid for five years. You can bring your spouse, children up to the age of twenty-one, other dependent children, grandchildren, parents, grandparents and great-grand-parents with you. After working here for four years, you and all these family members may be allowed to settle here. The provisions about work will not apply to Spanish and Portuguese citizens until 1 January 1993, but they can now come for business or self-employment.

Everybody else is subject to full immigration control and can only come here with permission from an immigration officer and if they qualify under the immigration rules to enter for a specific purpose. If you are coming to stay permanently or to work you have to get permission from a British Embassy or High Commission abroad before travelling; this is called *entry clearance* and could be either a visa, an entry certificate or a letter of consent. Citizens of some countries (these are listed in the immigration rules) are 'visa nationals' which means you must always get permission before travelling, whatever you are coming for.

10.2   Coming to settle

Normally only the *close relatives* of people already settled here
(allowed to stay permanently) will be allowed to settle with them.
You must get entry clearance and satisfy other conditions before
travelling. Particularly in the Indian subcontinent, long queues
have grown up of people waiting for interview there. Many people
will only be allowed to come if their relatives can show that they can
be supported and accommodated 'without recourse to public funds'.
Public funds for immigration purposes are *only* income support,
housing benefit, family credit and re-housing under Part III of the
1985 Housing Act; claiming any other benefits cannot be used
against a person.

Husbands and wives

You have to prove to an entry clearance officer that:

- you are the husband or wife of the person you are coming to
  join and she/he is settled in the UK;
- you did not get married mainly in order to come to Britain;
- you intend to live together permanently as husband and wife;
- you have met each other;
- you have adequate accommodation for yourselves and any
  dependants in the UK;
- you will be able to support yourselves without relying on
  public funds.

There are particular difficulties for people from the Indian
subcontinent. Many wives in Bangladesh, who may have been
married decades ago to men settled in the UK, may not have
marriage or birth certificates to prove relationships and are
questioned in great detail about family matters in order to bring out
'discrepancies' which could lead to refusal. Over half the men
applying to come here in 1987 from the Indian subcontinent were
refused because they could not satisfy the entry clearance officer
that they had not married mainly to come here; this rule is used
mainly against arranged marriages.

If the application is successful, you will be allowed in for a year when you arrive. Before the end of that year, you must apply to the Home Office for permission to stay permanently. The Home Office must be satisfied that you and your spouse still intend to stay together and can support and accommodate yourselves without relying on public funds before this is granted.

Fiancés and fiancées

To come here to get married you have to prove all the same things as husbands and wives and show that you intend to get married soon after your arrival in Britain. If you are granted entry clearance, you will be allowed in for six months, forbidden to work here, and you are expected to get married within this time. You can then apply to the Home Office for permission to stay for a year, and then for settlement at the end of the year.

Children

Children under eighteen may be allowed to join parents here (or to join one parent if the other parent is dead) if:

- you get entry clearance;
- both your parents are settled here;
- your parents have adequate accommodation for you here;
- your parents can support you here without having to claim public funds.

If children are coming to join one parent and the other parent is still alive but not coming to live here, or coming to join a relative other than a parent, you *also* have to prove *either*

- the parent living here has had the sole responsibility for your upbringing; *or*
- there are serious and compelling family or other considerations making your exclusion from the UK undesirable.

These rules are very difficult to satisfy. In practice, they are not interpreted so strictly for children under twelve coming to join their mothers but this has never been written into the rules. Special consideration can also be given to daughters (but not sons) between the ages of eighteen and twenty-one.

Adopted children will only be allowed to come if it can be shown that the adoption was necessary because the natural parents were unable to care for the child, not if the reason for the adoption was for a childless couple to bring a child here.

Parents and grandparents

You may be able to join your children settled here if:

- you get entry clearance;
- if a couple, that one of you is over sixty-five; if a widower, you are over sixty-five, or a widowed mother of any age;
- you can be supported and accommodated by your children here without needing to rely on public funds;
- you were financially dependent on your children here while living in your country of origin;
- you have no other close relatives in your country of origin who could look after you there.

In practice it is very difficult to prove all this.

Other relatives

Any other relatives wanting to join family in the UK have to get entry clearance, have to show that they were financially dependent abroad, that they can be supported and accommodated here without recourse to public funds, and that they were living alone in the most exceptional compassionate circumstances, without other close relatives to turn to. This applies only to sons, daughters, sisters, brothers, uncles and aunts of people settled here, normally only when they are over sixty-five. It is very rare for anyone to qualify to come here under this rule.

COMING TO WORK

If you want to come to work here you need to get a work permit before you travel. The employer here needs to apply to the Department of Employment for permission to employ a foreign worker, and has to satisfy restrictive conditions about your skills and experience and show there is nobody already allowed to work here who could do the job instead.

If you get a work permit you will be allowed in for four years and will only be allowed to do the job for which you were given your permit. If you change jobs, the new employer must first get a new permit for you and all the original conditions must be satisfied again. Because work permit holders are not freely 'available for work' you do not qualify for income support if you have lost a job. After four years, you can qualify to settle.

The wife (but not husband) and the children under eighteen of a work permit holder may be allowed to come here to join him, as long as they can be supported and accommodated without recourse to public funds. They must get entry clearance before coming and will be allowed to stay for the same length of time as he is.

Some work can be possible without a work permit. If you are coming to do one of a specific list of jobs (which includes ministers of religion, missionaries, journalists working for overseas news-papers, servants of diplomats, people working for overseas govern-ments and international organizations) you do not need a work permit but still have to get permission before you come. You may be allowed to come here as a writer or artist if you can show that you can support and accommodate yourself from the proceeds of your art or writing, and any savings, without having to take any other work or to claim benefits. Employees of High Commissions and Embassies are not subject to immigration control. If you are very rich and have capital of at least £150,000, and satisfy other requirements, you may be allowed to come here to set up in business or be self-employed, or to live off your capital.

GENERAL

Once you have been allowed to settle there are no further immigration restrictions on what you can do here. You are able to work without needing any extra permission, you can claim any benefits without this having any effect on your right to remain. If you leave Britain, you will be allowed in again for settlement, provided you have not been away for more than two years and that you confirm you are returning to stay. People who were settled and have been away for more than two years may still be allowed to settle again in certain circumstances, for example, if you have lived here for the majority of your life. A visa national will always need a re-entry visa.

10.3   Coming for temporary purposes

If you want to visit Britain you need to satisfy an immigration officer that you are coming just for a visit, for a definite length of time and intend to leave at the end of it and that you can be supported and accommodated for the length of your visit without needing to work or to claim benefits. If you are a visa national, you need to get a visa in advance; if not, you can arrive at a port or airport and seek admission there. You may be bringing money with you or you may show that you can be supported by friends or relatives here. Six months is the longest time allowed to a visitor.

If you want to study, you may be allowed to come here if you can show that you have been accepted for a full-time course of study at a recognized college or independent (fee-paying) school, that you have the money to pay the fees and to live here without needing to work or to claim benefits and that you intend to leave Britain at the end of your studies. 'Full-time' normally means at least fifteen hours of daytime classes per week, studying one subject or related subjects. Overseas students have to pay fees which cover the full cost of their courses and you are not usually eligible for local authority grants. A student will normally be allowed in for a year or the duration of the course, whichever is shorter, and can apply to the Home Office to extend this time to continue a course. If you have not yet been accepted by a college you may be allowed in for two months in order to enrol and can then apply to the Home Office for an extension.

A student wanting a short period of post-qualification training or on-the-job experience may be allowed to stay on as a trainee, on the understanding that this is temporary and that a transfer to ordinary employment will not be allowed. If a student has spent more than four years on short (under two years) courses, or appears to be chopping and changing courses with no end in sight, or has not been attending studies regularly, an extension will be refused. The wife (but not husband) of a student and children under eighteen may be permitted to live here with him while he is studying, as long as they can be supported and accommodated but will have no right to stay on after he has finished his studies.

Students may be permitted to take part-time or holiday jobs, provided the college does not object and provided the employer obtains a permit from the Department of Employment. Students' wives are normally allowed to work.

REGISTRATION WITH THE POLICE

If you are not a Commonwealth or EEC citizen and not allowed to stay permanently but are permitted to stay in Britain for more than six months, you have to register with the local police. The police have to be informed of your name, date of birth, nationality, marital status, address and occupation and of any change in any of these in the future. This requirement will only be lifted if you are later allowed to stay permanently.

10.4   Enforcement of immigration control

If you are refused entry clearance abroad, you have the right to appeal against this. If you had obtained entry clearance before travelling, but are refused entry here you have a right of appeal in this country and can remain here while the appeal is pending. Immigration officers have the right to detain you while this is going on; after seven days you can apply to the immigration authorities for bail. If you are refused entry and did not have entry clearance you can be sent straight back, and can only appeal after you have left; you can be detained at the port until there is a flight back, or while any representations made on your behalf are under consideration, and you have no right to apply for bail.

If you have been allowed in for a temporary period and you are refused permission to stay longer you can appeal against this *only* if your application was made to the Home Office before your permission to stay here ran out. If the application was made late there is no right of appeal and you are in Britain illegally. All immigration appeals are heard in Britain, even when the appellant is abroad. An appeal is made first to a single adjudicator and then, if leave is granted, usually on a point of law only, to a three-person Tribunal. Adjudicators used to be appointed by the Home Office but now both they and Tribunal members are appointed by the Lord Chancellor's department. You may be represented, but legal aid is not available; few appeals succeed.

Police constables and immigration officers have the power to arrest, without warrant, anyone who has or who they suspect has committed an immigration offence. This very wide power leads to frequent questioning of black people about their immigration status when they come into contact with the police for any other reason, often when there is no rational cause for suspicion. The Police and Criminal Evidence Act provides for codes of practice for the police in connection with the detention and questioning of people and searches of premises, but in law these do not apply to immigration officers, though they have agreed to follow them voluntarily.

If you knowingly remain longer than you have been allowed by the immigration officers or the Home Office without asking permission you have become an overstayer and are committing a criminal offence. It makes no difference whether you have overstayed for many years or for a few days. You can be arrested and appear before a magistrates' court charged with this; if found guilty, you can be fined up to £500, imprisoned for up to six months and recommended for deportation.

If you are not a British citizen, or a Commonwealth citizen with the right of abode, or a Commonwealth or Irish citizen who was settled here before 1 January 1973 and who has lived here ever since, you can be recommended for deportation by a court if you are convicted of any crime for which the penalty could be imprisonment, even if you were allowed to stay in Britain permanently. You can appeal against this as part of the sentence and it is then up to the Home Office whether to carry out the recommendation. Unless the court specifically directs your release, you will be detained while the Home Office decides what to do, which could be several weeks.

The Home Office can also make its own decision to deport people for overstaying or for breaking other conditions of stay, for example, working without permission. If it makes a decision to deport you, there is a right of appeal to the immigration appeal authorities. If you have lived here for more than seven years, compassionate aspects, as well as the law, can then be considered. If you have been here less than seven years, the appeal is only on the facts – i.e., whether or not you are an overstayer. The Home Office has the power to detain people it has decided to deport, even while an appeal is pending. If a man is being deported a decision to deport his wife and his children under eighteen can also be made, solely on the grounds of their relationship.

The Home Office can also decide to deport you on the grounds that your presence is 'not conducive to the public good', a very vague term which can include people who have been convicted of a criminal offence but whom the court did not recommend for deportation, or people who are alleged to have made a marriage of convenience. You do have a right to an immigration appeal, but if the Home Secretary decides that your presence is non-conducive on the grounds of national security there is no appeal, you do not have the right to representation or even to know the grounds of the Home Office's decision. You can only put your case to three 'advisers', chosen by the Home Office, who may make a secret recommendation to the Home Secretary, but this recommendation does not have to be followed.

Once all appeals have been exhausted, the Home Secretary can sign a deportation order against you and you can be sent out of the country. While the order is in force, you cannot return here. You can apply for the order to be revoked, either to the British post in your own country or to the Home Office, but this is not normally done until the order has been in force for at least three years. If the order is revoked that does not entitle you to return, but to apply to return if you can satisfy the immigration rules.

If the Home Office claims that you entered the country illegally, you have no right of appeal until after you have been sent out of the country. You can be treated as an illegal entrant either because you entered the country without being questioned by immigration officers at all or because it is alleged that you misled immigration officers, or did not tell them information that was relevant, and therefore, should not have been allowed in. People alleged to be illegal entrants have *no* rights; they can be arrested and detained solely on the decision of an immigration official and can be held for an indefinite length of time. The Bail Act does not apply to them and they have no right of appeal until after they have been removed from the country. They may also be removed very quickly, without being given the chance to seek advice. Judicial review of the decision may be sought but it is rare for the court to reverse the Home Office's decision.

There are also provisions in the law for fares to be paid for people settled here who want to return to their countries of origin if it is 'in that person's interest to leave the UK'. People receiving in-patient treatment in mental hospitals may be sent back, under the provisions of section 90 of the Mental Health Act, to receive treatment in their country of origin, again if it is 'in the interests of the patient to remove him'; no definition of this is given, and there are no legal safeguards against these powers.

10.5   Refugees

The immigration law and rules do not give refugees any specific rights. Almost as an afterthought, the immigration rules instruct officers to refer to the Home Office any instance where a person is seeking entry but does not qualify under the rules and 'the only country to which (he) could be removed is one to which he is unwilling to go owing to well-founded fear of being persecuted for reasons of race, religion, nationality, membership of a particular social group or political opinion'. The rules also state that nothing should be done contrary to the provisions of the United Nations Convention and Protocol on the status of refugees. However, this still leaves it to the Home Office to decide whether or not you are a refugee and, therefore, entitled to this protection.

During the 1980s the Home Office has shown increased unwillingness to accept claims for asylum from people from Third World countries. Tamils from Sri Lanka in particular have been detained for long periods while their applications are being considered. The Immigration (Carriers' Liability) Act was rushed through Parliament in March 1987 in order to penalize airlines by fining them £1,000 for bringing any asylum-seeker to Britain without the correct documents. The Home Office has also removed people very quickly after their applications have been refused, in some cases while the person is still attempting to have the refusal reviewed in court.

It is up to you, if you are claiming asylum, to satisfy the immigration officers about your well-founded fear of persecution and any evidence to show the danger you would face is important, but the decision will be made mainly on the basis of a detailed interview with you. It is more difficult for people from Third World countries to convince the Home Office that they are genuinely refugees from danger, rather than travelling for economic reasons. If asylum is granted, you will normally be allowed to stay for four years and can then apply for settlement. If the Home Office does not believe that asylum is justified but also thinks that you should not have to return at present, 'exceptional leave to remain' may be granted, usually for periods of two or three years. After seven years' exceptional leave to remain, you may apply for settlement. However, you have no right to do so and this will be entirely up to the Home Office.

If you are applying for asylum here, you are entitled to claim 'urgent cases' rate of income support to live on while waiting for a decision. The Home Office has stated that they will give permission to work if no decision has been made on your application within six months. If asylum or exceptional leave is granted, you are then free to work and will be treated as a home student for the purposes of fees and eligibility for grants.

10.6   Rights to British nationality

The British Nationality Act 1981 came into force on 1 January 1983. It defines who is British by birth and how people may become British, through naturalization or registration. Some limited rights under the previous 1948 British Nationality Act remain; if you are a Commonwealth or Irish citizen who was settled in Britain before 1973 and who has continued to live here since then and you were under eighteen on 1 January 1983, you have an automatic right to become British if you apply for it within five years after your eighteenth birthday. However, the fee for exercising this right is currently £60.

Other people who are settled here may be eligible to apply for British citizenship by naturalization. If you are married to a British citizen it is easier to be granted citizenship. In this case, you must show:

- that you are settled here;
- that you have lived here legally for at least three years and not been out of the UK for more than 270 days in that period, nor more than ninety days in the year before the application;
- that you are of good character.

You have to pay a fee (£60 in September 1988) and acceptance of the application is at the discretion of the Home Office.

If you are not married to a British citizen you have to show:

- that you have been settled here for at least a year;
- that you have lived here legally for at least five years and not been out of the UK for more than 450 days in those years, nor more than ninety days in the year before you apply;
- that you are of good character;
- that you have a sufficient knowledge of the English, Welsh or Scottish Gaelic language;
- that you intend to continue to live in Britain.

The fee for this is now (September 1988) £170. The application is at the discretion of the Home Office, which also decides the standard of knowledge of language and what being 'of good character' means; these have not been publicly defined. The Home Office does not have to give any reasons for refusing an application and there is no right of appeal against refusal.

People who were born in Britain before 1983 were automatically British citizens by birth. The only exception to this was children whose fathers were working here as diplomats at the time they were born. If you were born here after 1 January 1983 you are only automatically British if at the time of your birth:

- either of your parents was a British citizen; or
- either of your parents was allowed to stay here permanently.

If your parents were not married, only your mother's status counts. There are no plans to remove this discrimination against non-marital children.

If your parent later becomes settled, she/he can then apply for you to become British. If you are not able to inherit a nationality from either of your parents and are born stateless, and if you live here for the first ten years of your life without gaining any nationality, your parents can apply for you to become British.

10.7   More information

USEFUL ORGANIZATIONS

British Refugee Council, Bondway House, 3–9 Bondway, London SW8 1SJ (01-582 6922)

Joint Council for the Welfare of Immigrants, 115 Old Street, London EC1V 9JR (01-251 8706)

National Union of Students, 461 Holloway Road, London N7 6LJ (01-272 8900)

UK Council for Overseas Students' Affairs, 60 Westbourne Grove, London W2 5FG (01-229 9268)

UK Immigrants' Advisory Service, County House, 190 Great Dover Street, London SE1 4YB (01-357 6917)

UK Immigrants' Advisory Service Refugee Unit, address as above (01-357 7421)

United Nations High Commission for Refugees, 36 Westminster Palace Gardens, Artillery Row, London SW1P 1RR (01-222 3065)

For local law centres, Citizens' Advice Bureaux and other advice centres, consult your local telephone directory.

BIBLIOGRAPHY

J. Bhabha etc. (eds.), *Worlds Apart: Women Under Immigration Law*, Pluto Press, 1985.

A. Dummett and I. Martin, *British Nationality: The Agin Guide to the New Law*, NCCL, 1984.

L. Grant and I. Martin, *Immigration Law and Practice*, Cobden Trust, 1982 (supplement 1, 1985).

Immigration Law Handbook, Handsworth Law Centre, 1985.

F. Klug and P. Gordon, *British Immigration Control: A Brief Guide*, Runnymede Trust, 1985.

I. Macdonald, *Immigration Law and Practice in the United Kingdom*, Butterworth, 1987.

A. Owers, *Families Divided: Immigration Control and Family Life*, Church of England Board of Social Responsibility, 1984.

Publications from the Joint Council for the Welfare of Immigrants, Immigration Widows Campaign, Divided Families Campaign.

11 The rights of mental patients

This chapter covers:

Nearly half of all hospital patients are there because of some mental disorder. Anyone can apply voluntarily for treatment and may be admitted to hospital informally. Most patients are admitted to hospital in this way and they are entitled to leave at any time although, as an informal patient, they may be faced with the possibility of being compulsorily detained by one of the methods set out below, if they do try to leave. Some patients, however, are compulsorily detained. This chapter is mainly concerned with the position of compulsory patients and the rights of their relatives, as covered by the Mental Health Act 1983.

There are four categories of mental disorder which may result in detention in hospital or under special care. These are *legal* and not medical categories:

- *Mental illness*: this means any mental disorder not included in the three categories below. It includes illnesses such as schizophrenia or paranoia which may last a relatively short time, or permanent brain damage resulting from an accident.
- *Severe mental impairment*: this means arrested or incomplete development of mind, which includes severe impairment of intelligence and social functioning and is associated with abnormally aggressive or seriously irresponsible conduct on the part of the person concerned.

- *Mental impairment*: this means arrested or incomplete development of mind which includes significant impairment of intelligence and social functioning and is associated with abnormally aggressive or seriously irresponsible conduct, but which does not amount to severe mental impairment.
- *Psychopathic disorder*: this means a persistent disorder or disability of mind, which may or may not include significant impairment of intelligence, and which results in abnormally aggressive or seriously irresponsible conduct.

Before the 1959 Mental Health Act it was quite common for people to be detained in mental institutions because of promiscuity or other 'immoral' conduct. Such behaviour by itself may not now be considered a form of mental disorder. Nor may sexual deviancy or dependence on alcohol or drugs. Such people should be detained in hospital only if they appear to be suffering from a disorder so severe that it warrants assessment or treatment and it would be necessary for their health or safety or for the protection of others that they should receive treatment and that it cannot be provided unless they are detained.

11.1   Applications for compulsory detention

An application for someone to be compulsorily detained in hospital may be made by that person's nearest relative or by an approved social worker. Except in an emergency (see below), the application must be supported by the recommendation of two doctors one of whom must be acquainted with the patient. The two doctors must not have family or business connections with the patient or with each other and one of them must be approved by the local authority as having experience in dealing with mental disorder. If the application is successful, the applicant may authorize anyone to take the patient to hospital, by force if necessary.

There are three kinds of applications: assessment, treatment and emergency.

ADMISSION FOR ASSESSMENT

An admission for assessment may be made in cases where the disorder justifies detention to enable the doctor to decide what treatment is needed, if any, and that detention is necessary for the patient's health or safety or for the protection of others.

The patient may not be detained for assessment for more than twenty-eight days and the application cannot be immediately repeated. A patient may appeal within fourteen days to a mental health review tribunal (see below).

ADMISSION FOR TREATMENT

An application may be made for admission for treatment of a person outside hospital or a patient already admitted for assessment. An approved social worker may not apply for admission for treatment until the nearest relative has been consulted, if that relative is readily available. The approved social worker cannot make the application if the nearest relative objects. Although it is not essential, it is advisable for the nearest relative to make any objection in writing to the local health authority or the approved social worker. In an extreme case, the approved social worker can challenge the nearest relative in a court of law.

The grounds for such admissions are that the person is suffering from a disorder so severe that it warrants treatment and it is necessary for that person's health or safety or for the protection of others that such treatment should be given and that it cannot be provided unless they are detained. If they are suffering from psychopathic disorder or mental impairment it is also necessary for the disorder to be susceptible to treatment.

An admission for treatment is valid for a maximum of six months. The responsible medical officer (i.e., the psychiatrist in charge of the patient) may then renew it for another six months and after that for periods of a year at a time. Patients suffering from psychopathic disorder or mental impairment must be released from hospital on reaching the age of twenty-five unless the responsible medical officer reports that they are dangerous.

EMERGENCY ADMISSION

In an emergency, the nearest relative or an approved social worker may apply for admission for assessment with only one medical recommendation. A patient cannot be detained in this way for more than seventy-two hours unless within that time a second doctor recommends it, in which case the admission becomes an admission for assessment.

Anyone who is voluntarily in hospital can be detained for seventy-two hours on a recommendation by the doctor in charge of the patient. A nurse can also detain such a patient for a period not exceeding six hours if a doctor is not immediately available and 'the patient is suffering from mental disorder to such a degree that it is necessary for his health or safety or for the protection of others for him to be immediately restrained from leaving the hospital'.

A policeman who finds a person in a public place who appears to be suffering from mental disorder and to be in need of care or control can take him or her to a safe place. Such detention must not be for more than seventy-two hours and during that time an application may be made for admission for assessment or treatment.

A magistrate may issue a warrant authorizing a policeman to enter any premises, by force where necessary, in which it is believed someone suffering from mental disorder is living alone and unable to care for himself or who is being neglected or ill-treated. The policeman may then remove such a person to a safe place for not more than seventy-two hours.

DISCHARGE FROM HOSPITAL

The responsible medical officer or the nearest relative may discharge a patient at any time, but the medical officer may forbid discharge by the relative on the ground that the patient is detained for treatment and is potentially dangerous to himself or others. If that happens, the relative can appeal, within twenty-eight days, to a mental health review tribunal.

Leave of absence from a mental hospital may be granted indefinitely or for a specific period. A patient is automatically discharged if leave has been continuous for six months and at the end of that time he is not absent without leave and has not been transferred to guardianship (see p. 251).

Patients who are absent without leave may be detained and forcibly returned to hospital, unless they have been absent for twenty-eight days in which case they are automatically discharged.

THE NEAREST RELATIVE

The nearest relative is the first of the following who is over eighteen and resident in the UK, the Channel Islands or the Isle of Man: a legally appointed guardian, a relative the patient ordinarily resides with, husband or wife, child, father or mother, brother or sister, grandparent, grandchild, uncle or aunt, nephew or niece, anyone, other than a relative, with whom the patient has been ordinarily residing for five years if the patient is separated from his or her spouse.

The major exceptions to this rule are:

- A husband, wife or parent need not be over eighteen.
- A person who has been living with the patient for six months *as a spouse* will be regarded as such if the patient's real spouse is permanently living apart.
- If the rights and powers of a parent have been taken away under the Child Care Act 1980, the local authority or guardian will act as the nearest relative, unless the patient is married.
- An adopted child is treated as the child of the adopters.
- An illegitimate child is treated as the legitimate child of its mother.

Anyone who is a relative or spouse of the patient, or an approved social worker, may apply to a county court for an order depriving the nearest relative of all rights concerning the patient and appointing someone else. This can be done on a number of grounds, the most important of which is that the nearest relative objects unreasonably to the patient being admitted to hospital or misuses the power to discharge.

If an order has been made displacing the nearest relative and somebody else wishes to take over the responsibilities of nearest relative, he or she may apply to the court to vary the order. This might happen if, for instance, a relative reached the age of eighteen or returned from abroad and therefore became eligible to act as the nearest relative.

APPEALS

A patient can appeal to a mental health review tribunal:

- at any time within six months of admission for treatment;
- within twenty-eight days when reclassified from one form of mental disorder to another;
- at any time when the order for detention has been officially renewed;
- within twenty-eight days if not released at the age of twenty-five and the patient is classified as suffering from psychopathic disorder or mental impairment.

A patient's nearest relative can appeal:

- within twenty-eight days when the doctor has overruled the relative's order for discharge;
- within twenty-eight days if the patient's disorder is re-classified;
- within twenty-eight days when a patient suffering from psychopathic disorder or mental impairment is not released at the age of twenty-five.

The Managers of a hospital must refer a patient's case to a tribunal if:

- the patient does not apply within six months of admission for treatment;
- the patient does not apply within six months of being transferred from guardianship to hospital;
- a tribunal has not considered the case during the previous three years.

GUARDIANSHIP

A person over sixteen who is suffering from mental disorder may be put into the care of a guardian instead of being detained in hospital. The guardian may be the local health authority or anyone else. An application for guardianship should be made to the local health authority or anybody accepted by them. Patients can be transferred from hospital to guardianship and vice versa. But a transfer from guardianship to hospital needs two medical recommendations, and the patient can appeal to a tribunal within six months of the transfer.

The nearest relative has an absolute right of discharge from guardianship unless the patient has been transferred to hospital.

A patient suffering from psychopathic disorder or mental impairment must always be discharged from guardianship at the age of twenty-five.

11.2   Detention of offenders

DETENTION BY COURT ORDER

When a person is convicted of an offence punishable by imprisonment, the court may make a hospital order, on the evidence of two doctors, that the person suffers from mental disorder needing treatment. In that event, the court may not impose any sentence of imprisonment or fine nor make a probation order.

A patient may appeal to a tribunal within six months of the order and then has the same rights of appeal as someone detained without a court order. The nearest relative can appeal after six months and then every twelve months.

Restriction orders

When a Crown Court makes a hospital order, it may also make a restriction order if it considers it is necessary to do so to protect the public from serious harm. A magistrates' court may not make a restriction order but may refer a case to the Crown Court for that purpose.

If this happens, the Home Secretary can release the patient at any time either absolutely or subject to conditions. The patient has the right to apply to a tribunal once in each year while detained or once in each two-year period while conditionally discharged. If a person is conditionally discharged and then recalled to hospital, the Home Secretary must refer the case to a tribunal within one month of the recall.

DETENTION BY DIRECTION OF THE HOME SECRETARY

A person serving a prison sentence may, on the recommendation of two doctors, be transferred to a hospital by direction of the Home Secretary. When making a transfer direction, with or without a time limit, the Home Secretary may also make a restriction direction. This has the same effect as a restriction order made by a court, with one exception: it lapses at the end of the prison sentence. After that occurs, the patient is in the same position as if he or she had been admitted for treatment (see above).

11.3   Mental health review tribunals

Mental health review tribunals hear appeals by mental patients or their nearest relative for the discharge of patients from hospitals and institutions and from guardianship. Application forms can be obtained from the patient's hospital, from the tribunal's office or from the local health authority if the patient is in the care of a guardian (see above).

The tribunal consists of three members chosen from three panels consisting of lawyers, doctors and lay members with administrative or social work experience. All three must be independent of the hospital and the local health authority concerned in the case.

POWERS OF THE TRIBUNAL

The tribunal must discharge a patient detained for assessment (see above) if satisfied that he or she is not suffering from mental disorder severe enough to justify detention for assessment, or that detention is not necessary for the patient's health or safety or the protection of other persons.

In all other cases (except restricted patients) the tribunal must discharge a patient if satisfied he or she is not suffering from mental illness severe enough to justify detention for treatment, or that it is not necessary for the health or safety of the patient or the protection of other persons that such treatment should be given.

In addition to the requirements set out in the previous paragraph, a restricted patient cannot be discharged unless the tribunal is satisfied that it is not appropriate for the patient to be recalled to hospital for further treatment. If the tribunal is not satisfied on this last point but is satisfied on the others, it must direct the conditional discharge of the patient.

The only appeal against a decision of a tribunal is on a point of law.

PROCEDURE OF THE TRIBUNAL

The hearings are normally held in private at the patient's hospital. The applicant may ask for a public hearing but this may be refused if it would be harmful to the patient's interests. The applicant and the hospital representative (usually the consultant responsible for the patient) are both present and give evidence. They can question each other and any other witnesses. The applicant can also address the tribunal but otherwise the tribunal conducts the proceedings as it thinks best.

The tribunal has power to take evidence on oath, to order witnesses to appear and to produce any documents. The medical member examines the patient before the hearing date and inquires into all relevant aspects of his or her health and treatment.

ADVICE AND REPRESENTATION

It is most important that a patient should receive advice and representation when appealing to a tribunal. This can be given by a solicitor under the Legal Aid Act by using the scheme known as 'advice by way of representation' (see 7.1, p. 162).

Expenses may be paid to the applicant, witnesses and their representatives unless the representatives are lawyers. Expenses consist of rail fare, subsistence and any loss of earnings agreed by the tribunal.

11.4   Rights in mental hospitals

CONSENT TO TREATMENT

A patient in any hospital cannot be treated without a legally effective consent, except in cases of necessity. There are specific exceptions for mental patients, whose treatment is divided into three types:

- Psychosurgery and the implantation of hormones to reduce male sexual drive may be given only with the consent of the patient *and* a second opinion from a doctor.
- The administration of medicine for three months or longer and electro-convulsive therapy may be given only with the consent of the patient *or* a second opinion from a doctor.
- Any other treatment can be given if the doctor thinks fit.

These rules apply to treatment for the patient's mental disorder, not any physical illness he or she may have. They do not apply to treatment which is immediately necessary to save the patient's life, to prevent a serious deterioration of his or her condition, to alleviate serious suffering or, if it is needed, to prevent a danger to self or others. Treatment which is irreversible or hazardous cannot be given in any of these cases except the first (i.e., if it is necessary to save the patient's life).

These provisions apply to all mental patients except those detained under the various short-term powers in the Mental Health Act 1983. This includes voluntary patients except for the provisions relating to treatment requiring consent and a second opinion.

LETTERS

A postal packet sent *by* a detained patient may be withheld if a request to do so has been made by the addressee. If the patient is detained in a special hospital (Broadmoor, Park Lane, Rampton and Moss Side) it may also be withheld if it is likely to cause distress or danger to anyone.

Post sent *to* a patient in a special hospital may be withheld if it is necessary for the patient's safety or the protection of others.

No letters to or from the following people can be withheld under *any* circumstances: an MP, an officer of the Court of Protection, the various Ombudsmen, a mental health review tribunal, the managers of the hospital, a lawyer instructed by the patient or the European Commission or European Court.

INDEPENDENT MEDICAL EXAMINATION

A patient can be examined by an independent psychiatrist. The patient's medical notes must be shown if the psychiatrist wishes to see them. Any fee charged may be covered by the Legal Advice Scheme.

PROPERTY

A patient's property cannot be interfered with unless he or she consents or someone is authorized to do so by the Court of Protection.

The Court of Protection manages the property of people who, through mental disorder, are incapable of managing their own affairs whether or not they are in hospital.

VOTING

A detained patient cannot be entered on the electoral register. A voluntary patient in hospital can register to vote at his or her former address.

ACCESS TO THE COURTS

A person is not liable in any civil or criminal proceedings in respect of anything purporting to be done under the Mental Health Act, unless it was done in bad faith or without reasonable care. Civil proceedings need the permission of the High Court and criminal proceedings must be by, or with the consent of, the Director of Public Prosecutions.

This protection does not apply to the Secretary of State or a health authority.

MENTAL HEALTH ACT COMMISSION

A special health authority, known as the Mental Health Act
Commission, has been set up. Its duties include:

- to review the exercise of the powers granted by the Mental
  Health Act;
- to interview patients in private;
- to investigate complaints;
- to appoint doctors to give the second opinions required by the
  provisions dealing with consent to treatment (see above);
- to prepare codes of practice on treatment and admissions;
- to review any decision to withhold a patient's mail if the
  application is made to them within six months.

The existence of the Commission does not remove a patient's
right to complain to the hospital managers or the Health Service
Commissioner. The Commission has no powers of enforcement and
can do little more than report its findings.

11.5   More information

USEFUL ORGANIZATIONS

Mental After-Care Association, Bainsbridge House, Bainsbridge Road,
London WC1A 1HP (01-436 6194)

MIND (National Association for Mental Health), 22 Harley Street,
London W1N 2ED (01-637 0741)

National Council for Civil Liberties, 21 Tabard Street, London SE1
4LA (01-403 3888)

BIBLIOGRAPHY

L. Gostin, *A Practical Guide to Mental Health Law,* MIND, 1983.
L. Gostin *et al., Representing the Mentally Ill,* Oyez Longman, 1984.
National Council for Civil Liberties, *Fact Sheet Number 3,* January 1986.

12 The rights of young people

This chapter deals with:

12.1   Who has charge of children?

Until they reach the age of eighteen the law calls all children 'minors'. They have far fewer rights than adults to make their own decisions. The law generally assumes that they are under the control of an adult or adults – usually the parents.

The adults in charge are said by the law to have the 'parental rights and duties' to decide on all matters relating to the child's upbringing as well as the duty to look after the child and pay for his keep.

These parental rights and duties are given different names in different situations, e.g., custody, guardianship, adoption or care order. But they all boil down to the same thing: a holding of all or some of the parental rights and duties. With each of the different names the court has the power to change things if problems arise.

CUSTODY, CARE AND CONTROL

Married parents have joint custody of their children. If they separate, then the court may order that they still have joint custody (the right to participate in joint decisions about important matters in the child's life: schooling, religion, permission to marry etc.), but only one has 'care and control' which means day-to-day charge of the child. The court may give custody to one of the parents only but the non-custodial parent will still have the right to be informed and consulted about all important matters in the child's life. (The position where parents are unmarried is described in 12.4, p. 259.

Foster parents, child minders and babysitters are people who look after children but have no authority in themselves. They must do as they are told by the parents (or by the local authority if the child is in care – see the paragraph on care orders below).

12.2   Registration of births and naming a child

A child must be registered at the local registry office within forty-two days of birth. A short birth certificate will be issued free of charge showing the name, sex, date and place of birth. A longer form of birth certificate is available which costs £10 by post or £5 if personally collected. This gives more information.

Only a parent or someone present at the birth may register the birth of a legitimate child. Anyone can obtain a copy of a birth certificate from:

> Chief Registrar
> St Catherine's House
> 10 Kingsway
> London WC2B 6JP

If the parents are married when a child is born, then neither may change the child's name without the other's permission or a court order. If the child is over sixteen, then his/her consent is needed before a change of name. A change of name can be made formally by a deed poll or a statutory declaration. But the birth certificate itself can never be altered. If someone wants to change their name informally without legal documents, there is no law to stop them.

12.3   Citizenship and nationality

Any child who is a British citizen may come and go from the United Kingdom, Hong Kong, Gibraltar or the Falkland Isles as they please.

Anyone born in any of these places before 1 January 1983 is automatically a British citizen. If born after that date, a child is a British citizen only if one or both of the parents is a British citizen or lawfully settled here. For this purpose 'parents' include mother and father if they are unmarried but only the father if they are married. People who are not British citizens may apply to the Home Office for citizenship.

12.4   Illegitimacy

The mother has legal custody, which means all the parental rights and duties in relation to her illegitimate child. The father has rights only if he obtains a court order to say so. If the parents marry, then the child becomes legitimate and the parents have equal rights.

If an unmarried mother wants the court to make an official declaration about who is the child's father and/or order the payment of money (maintenance) for the child, they can apply to the magistrates' court under the Affiliation Proceedings Act 1957. From 1990 it is planned to bring in a new, simpler procedure using the Guardianship of Minors Act 1971.

If an illegitimate child is taken away from the mother by a local authority who says that she is not looking after the child properly, then the father may want to apply to take care of the child himself. It is very difficult for him to do this unless there is already a court order giving him at least some parental rights or duties.

If parents die without making a will, an illegitimate child can inherit from their estates just as a legitimate child can. An illegitimate child can also claim money from their estates if the parent was maintaining the child before death.

12.5   Religion

A child's parents can make the child a member of any faith they
wish and can make the child have religious instruction. They can
also change the child's religion. If there is a dispute, then a court
can make orders about the child's religious upbringing. The child's
wishes are usually taken into account. A child at a state school
must have religious instruction unless the parents specifically
withdraw him or her from it.

12.6   Travelling and passports

A child may travel on a parent's passport until the age of sixteen.
The child must be with the parent at the time of travel and his or
her name must be on the parent's passport. Alternatively a child
can have its own passport although the parent must apply for it on
the child's behalf if he or she is under eighteen.

12.7   Medical treatment and contraception

Until a child is eighteen the parents normally arrange for medical
treatment and must sign a form of consent before operations or
certain kinds of treatment are allowed.

After a child is sixteen he may refuse or consent to treatment by
himself. If the doctor thinks that a child under sixteen really
understands what the treatment means, then that child can give
consent. The doctor will want to inform or ask the parents as well,
especially if the child is asking for contraception or an abortion.
However, it is very unlikely that the doctor can tell the parents
about the treatment if the child insists that the parents are not to
be told.

The law does not stop a doctor from giving contraception to a
person under sixteen without the parents' knowledge. But the
General Medical Council have advised doctors that they should rarely
do so. If the parents cannot be consulted for some reason, or if it really
seems in the child's best interest, the doctor may provide treatment or
contraception anyway. If they cannot agree between themselves,
then the court can be asked for an order about medical treatment.

12.8 Leaving home

If a child wants to leave home and the parents agree, there is no problem so long as the child has enough money and somewhere suitable to live. If proper arrangements are not made, or if a child gets into trouble, the child may be taken before a magistrates' court to consider making a care order or to see that proper arrangements are made.

If the parents do not agree to the child leaving home, they may make a child a ward of court and ask for an order that the child stays with them. The court will listen to the child's own wishes and will do what the court thinks is in the child's best interests.

12.9 School and education

The law makes education compulsory for everyone from the age of five until sixteen. Most people go to school but parents have the right to educate their children themselves so long as it is 'efficient full-time education suitable to his age, ability and aptitude'. If the local authority thinks that a child's education is not good enough, then the magistrates' court can be asked to decide. A care order (see p. 264) can be made or the parents can be fined if the court agrees with the local authority.

The local authority will try to allow a child to attend the state school which he or his parents choose. If that is impractical, the parents must accept a different school. The school can make rules about what pupils do inside and outside school. They may also set homework, and junior and secondary schools can punish pupils who do not do it.

Moderate corporal punishment (hitting children) is not illegal (although it may be soon). Most local authorities have banned it. Pupils can be punished by being expelled but only if they have done something very serious. Parents can appeal to the Secretary of State if they think their child has been expelled unjustly from a state school. Suspension (temporary banning from school) is a lesser punishment for which each school has its own rules. But a child should always be told why, and for how long, they have been suspended.

12.10   Children and the courts

CRIMINAL CASES

Children under ten cannot be arrested or charged with any crime. The law considers them to be below the age of criminal responsibility. Children aged between ten and seventeen are called 'juveniles' by the criminal law. The police have their own juvenile bureau (a group of specially assigned police officers) which normally deals with children in trouble and decides whether to take them to court or not.

The rules for police questioning, searching and detaining juveniles suspected of crime are the same as those for adults (see chapter 6) but juveniles have extra rights. The police should not search or interview them without a parent or social worker being present (save in very special circumstances). The police should inform the parents or a social worker as soon as they detain a juvenile, and should normally wait for that person to arrive before they take any further action. Juveniles have the same rights as adults to have legal advice.

If the child is accused of a relatively minor crime, has been in very little trouble before and admits the offence, then the juvenile bureau may decide not to take the child to court but to 'caution' him or her. This means that a senior police officer will give the child a severe telling-off.

If the case does go to court, it is usually to the juvenile court which is a special part of the magistrates' court. A juvenile cannot be sent to prison but may be sentenced to detention in a young offender institution. The court can impose lesser punishments such as fines or they can make a care order.

CIVIL (NON-CRIMINAL) CASES

A child can start a civil court case or have one started against him. But it must be done through an adult (usually the parent) called a 'guardian *ad litem*' or 'next friend'.

Married and unmarried parents can apply to the court for orders about custody, access, maintenance or any other order about the child's welfare if they cannot agree. There are several other sorts of order which the civil courts can make to give people all or some of the parental rights and duties. First and paramount consideration is given to what is in the child's best interests.

Place of safety orders

This order can be made by any magistrates if the police or a social worker satisfy them that a child is in immediate danger and needs to be removed. The child is then taken into care for a maximum of twenty-eight days.

Custodianship

This is a custody order designed for people other than parents (e.g., grandparents, relatives, or foster parents). The child must have been living with them for at least three months (and usually longer).

Guardianship

A child's parents or the court can appoint a guardian. Normally, parents do it in a will to make sure that there is someone to care for the child if they die. The guardian must act in the child's best interests and can be removed by the court.

Adoption

This order gives all of the natural parents' rights to the adoptive parents. The child is then treated exactly as if he had been born to the adopters. An adoption certificate is issued. The child does not usually see the natural parents ever again and the natural parents have no rights or duties towards them and no right to know anything about the child. Adopted people have the right to see their original birth records once they are eighteen. This is done by applying to:

> Registrar of Births and Deaths
> 10 Kingsway
> London WC2B 6JP
> (01-242 0262)

Then the child can take steps to trace and meet his real parents. A child can be adopted only with his parents' consent, although the court can dispense with their consent in some special circumstances (e.g., if they are being extremely unreasonable).

Care and supervision orders

A *care order* gives a local authority nearly all of the parental rights and duties. The parents are still liable to maintain children, have to be consulted if the child might emigrate and they must still consent to any adoption (save in unusual circumstances). Normally the local authority will allow the parent to visit a child. If they stop all visits, the parent can apply to the magistrates' court for an access order.

To obtain a care order the local authority usually takes the child (rather than the parents) to the magistrates' court. The child will almost always have a representative (called the guardian *ad litem*) as well as a lawyer to tell the court what the child wants and what seems to be in the child's best interests. The parents attend the court-hearing and can have their own lawyers. The local authority have to prove that the child is being neglected or endangered in some particular way and that the child is in need of care and control which they are unlikely to receive unless an order is made. If the court is satisfied about that, then it will consider whether to make a care order. A care order usually means that the child goes to live with foster parents or in a community home.

Alternatively, the court may consider making a *supervision order*. This usually means that the child remains living at home but the parents must allow a social worker to visit the child, talk with the family and give advice. There can be extra conditions. The child might be required to attend for specific medical treatment or to reside with a specific person.

There are several other ways in which the local authority can obtain a care order. Any child or parent who discovers that the local authority are going to apply for a court order should seek legal advice immediately.

Wardship

In wardship proceedings the child is made a ward of court, which means that custody is given (technically) to the judges of the High Court. The court then makes a 'care and control' order and states where the child shall live. No important step can be taken in the child's life without the court's permission. The child remains a ward until the age of eighteen, or earlier if the court makes an order to end the wardship.

12.11   A summary of rights – year-by-year

From birth: a child can have a bank or building society account in their name; have their own passport and inherit goods or money.

five: must have full-time education; can drink alcohol legally (in private); can attend a U or PG category film (but the cinema manager has discretion over admission).

seven: can withdraw money from Post Office or TSB account.

ten: can be arrested and convicted of a criminal offence.

twelve: can buy a pet without a parent being present.

thirteen: can do part-time work for two hours a day (one on Sundays).

fourteen: must pay full fare on public transport; can consent to medical treatment, including abortion (if they properly understand it); can own an air rifle or (with conditions) a shotgun; can go into a pub to play dominoes, cribbage and drink soft drinks. Boys can be sent to detention centre and can be convicted of rape.

fifteen: can open a Post Office giro account (with a guarantor); can be sent to youth custody.

sixteen: can leave school; work full-time; join a trade union; marry (with parental consent); consent to sex (but sex between men is illegal until the age of twenty-one); claim social security benefits; drink alcohol (except spirits) with meals in pubs or restaurants; buy liqueur chocolates, fireworks and premium bonds; enter a brothel and live there; sell scrap metal; choose their own doctor and consent to medical treatment; have an abortion without parental consent; take part in public performances without a local authority licence, hold a moped or motorcycle licence.

seventeen: can become a street trader; hold a driving licence (except HGV); buy a firearm; have an air weapon in a public place; be sent to prison.

eighteen: can leave home or marry without parental consent; vote; sit on a jury; have a cheque or credit card; make a will; give blood; own land or shares; sue and be sued in their own name in the courts; buy drinks in pubs; place bets; emigrate.

twenty-one: can stand for Parliament; adopt a child; hold a bus or HGV licence.

12.12   More information

USEFUL ORGANIZATIONS

British Agencies for Adoption and Fostering, 11 Southwark Street, London SE1 1RQ (01-407 8800).

Brook Advisory Centre, 233 Tottenham Court Road, London W1P 9AE (01-323 1522). Advice for young people on contraception, pregnancy and abortion.

The Children's Legal Centre, 20 Compton Terrace, London N1 2UN (01-359 6251).

Citizens' Advice Bureaux. Consult your local telephone directory for addresses and telephone numbers.

Lesbian and Gay Youth Movement, BM/LGYM, London W1 (01-317 9690).

London Youth Advisory Centre, 26 Prince of Wales Road, London NW5 3LG (01-267 4792).

National Association of Young People in Care, Rooms 21–2, The Wool Exchange, Market Street, Bradford BD1 1LD (0274 728484) *and* 20 Compton Terrace, London N1 2UN (01-226 7102).

BIBLIOGRAPHY

G. R. Barrell, *Teachers and the Law,* Methuen, 1979.

Butterworth's Family Law Service, Butterworth. A loose-leaf encyclopedia, regularly updated.

M. Rae *et al., First Rights,* NCCL, 1986.

13 The rights of workers

This chapter deals with:

Central to any system of civil liberties is a recognition of the importance of workers' rights. In the UK, there was grudging acceptance of workers' rights in the form of the Trade Union Act 1871, which allowed trade unions to exist when hitherto they had been illegal. The expression of trade union rights in the form of calls for industrial action was made lawful by the Trade Disputes Act 1906. The foundation of modern workers' rights lies in those two statutes, now repealed, and it was not until the 1960s that attention was given to the rights of workers as individuals, with the passing of legislation on minimum periods of notice and redundancy pay. Ironically, the first comprehensive statute dealing with individual and collective workers' rights – the Industrial Relations Act 1971 – lasted only three years before it was defeated by trade union opposition and the passing of the Trade Union and Labour Relations Act 1974, the starting point for the basic freedoms of people at work. Since then, a general expansion of individual rights, as contained in the Employment Protection (Consolidation) Act 1978 (EPCA), the Sex Discrimination Act 1975, the Race Relations Act 1976 and the Equal Pay Act 1970 (which became effective at the end of 1975), has been trimmed back both by the decisions of tribunals and courts, and by a series of administrative measures and statutes imposed since 1979. These include the Employment Acts 1980, 1982, 1988 and 1989 the Trade Union Act 1984, the Wages Act 1986, the Social Security Act 1986 and several codes of practice issued by the Department of Employment.

On the other hand, European Community law has had a noticeable impact in the fight for women to achieve equal pay for doing work which is the same as, or of equal value to, a man's, and in challenging other forms of discrimination on the grounds of sex.

European law applies throughout the UK. Employment legislation applies in England, Wales and Scotland, and most of it applies (in the form of parallel Orders) in the six counties of Northern Ireland. The Scottish and English laws of contract have different terminology but similar substance.

This chapter deals principally with the rights contained in the Acts, codes and cases arising since 1974. From the outset it is important to recall that the courts have been hostile to the concept and practice of workers' rights, particularly when these rights are advanced by way of industrial action by trade union members. Because union membership is the key to enforcing workers' rights at workplace level through collective bargaining and industrial action, union rights are dealt with first.

13.1   Unions

WHY JOIN?

Employment law has traditionally viewed workers' problems as definable in individual contracts of employment. In reality, your rights as an individual worker are largely determined by the negotiating position you have with your employer, and individuals have little opportunity to influence the specific terms and conditions of employment, whereas collectively workers can and do. Further, although just less than half of the twenty-one million or so people in employment are members of trade unions, two-thirds have their terms and conditions affected by collective bargaining between their employer, or a group of employers, and trade unions.

RIGHTS AGAINST EMPLOYERS

You are protected by the EPCA against dismissal and victimization short of dismissal on the grounds of your trade union membership. This includes seeking to become a member and taking part, at an appropriate time *outside* working hours but on your employer's premises, in the activities of the union. You are not protected against discrimination at the point of hire – the protection applies only to current or dismissed employees. Nor are you protected if the grounds of your dismissal or victimization are your trade union membership in the past, for example, when you were working for another employer.

The rights entitle you to recruit members, hand out literature, collect subscriptions and hold meetings during the times when you are not working. If management allows you to talk while you are at work, you are also allowed to talk about trade union membership and to encourage people to join.

Anything which prevents or deters you from being a member, or taking part in the union's activities, or which penalizes you for so doing, is unlawful. This includes the refusal to give members of one union the same pay rise as another and refusing to allow representation by a union official in accordance with agreed procedures. Any form of disadvantage is unlawful, so long as the target of the management action is genuinely 'trade union activity'. That includes the presentation of, for example, a complaint or grievance relating to health and safety, and does not mean simply the activities of a group of individuals who happen to be union members. The union flavour of the issue must be clear, and the management action must be taken against you as an individual, and not as a form of retaliation against the union which may be seeking to organize.

You can make a claim to an industrial tribunal (see 13.8, p. 295). Unlimited compensation is available for victimization, and compensation for dismissal of up to £27,560 (1989), with unlimited further compensation available if management refuses to comply in full with an order made by the tribunal. The most important remedy for dismissal is an order for reinstatement. In order to make a claim, you should use the 'interim relief' procedure available while you are under notice or during the first seven days afterwards, which requires a certificate from a union official confirming that in their opinion you were dismissed because of your trade union activities *and* are likely to win a claim for unfair dismissal on those grounds. A very quick hearing will then be arranged by the tribunal which has power to order management to continue your contract until the full hearing of the case.

With the exception of the requirement of a union official's certificate, all of the above rights and procedures apply to someone who has been victimized or dismissed on the grounds that they *refused* to join, or take part in the activities of, a trade union.

UNION RECOGNITION

Recognition means that management is prepared to negotiate with an independent trade union or unions over terms and conditions of employment. Negotiation is stronger than consultation, which is essentially a one-way process, and the mere right to represent individuals in, say, grievance or disciplinary hearings. Recognition has the advantage that the union has negotiated a procedure for the settlement of disputes, and also some legal advantages flow from it.

These are:

- the duty to deal with and give facilities to safety representatives appointed by the union under the Health and Safety at Work etc. Act (see 13.4, p. 284);
- consultation on occupational pensions;
- consultation on redundancies, on take-overs and mergers, and the automatic transfer of collective agreements (see 13.6, p. 292);
- disclosure of information for the purposes of collective bargaining, with a legally enforceable right to obtain better terms and conditions if information is denied;
- time off with pay for union representatives carrying out duties or training connected with collective bargaining, or without pay for union members attending internal union activities;
- time and facilities for carrying out workplace ballots.

The right to time off can be enforced by a claim to a tribunal (see 13.8, p. 295). It is available to shop stewards, staff representatives and other labour representatives. It enables them to prepare for negotiations, draw up plans, consult other members and officers, and negotiate. The amount of time off is that which is 'reasonable' for carrying out duties and training in connection with their industrial relations functions.

Quite separately, union *members* have the right to take time off for union activities, such as voting, attending union conferences and other matters of internal organization. This right does not attract pay.

Union membership agreements, or closed shops, can be negotiated with management but since the Employment Act 1988, dismissal or victimization for not being a member of the union is unlawful. Following the 1988 White Paper 'Employment for the 1990s' it is likely that the closed shop will be outlawed by legislation in 1989/90.

All companies with 250 employees must include in their annual report a statement of the measures taken to provide information to, and to consult with, employees on matters of concern to them (Companies Act 1985).

RIGHTS WITHIN THE UNION

The relationship between you and your union is governed both by the union rule-book and by statute. The rule-book, together with custom and practice, sets up contractual rights entitling you to the benefits and the procedures contained in it. In addition, the rules of natural justice will generally apply to any disciplinary hearing within the union. These are the right to be given notice of the allegation made against you, the opportunity to state your case and to be heard by an impartial body within the union.

You have the right under the Employment Acts 1980 and 1988 to resign, and not to have unjustifiable disciplinary action taken against you. You can complain to a tribunal (see 13.8, p. 295) which can set aside the decisions of the union and award compensation.

Discipline is unjustifiable if it is on the grounds of failing to participate in or support industrial action, even if a majority of the members involved voted in favour. Similarly, disciplinary action for refusing to break your contract of employment, or for following calls for action in breach of the union's rules, is unjustifiable. Disciplinary action means expulsion, fines, deprivation of benefits or any other detriment. It also includes advising another union not to take the person into membership because of, for example, refusing to support industrial action by the first union.

There is no general right to join a trade union. Such a right does exist if it is the practice within, say, an industry or section of industry for employees to belong to a particular union in accordance with a union membership agreement. In that case, if you are or are seeking to be employed (even if you do not have a job or a job offer), you have the right not to be unreasonably excluded or expelled from membership. You can complain to a tribunal if you are refused.

The Independent Review Committee of the TUC also operates to protect you if you have been expelled from your union and lost your job as a result. Such situations will be very rare, but the Committee works by pressure upon unions and the internal power of the TUC to enforce compliance.

POLITICAL ACTIVITIES

A union may resolve to have a political fund, and to require its members to pay contributions, part of which go into the fund. Activities of a party political nature must be paid for out of the political fund, and not out of the general fund of the union. You have an absolute right to refuse to contribute to the fund, and must not be disadvantaged for so doing (Trade Union Act 1913). Ballots were held in all unions which had political funds, pursuant to the Trade Union Act 1984, and all passed resolutions favouring the continuance of such funds.

In Northern Ireland, the system is reversed, in that all members are contracted out of the political fund, and it requires a positive statement by an individual to join in the fund.

ELECTION OF OFFICERS

Since the Trade Union Act 1984 and the Employment Act 1988, all officials who have voting rights, or who attend and speak at the governing bodies of trade unions, must be elected by secret postal ballot every five years.

13.2   Contracts of employment

Not everyone who works has a contract of employment. But
employment law protects only employees and in some cases, such
as discrimination, people applying to become employees. A distinction is most frequently drawn between employees and the self-
employed. It is easier to see than to define. It does not matter what
label is used, nor what the parties to the contract intended. The
purpose for which the work is done is not conclusive.

EMPLOYED OR SELF-EMPLOYED?

You will generally be an employee, and not self-employed, if the
economic reality of the relationship is that you are *not* in business
on your own account. You and your employer owe each other
obligations which include, on your part, the requirement to obey
instructions, to work for no other employer, and to do the work
yourself; and on your employer's part to provide work and to
accept the work done. Once a self-employed person completes the
work, the contract ends, even if a subsequent identical contract is
given and there is in fact no break in the relationship. Since there
are tax advantages to the worker, and tax and other advantages to
the employer, in establishing self-employed status, there are super-
ficial temptations. However, self-employed workers are denied
access to employment protection legislation, and are unprotected
by the employer's compulsory insurance against industrial injuries.
Unless you genuinely want to go into business on your own
account, taking the risks inherent in such a practice, you should
resist offers to become self-employed, and in any event the courts
are more likely to find that you have a contract of employment.

Certain categories of worker are given employment protection
rights although strictly they are not employees. For example,
apprentices enter into fixed-term contracts which impose particular
obligations upon the apprentice and the employer. Termination
generally requires the apprentice's parents' consent, and there is a
strict obligation to give and accept instruction in the trade.

Civil servants work under terms of service with the Crown and do not have contracts of employment. This includes some National Health Service workers. Nevertheless, they have access to most of the employment legislation, and where they are excluded, they have their own arrangements, for example, in relation to redundancy pay.

People who *hold office* may or may not be employees, depending on the nature of the relationship with their 'employer'. Directors of companies, for example, may be office holders under company law and also be employees of their companies. Trade union officers hold office by virtue of their election, in some cases, and are also employees of their union. Police officers hold office and are not employees.

Homeworkers may or may not be employees, depending on the nature of the relationship, and upon whether they are engaged in business on their own account, applying the 'economic reality' and 'mutual obligation' tests.

Casual workers may be employees only for the time when they are engaged, even though they continue to work day after day for the same employer and take on all the appearances of a regular employee. If you can establish that all your contracts as a casual worker are linked under an 'umbrella contract', spanning a period long enough to entitle you to bring a claim under the employment legislation, you will be able to take advantage of your rights.

Trainees on Training Agency schemes may or may not be employees, depending on the type of scheme and the arrangements for pay, but are covered by health and safety and discrimination legislation.

WHAT'S IN A CONTRACT?

Every employee has a contract of employment. For most people, this means a written statement of the main terms given to you shortly after you started work. Nevertheless, you are still an employee, working under a contract of employment, even if nothing is written down. The fact that you have agreed to work, and your employer has agreed to pay you, constitutes a contract of employment. True, if a dispute arises as to the rate of pay, or entitlement to bonus, it will be more difficult for you to prove your version is correct, but that does not detract from the fact that you have contractual rights.

A contract will generally consist of terms and conditions which may be identified in any of the following forms:

Written statement

Within thirteen weeks of your starting work your employer must provide you with a statement, in writing, of the particulars of your terms of employment (EPCA 1978). These must include: the date your employment started, and whether any previous employment is regarded as continuous with it; rate of pay or the method of calculating it and how often it is paid; hours of work; entitlement to holidays, holiday pay, sick pay, and whether or not a pension scheme exists; the length of notice required to be given by each side; job title; any disciplinary rules which apply to you; and the name of any person to whom you can apply if you have a grievance, or are dissatisfied with any disciplinary action, and the procedure which you must follow. For all of these, cross-references can be made to more detailed documents, such as those described below. If you are not given a written statement you can make a claim to a tribunal (see 13.8, p. 295).

The written statement provides strong evidence of what the agreed terms are, but does not in itself constitute the contract of employment. That is much broader than the written statement, so you can challenge the terms in it if they are not those you agreed. Do not sign that the terms in a statement are correct. By all means give a written receipt, but only agree that you have received the document and not that you accept its contents as being true.

Collective agreements

Frequently many of these rights will be determined by agreements negotiated by trade unions on your behalf. The fruit of the negotiations between unions and employers are incorporated automatically into your contract of employment, since either your written statement or the custom and practice at your work place will generally say so. Collective agreements generally set substantive terms and conditions such as wages and hours, and will also provide the machinery for the resolution of disputes, discipline and grievances.

Itemized pay statement

Every time you are paid you are entitled (EPCA 1978) to a written statement setting out the gross pay, any variable or fixed deductions, net pay and, if not all the pay is paid in the same way, the method of payment for each part, for example, where a bonus is paid less frequently than basic pay. If you have fixed deductions for each pay period, it is sufficient for management to give you a statement in advance of what the fixed deductions are, and they must reissue it at least annually. If you are not given an itemized pay slip then you can make a claim to a tribunal (see 13.8, p. 295).

Works rules

Management may publish on notice-boards or in employee hand-books a set of works rules. These do not necessarily form part of your contract, so that if you break any of them you may not automatically be breaking your contract of employment. At most, they are management's instructions about how the job is to be done, and are not to be treated as rules cast in stone – they can be challenged if you make a claim to a tribunal arising out of, for example, your dismissal for breaking one.

Wages Council orders

Since 1909 protection has been given to workers in industries where there is low trade union organization and where workers are notoriously prone to exploitation. The Wages Act 1986 cut down the rights of workers engaged in a range of industries including catering, garment manufacture and retailing. Minimum basic wages, whether by time or piece-work, are set for all workers aged twenty-one and over – there is no protection for those under twenty-one.

Wages Council orders take effect as part of the contracts of workers covered by them. Protection is given not only to employees but to anyone engaged in the industry, including, therefore, self-employed homeworkers and casuals. If you are not paid the minimum rate, wages inspectors employed by the Department of

Employment can prosecute your employer, who is obliged to keep records and publish the Wages Council orders. A court can order the employer to pay fines and to make payments of arrears of wages, or repayment of deductions unlawfully made (e.g., for accommodation). In addition, proceedings can be brought either by you or the wages inspector in the civil courts.

A similar system exists for workers engaged in agriculture.

Breach of contract

Since it takes two to make a contract, changes to it must be agreed by both. Otherwise there is a breach of contract which, if it is sufficiently serious, entitles you to say the contract is at an end and to walk out. Alternatively, you can refuse to accept that the serious action or omission by your employers has brought the contract to an end, and can continue to work, while reserving your rights to make a claim in the courts for breach of contract. A breach occurs when either party fails to carry out the agreed terms, or terms which have been implied by custom and practice, or when you are dismissed with no, or insufficient, notice, unless you have committed 'gross misconduct' (see p. 289).

A sufficiently serious breach of contract will also entitle you to bring a claim of unfair dismissal (see 13.5, p. 288).

Contractual obligations

This paragraph contains the main contractual obligations between you and your employer. The method and frequency of wages or salary are as set out in your written particulars. You are not obliged to accept cashless pay unless this has been agreed. If you were employed before 1987 (when the Wages Act 1986 took effect) and were entitled to be paid in cash, management must obtain your agreement before changing to other forms of pay.

If *deductions* are made unlawfully from your pay you can make a claim to a tribunal (see 13.8, p. 295). Deductions are lawful only if you have given your consent in writing, or if this is provided for in your contract. However, there are exceptions allowing management to make deductions in respect of: overpayment of wages and expenses; payments by law to public authorities; payments to third parties e.g., trade unions; or deductions following a strike or other industrial action. The 1986 Act applies not just to employees but to all workers.

Hours of work are determined by agreement either with you or with trade unions. There are no restrictions on the maximum or minimum number of hours to be worked by men or women, or the times of the day and days of the week when work may take place. There are some restrictions on the hours of young people below the age of eighteen. There is no definition of 'part-time worker' but in order to claim rights under the employment legislation you need to have worked for at least sixteen hours a week, or alternatively for eight hours a week for more than five years.

There is no statutory obligation to offer *holidays*, or to pay for them, or even to offer or pay for bank holidays.

As long as management pay you they have no obligation to *provide work*. The right to work may be enforced only by:

- employees who are offered the opportunity to earn commission or a bonus (and therefore cannot achieve this if they are denied the right);
- artists, actors, singers and performers whose careers are advanced by exposure; *and*
- highly-skilled craft workers who need to keep their hand in.

Although management is under an obligation to provide adequate storage accommodation for your *personal property* if you work in a factory, they are not generally liable to recompense you for losses unless they are aware of a history of thefts and have done nothing, or they know you are required to bring tools or clothing to work in order to carry out your job. In that case, it is more likely that you can claim. There is no *right to search*, for example, on leaving the work premises, unless you have agreed this in your contract or accepted it by long-standing custom and practice. Security officers have no general powers to search or to detain you. If you damage your *employer's property* you may be liable to compensate them if the damage is caused by your lack of care. In practice, damage to property or injury to fellow workers does not result in claims against workers.

If you are injured at work you can claim that your employer has not provided a *safe system of work.*

Management have no right to impose a *suspension* or *lay-off* without pay and without your agreement. Suspension with pay pending the investigation of an allegation of misconduct against you is often provided for in agreements, but unilateral suspension without pay for economic or disciplinary reasons is unlawful. If you accept that management's needs have diminished, you can claim redundancy pay (see 13.6, p. 292) if you are suspended, or reduced to less than half pay, for more than four weeks. You can also claim a guarantee payment of £11.85 per day (1989) for up to five days a quarter (EPCA 1978).

You are entitled to see *personal data* held by your employer on computer or in a form other than manual records (Data Protection Act 1984). If the data is inaccurate, you can apply to a County Court or the High Court for its rectification or removal, and can claim damages for loss you have suffered and for distress caused to you. Your employer must comply with a request for the data within forty days (see also 4.1, p. 72).

You owe a duty of *fidelity* to your employer while you work, and some aspects of that survive your leaving. While you are employed, you must not disclose confidential information, but you can use it after you leave unless there are clear written restrictions in your contract – known as restrictive covenants – forbidding this. Then, such restrictions will be upheld provided they do not stop you earning a living, and they are reasonable for the protection of your ex-employer's interests. A covenant is unreasonable if it restricts you for too long, or to too narrow a geographical area, or if it excludes you from your main types of work. Information relating to your employer's specific trade secrets must be kept confidential even after you leave.

While employed, you must work only for the one employer during your working hours, but, in the absence of some implied restriction on your working for others, you can work in your own time as you wish. Any money you make arising out of your employment belongs to your employer and you must account for it. If you produce written material for publication, your employer has the copyright over it (Copyright Act 1956). If you make inventions or create patents management gets the benefit provided your normal duties include the likelihood of your making inventions. If you invent something of outstanding benefit to management, you can claim a fair share of the profits (Patents Act 1977).

You are under a duty to *obey instructions*, provided these are lawful, reasonable and within the scope of the contract you have agreed. Other instructions will constitute breaches (or even the tearing up by your employer) of the contract, for example, if you are instructed to do something which is against the criminal law, or which is unsafe, unreasonable or outside the scope of the duties you have agreed to perform. If your contract is in any way illegal (e.g., because of your intention to avoid tax by being paid cash in hand), you can claim *no* rights under it or the employment legislation.

You are under no obligation to disclose *previous convictions*, unless you are applying for a job in certain professions or occupations where disclosure is obligatory. You are entitled to answer 'no' to questions aimed at probing convictions which have become 'spent' after periods of time, e.g., five years for a fine (Rehabilitation of Offenders Act 1974, see 7.7, p. 170). Answering negatively is neither a lie nor grounds for dismissal.

Discrimination is unlawful on the grounds of race, gender, and being married. In Northern Ireland, race is not protected, but discrimination on the grounds of religious belief and political opinion is (see 15.1, p. 322).

On leaving, management is not obliged to give you a *reference*, but anything they do say must be honest, accurate and carefully written.

You have a right to *time off* without pay to be a member of a local council, health authority, school or college governing body, water authority or magistrates' bench. If this right is denied you can claim to a tribunal (see 13.8, p. 295) (EPCA 1978). The amount of time off is that which is 'reasonable' taking into account the effect of your absence on your employer's business.

13.3   Women

The Equal Pay Act 1970 and the Sex Discrimination Acts 1975 and 1986 give women (and men) the right to equal treatment and opportunities. Most of the progressive developments have come, however, from European legislation – Article 119 of the Treaty of

Rome and the Directives on equal pay and equal treatment. The UK government changed the law in 1983 and 1986 to comply with rulings of the European Court, which also extended women's rights through the case law. Pay and matters governed by your contract are dealt with in the Equal Pay Act; non-contractual benefits and opportunities are dealt with by the Sex Discrimination Act. (For other aspects of sex discrimination see 9.2, p. 207.)

EQUAL PAY

You are guaranteed equal pay if you are doing work which is the same as, or broadly similar to, that of a man, or if you are covered by a job-evaluation scheme which gives you similar scores to a man doing different work, or if you are doing work which you consider to be of equal value to a man's. In addition, the Treaty of Rome enables you to claim in an industrial tribunal for discrimination in contractual matters which is overt and direct, even if you cannot point to a male worker. For example, a contractual entitlement to redundancy payment which differs as between men and women is unlawful even though there may be no man with whom you can compare yourself.

Pay is widely defined and includes all aspects of remuneration including pension contributions. In making comparisons you must look at the whole package of conditions available to you and your male comparator.

If a job-evaluation scheme exists you will have to prove that it is discriminatory either by showing that it was compiled at a time when discrimination between men and women was lawful (i.e. pre-1976), or that it gives undue weight to characteristics and abilities commonly possessed by men, or undervalues those of women.

You can also compare yourself with a man who is doing work which is of 'equal value' to yours. You make your claim to a tribunal (see 13.8, p. 295) which will decide whether to refer your claim for analysis to an independent expert appointed under the Equal Pay Act. Unless your employer can convince the tribunal that there are no 'reasonable' grounds for making the comparison, your claim is then assessed in a lengthy and cumbersome process which involves examining the work you do and that done by your comparator(s). The tribunal may accept or reject the expert's report.

Management may defend the inequality in a claim under any part of the Equal Pay Act by saying that the difference is genuinely due not to sex but to a 'material factor'. This may include additional responsibility, the pressure of market forces, seniority or the 'red circling' of a particular comparator on the grounds of prior employment history.

If you win, the tribunal can award arrears of pay for up to two years prior to the making of the claim, and can change the terms of your contract to give you equality.

SEX DISCRIMINATION AT WORK

The Sex Discrimination Acts 1975 and 1986 outlaw discrimination at work on the grounds of sex or the fact of being married. It is *direct* when management treat you less favourably than they treat a man, or would treat a man if there were one in your place. It is *indirect* when a requirement applies equally to men and women but is such that the proportion of women who can comply with it is considerably smaller than the proportion of men who can, and which management cannot justify and which is to your detriment because you cannot comply. For example, an age barrier to recruitment or promotion might unfairly prejudice women who have been out of the economy for the purpose of child care. Or reserving certain benefits and opportunities to full-time workers could prejudice women if they form the majority of part-time workers.

Discrimination can occur at the recruitment stage, in advertisements and in the terms and conditions which are offered. If you are denied transfer, promotion, training, benefits, facilities and services, or if you are dismissed or subjected to any other detriment, you can make a claim to a tribunal (see 13.8, p. 295).

You cannot claim if the discrimination relates to provisions made for pensions or death, but a requirement that women retire at a different age from men is unlawful.

Certain jobs may lawfully be reserved for men, if management proves that being a man is a 'genuine occupational qualification' for the job. These are narrowly defined and include jobs requiring authenticity, for example, acting, physical strength, physical contact with men, or working in a country whose laws and customs make it ineffective for women to do the work.

Special procedures exist for seeking information before you make a claim (see p. 296).

MATERNITY

A pregnant worker has three rights – to maternity leave, to statutory maternity pay and not to be dismissed on account of her pregnancy.

Maternity leave

Provided you have been employed for two years by the eleventh week before your expected week of confinement, you are entitled to your job back at any time up to the twenty-ninth week after confinement (EPCA 1978). You go back to terms and conditions not less favourable than would have applied if you had not been absent. You have full continuity of employment.

You must notify management in writing twenty-one days before the start of your leave, and at the same time confirm that you intend to return. You can also be asked in writing after your confinement to confirm your intention to return. In any event, you must give twenty-one days' written notice of the date on which you intend to return. Your employer can seek medical confirmation, and you yourself can postpone the date of return by up to four weeks on medical grounds.

Maternity pay

You may be entitled by your contract or collective agreement to be paid while you are on leave, and to be paid above the minimum statutory maternity pay (SMP) levels. You can take advantage of whichever is better. SMP is available if you have been employed for twenty-six weeks including the fifteenth week before the expected week of confinement, and have average weekly earnings above the lower earnings limit for the purposes of social security contributions (EPCA 1978 and Social Security Act 1986). You need not be working at the fifteenth week, providing your contract continues into it. Pay is available from the eleventh week before confinement and lasts for eighteen weeks.

You do not get SMP if your pay is below the lower earnings level. You are entitled to pay at a higher rate for the first six weeks of absence provided you have been employed for two years at sixteen hours per week (or for five years at eight hours per week) by the fifteenth week before confinement. You then receive twelve weeks' pay at the lower rate (£32.85 in 1988) for twelve weeks.

No dismissal

It is automatically unfair to dismiss you on account of pregnancy, or to fail to offer you a suitable available vacancy. If a redundancy has occurred during your maternity leave and it is not reasonably practicable to give you your old job back, suitable alternative employment must be offered. Otherwise you can claim unfair dismissal (see 13.5, p. 288). If it is not reasonably practicable for other reasons to give you your old job back, you must be offered suitable alternative employment on no less favourable terms. However, if the number of employees at the time of your taking leave is five or less, including you, management can refuse to take you back on the grounds that it is not reasonably practicable to offer you a suitable alternative vacancy.

Claims

If you are denied any of the above rights you may make a claim to a tribunal. Employers can recoup the total cost of statutory maternity pay from their social security contributions.

13.4   Health, safety, sickness and disability

HEALTH AND SAFETY AT WORK ETC ACT 1974

This Act imposes duties on all employers to ensure so far as is reasonably practicable the health, safety and welfare of their employees. This means providing safe plant and systems of work, and making arrangements for the safe handling, storage and transport of all articles used at work. Information, instruction, training and supervision should be provided so as to ensure employees' health and safety.

If management break these obligations, the Health and Safety Executive inspectors can issue prohibition or improvement notices requiring the work to be stopped, or the machinery to be improved, and they also have power to prosecute.

If your trade union is recognized for collective bargaining (see 13.1, p. 268), you have the right to appoint union safety representatives who are given rights under the Act to time off with pay, and to carry out inspection of the work-place and of relevant documents. Claims for time off can be made to a tribunal, or complaints about safety can be made to the Health and Safety Executive.

Regulations and a code of practice set out employers' obligations to provide first-aid facilities, including first-aid boxes and trained first-aiders, the number depending on the nature of the risk and the number of employees. In hazardous work-places there should be one qualified first-aider where more than fifty persons are employed, and two where more than 150 are employed.

Accidents and industrial diseases causing the loss of more than three days' working time must be notified to the Health and Safety Executive.

The Fire Precautions Act 1971 requires a fire authority to give a certificate to the occupiers of any work-place. This imposes duties on employers to ensure that fire precautions and means of escape are provided and maintained.

SPECIFIC WORK-PLACES

While the previous paragraphs apply to all work-places, specific work-places and processes are covered by their own additional regulations.

Factories

Employers must keep factories clean, at a reasonable temperature (60°F minimum – there is no maximum), free from humidity, well ventilated, well lit, well provided with toilets and clean floors. Dangerous machinery must be fenced, cranes must be kept in good mechanical order and be regularly inspected. If you are working on processes involving danger to your eyes you must be provided with, and wear, eye protection. Adequate drinking water and washing facilities must be provided. The atmosphere must be kept free of harmful dust and fumes.

Some of these obligations apply in all circumstances – they are 'absolute' duties and any breach of them will be a breach of the law. On the other hand, some depend on what is 'reasonable' or 'reasonably practicable', in which case a lesser standard will suffice.

Offices and shops

Similar obligations apply to these premises with the addition of adequate seating.

Mines and quarries

Extensive protection is given to workers in these industries. Inspectors may be appointed by a union under the Mines and Quarries Act 1954; they are given specific powers and duties to enforce the legislation.

Construction sites

These must be kept safe, excavations and demolitions must be fenced or secured and machinery must also be fenced.

Agriculture

Agriculture, forestry and nurseries are covered by the Agriculture Act (Safety, Health and Welfare Provisions) 1956 and regulations made under it.

Other industries

Specific regulations cover, for example, working with asbestos, wood, civil engineering, lead, nuclear radiation and in foundries.

Sanctions

For breach of any of the above, the Health and Safety Executive may bring proceedings in the criminal courts, and may issue prohibition and improvement notices.

COMPENSATION

In addition to possible prosecution, many breaches of the above laws give rise to claims by an injured worker, for breach of statutory duty or negligence. Every employer is under an obligation to provide:

- a safe system of work;
- competent staff, i.e., if another worker is careless you can sue the employer for failing to supervise him/her;
- a safe place of work;
- safe and adequate plant, machinery and materials, and adequate supervision.

A civil claim is made in either the county court or the High Court, depending on the seriousness of the injury or the disease you have contracted. Legal aid is available. You must claim within three years of the injury or disease, although you can sometimes claim later if you did not know that you were suffering from an injury or disease which is attributable to your employer's negligence. If successful, you will be awarded damages to compensate you for your injury, and for financial losses such as loss of wages and expenses.

SICK PAY

Many contracts and collective agreements contain arrangements for payment during times of sickness. If these are better than the minimum statutory sick pay (SSP) you are entitled, by your contract, to them. If you have made sufficient social security contributions you will be entitled to SSP, payable by your employer and fully reimbursable from the State. Provided you earn more than the lower earnings level you qualify for SSP for the first twenty-eight weeks of absence, excluding the first three days. You get SSP at the higher or lower rate according to your average weekly earnings, but you are entitled to no more than twenty-eight weeks' SSP in any three-year period.

DISABILITY

In July 1986 the EEC made a recommendation to member States that they should take all appropriate measures to promote fair opportunities for disabled people in the field of employment. It sets out a programme of positive action and encourages member States to deal positively with disabled people. It is not the law either in the UK or in Europe, but represents an approach which could be adopted.

The Disabled Persons (Employment) Acts 1944 and 1958 and Regulations prescribe a quota of three per cent of the workforce to be registered disabled persons. This applies to an employer of twenty or more employees. For some jobs, priority is given to persons holding 'green cards' and you need a special permit before a non-disabled person can be employed. In fact, there is little regard for and even less enforcement of these laws. Long before the law on unfair dismissal was enacted, it was a criminal offence to dismiss a registered disabled person, unless the employer could show a reasonable cause.

The Companies Act 1985 requires companies with 250 employees to make a statement in their annual report concerning the employment of disabled people.

13.5   Dismissal

The termination of a contract of employment by the unilateral act of your employer is a dismissal. It can take many practical forms. You may be dismissed with or without or with less than your contractual notice. You may be made redundant or offered early retirement. You may resign in protest at your employer's words or behaviour – this is called constructive dismissal. You may be given an ultimatum in which you can either resign or be dismissed. You may be the victim of a process of 'squeezing-out' over a period of time. If you are on a fixed-term contract, management may refuse to renew it on its expiry. Or they may refuse to take you back after a strike, or to re-engage you after your dismissal during a strike. Or they may refuse to offer you a job after you have been on maternity leave.

In reality, there are only two kinds of dismissal in law upon which you can take action. You can either claim *wrongful dismissal*, which is when you are given less than your contractual period of notice or denied access to agreed procedures (that is *all* it means); or you may claim an *unfair dismissal* because the reason given by your employer, or found by a tribunal on your claim, is insufficient, and management acted unreasonably in dismissing you for that reason in all the circumstances (EPCA 1978).

NOTICE

You are entitled to periods of notice depending on your length of service, and the written statement (see 13.2, p. 274) must include a note of your contractual entitlement. After one month's service you are entitled to one week's notice and thereafter at the rate of one week for each year of service up to a maximum of twelve. Of course, your contract may provide for longer periods than this, but if nothing is said, you are entitled to a 'reasonable' amount of notice which may exceed the statutory minima.

If you do not get your contractual or statutory notice, you can sue for breach of contract in the county court or the High Court, depending on your claim. If you have been denied access to a contractual procedure for challenging dismissal, your notice period is extended by the notional period during which you would have pursued your rights internally.

You lose your right to notice if you are dismissed for gross misconduct, a term not defined in any statute but taken to mean conduct by you which shows that you no longer intend to be bound by the contract, and which, if proved, deprives you of your rights.

REASONS FOR DISMISSAL

Provided you have been employed for two years at the date of dismissal, you are entitled to particulars, in writing, of the reasons for your dismissal. Following a written request, management must provide them within fourteen days. If this is not forthcoming, you can claim to a tribunal (see 13.8, p. 295), which has the power to declare the reason for your dismissal and to award two weeks' pay. If you are claiming unfair dismissal, you should seek written particulars in any event, and add this to your claim if management do not comply.

UNFAIR DISMISSAL

In order to claim unfair dismissal you must have worked for *two years* at sixteen hours per week, or for *five years* at eight hours per week (minima), unless you are claiming on the basis of race, sex or trade union discrimination. You can claim at any stage up to the age of sixty-five, unless there is a lower normal retirement age at your workplace.

If you bring a claim in the tribunal (see 13.8, p. 295) management must show what the reason was for your dismissal. It must fit into one of the following categories: conduct, capacity, redundancy, a legal restriction (e.g., not having proper working papers) or 'some other substantial reason' which could justify the dismissal. Few employers have difficulty putting forward a reason. So the main dispute focuses on the reasonableness of the employer in deciding to dismiss for that reason. Since the circumstances in which dismissal arises are numerous and varied, there is not space here to deal with this complex area of the law. Clear rules have emerged for dealing with sickness, reorganizations, criminal acts committed within the employment context, poor performance and refusal to obey instructions. Nevertheless, each case is to be treated on its own merits and tribunals on the same facts could reach quite different conclusions.

Remedies for unfair dismissal

If you win your case, the tribunal must first consider whether you wish to be reinstated and, if so, must decide whether it is just and equitable to order that. If not, compensation should be awarded to take account of the losses you have suffered up to the date of the hearing, and the amount of time you are likely to be unemployed, or if you have a job, to compensate you for any loss in pay in the new job. If you have claimed unemployment benefit, your losses are calculated after taking account of what you have received.

In addition, you should also get a payment equivalent to a redundancy payment (see 13.6, p. 292) which is called a basic award.

After dismissal, you must take steps to try and find alternative work, and if you do not your compensation may be reduced by a percentage. Also, it may be reduced, and the tribunal may refuse to order reinstatement, if you have contributed to your dismissal by your own actions.

In 1986/87, only one in three applicants who reached a tribunal hearing succeeded. The median award of compensation was £1,805. Reinstatement was awarded in less than three per cent of cases.

BREACH OF PROCEDURE

The existence of a disciplinary procedure in your contract of employment or collective agreement is important for both unfair and wrongful dismissal. If you are denied your rights, you may claim an injunction (or in Scotland an interdict) in the High Court to prevent management acting upon your dismissal or taking other disciplinary action until the procedure has been exhausted. This means you are to be treated as still employed, although perhaps not being required to work, until the full trial of your case for wrongful dismissal. You can get legal aid for this. Also, in unfair dismissal proceedings a failure to go through either the agreed procedure, or to adopt the rules of natural justice (giving notice of an allegation, an opportunity for you to say what you think, and an open-minded management) may result in the dismissal being unfair. In other words, a potentially fair dismissal can be made unfair if proper and reasonable procedures are not followed.

13.6   Redundancy

Redundancy occurs when management's requirements for work of the particular kind you are employed to do has ceased or diminished, either temporarily or permanently. If you are dismissed for this reason, or put on short-time working (receiving less than half-pay), or are laid off for four weeks or more, you can claim a redundancy payment (EPCA 1978).

The payment is based on your age, length of continuous service and weekly pay. You are entitled to one and a half weeks' pay for each year of continuous employment when you are aged between forty-one and sixty-three inclusive, one week's pay between the ages of twenty-one and forty inclusive, and half a week's pay for each other year.

Weekly pay does not include all your earnings and so, for example, voluntary overtime is excluded but regular commission and bonuses are included. The maximum weekly pay allowable for redundancy purposes is £172 (1989).

You lose your right to a redundancy payment if you turn down an offer made by your employer to re-engage you on a new contract if the offer is of suitable alternative employment – the kind of work which would be regarded as suitable for you – *and* you have unreasonably refused to take it. The unreasonableness is judged by what your own circumstances are.

Before you are made redundant, you have a right to claim a reasonable amount of time off with pay in order to look for work or to re-train. And, if you accept an offer of new employment with the same employer or one of its associates, you have the right to a four-week trial period during which time you can quit the job and be regarded as redundant. In other words, you do not prejudice your rights by taking the job for a trial period.

As with unfair dismissal, you need *two years'* continuous employment. Your entitlement to redundancy pay is reduced if you have reached the age of sixty-four.

If management dispute that there is a redundancy situation, for example, by claiming that there has simply been a reorganization of the business without any lessening of the requirements for employees, or if you dispute the amount of money paid to you, you can make a claim to a tribunal (see 13.8, p. 295). If your employer has gone bust, you can make a claim for redundancy pay and other outstanding debts including notice and holiday pay to be made by the Secretary of State (EPCA 1978 and Insolvency Act 1986).

CONSULTATION

If your union is recognized for collective bargaining, management are under an obligation to consult it at the earliest opportunity about a proposal to make any dismissal (Employment Protection Act 1975). There is a minimum consultation period: thirty days if ten or more employees are to be dismissed, ninety days if a 100. If the union claims there has been no, or inadequate, consultation, it can make a claim to a tribunal which can then make a 'protective award' of compensation in favour of the employees who have been dismissed without the necessary consultation having taken place.

TAKE-OVERS, MERGERS AND TRANSFERS

If the business in which you work is transferred as a going concern to another employer, the Transfer of Undertakings Regulations 1981 protect your terms and conditions with the new employer. Recognition of your union and all your contractual terms go over to the new employer. If you are dismissed as a result of the transfer, you can claim unfair dismissal which will be automatically unfair unless management proves that the dismissal was on account of an organizational or technical reason associated with the transfer.

PAYMENT

The total amount of any redundancy payment is to be paid by your employer, without reimbursement from the State. You are entitled to a written statement of the calculation.

13.7   Industrial action

There is *no right to strike* in the UK. What is regarded as a fundamental or constitutional right in other countries becomes an immunity from some forms of civil action in the courts in the UK. Persuading people not to work, and to break their contracts, has always been unlawful in common law. If it is done in contemplation or furtherance of a trade dispute, as narrowly defined by the Trade Union and Labour Relations Act 1974, and if a ballot in favour of the action has been held, union leaders are 'immune' from normal civil liability.

Restrictions on the freedom to strike are placed on police officers, apprentices (who must make up the time) and merchant seafarers; limited action by postal workers is also restricted by law.

A *trade dispute* is a dispute between workers and their *own* employer about terms, conditions, suspension, duties, engagement of workers, allocation of work, discipline, union membership, negotiating procedures and union facilities. In the course of such a dispute you can persuade people not to work. But if you do it on behalf of the union, because you are a lay or full-time officer, or if the union adopts your actions, the union must conduct a ballot, and such calls for action will only be lawful if taken within four weeks of the result of a successful ballot. The ballot must ask all those likely to be asked to break their contracts whether they are in favour.

It does not matter what form the *industrial action* takes – it can be a strike, work to rule, ban on overtime (whether it is voluntary or compulsory), withdrawal of cooperation, boycotts – they are all forms of industrial action and involve breaches of contract. As such, all those engaged in action are liable to their employers for breach of contract. In practice, employers do not sue their workers for the losses suffered by them as a result of each worker's breach of contract. More likely is an action against the union. Unions can be sued in their own name for damages if industrial action is taken which is unlawful. Much 'secondary action', that is action taken against an employer who is not a party to the main trade dispute, is unlawful. If the union has organized this, an injunction (or in Scotland an interdict) can be granted to prevent it, and claims for damages of up to £$\frac{1}{4}$ m., depending on the size of the union, can be awarded.

Equally likely is that employers may *dismiss* all of those engaged in industrial action. If all of you who take industrial action at the same work-place are dismissed, and none is re-engaged within three months, none of you has any claim. After the three-month period, selective re-engagement is permissible. This means that you are always at risk whatever form of action you take.

Employers sometimes *withhold pay* for all or part of the time that you have been engaged in limited industrial action. They are entitled only to deduct a proportion of pay representing the proportion of your time lost by your action.

Since the Employment Act 1988, *ballots* in favour of industrial action must be taken at each work-place where workers are to be called upon. Action in pursuit of union membership agreements (see p. 271) is always unlawful.

Picketing of your own work-place (but nowhere else) during the course of a dispute is lawful provided that your purpose is peacefully to persuade people not to work, or to communicate information. A code of practice (and one court decision) recommends that there be a limit of six pickets on each entrance, but different numbers may be appropriate in different circumstances. Offences under public order legislation (see 11.1, p. 14) are the most likely criminal charges to arise out of picketing.

13.8   Claims

Most claims in this chapter are brought before industrial tribunals. Legal aid is not available, but an extension to the green (pink in Scotland) form for preparation and/or counsel's advice can be granted. Legal aid is available if you are taking a case such as an injunction or interdict to the High Court. Help can be obtained from the Equal Opportunities Commission, the Commission for Racial Equality or, in certain cases, from the Commissioner for the Rights of Trade Union Members.

CLAIMS IN TIME

The first point to check is whether you are in time to bring a claim. Deadlines are strict, usually three months from the action complained of. Make sure you fill in, or have filled in on your behalf, the 'Originating Application to an Industrial Tribunal' form (IT 1) and that it reaches the Central Office of Industrial Tribunals for

England and Wales, or for Scotland, or for Northern Ireland, within the appropriate time.

DOCUMENTS

The organization against which you are claiming – usually an employer but sometimes a trade union – will reply in a set form. You may ask for further particulars of any matter they raise, and you can also be asked to give particulars. Before commencing proceedings in a race relations or sex discrimination claim you may issue a questionnaire seeking to obtain information from your employer about the actions and policies you are challenging. If you have been dismissed, write a letter seeking particulars, in writing within fourteen days, of the reasons for your dismissal.

An important step in the proceedings is the 'discovery of documents'. You are entitled to see all documents relevant to your claim, including internal notes and minutes, which are particularly important in respect of claims for discrimination. If the employers do not provide documents, you can seek an order from the tribunal to this effect.

REPRESENTATION

You can be represented at a tribunal by anyone you like. If you are claiming unfair dismissal, the employers start the case and bring their witnesses. Otherwise you start.

If you think the hearing is likely to last more than one day you should tell the tribunal so that they can fix a block of time for it. Otherwise the case will be adjourned with an interval in between.

The case is generally conducted by the Chairman (the statutory term), but the tribunal consists of a lawyer, a person nominated by employers' organizations and one by employees' organizations. They have an equal say in the decision.

AWARDS

Tribunals can award compensation, make recommendations of

reinstatement or re-engagement, and order employers to rectify discriminatory acts and policies.

APPEALS

Appeals on points of law go to the Employment Appeal Tribunal (EAT) in London or Edinburgh, or to the Northern Ireland Court of Appeal. The EAT consists of a High Court judge and a person nominated by employers and one by employees. Legal aid is available. You may be represented by anyone you like at the EAT, and appeal from its decisions lies to the Court of Appeal, the Court of Session in Scotland or the House of Lords. This can only be on a point of law, and you must have the permission either of the EAT or the Court of Appeal or Court of Session in order to take the case further.

13.9   More information

USEFUL ORGANIZATIONS

The best source of advice is your trade union. The *TUC*, Congress House, Great Russell Street, London WC1B 3LS (01-636 4030) will direct you to an appropriate union.

Advisory Conciliation and Arbitration Service – Regional Offices in Newcastle, Leeds, London, Bristol, Birmingham, Nottingham, Manchester, Liverpool, Glasgow, Cardiff and the Labour Relations Agency in Belfast.

Commission for Racial Equality, Elliott House, 10–12 Allington Street, London SW1E 5EH (01-828 7022)

Commissioner for the Rights of Trade Union Members, Sunley Building, Piccadilly Plaza, Manchester M60 7JS (061-832 9111)

Equal Opportunities Commission, Overseas House, Quay Street, Manchester M3 3HN (061-833 9244)

Equal Opportunities Commission for Northern Ireland, Chamber of Commerce House, 22 Great Victoria Street, Belfast BT2 2BA (0232 242752)

Fair Employment Agency, Andras House, 60 Great Victoria Street, Belfast BT2 7BB (0232 240020)

Health and Safety Commission, 1 Baynards House, 1 Chepstow Place, London W2 4TF (01-221 0870)

Labour Relations Agency, Windsor House, 9–15 Bedford Street, Belfast BT2 7NU (0232 321442)

BIBLIOGRAPHY

J. McIlroy, *Industrial Tribunals*, Pluto Press, 1982.
J. McMullen, *Rights at Work*, Pluto Press, 1983.
D. Pannick, *Sex Discrimination Law*, Oxford University Press, 1986.
M. Rowland, C. Kennedy and I. McMullen (eds), *The Rights Guide to Non-means-tested Benefits*, Child Poverty Action Group, 1989 (and annually).
Lord Wedderburn, *The Worker and the Law*, Penguin, 1986.

14 The rights of travellers

This chapter deals with:

14.1   The right to travel

As with most other rights under English law, you are free to do
what you are not prevented from doing by criminal or civil law. As
a traveller, you are subject to the same laws as anyone else, even if
those laws may be enforced differently in different parts of the
country and in different places. So you have the right to pass and
repass on the highway, but no special right to stop and park your
caravan or other vehicles. As will be explained later, however,
special extra laws may apply to you if you are defined as being a
'gypsy' (see 14.3, p. 303).

14.2   The right to stop

Where can you stop, legally, and park and live in a caravan? The
answer to this is: a legal site. But what is a legal site?

- A piece of land you own, which has any necessary planning
  permission. You are the owner and occupier.

- A piece of land owned by someone else, including a local council, which is laid out as a site, with any necessary planning permission, site licence, and where the site operator and yourself have agreed you can stay. You are a licensee, with very limited rights if it is a local authority Gypsy Caravan Site.
- A piece of land, not necessarily laid out as a site, where no planning permission or site licence for the parking of an inhabited caravan is required, because you are doing seasonal agricultural or forestry work for the landowner (usually a farmer), or in a limited number of other cases where you are staying for short periods on open fields.

There is one other type of land which you cannot be moved from, although it is not usually called a 'legal site'. That is land which has been continuously occupied by caravans since before the end of 1963, which you own, or where no one else has a better title to it. In these cases, you may apply for an Established Use certificate from the local planning authority, to make your status and rights clear.

Other than the four cases above, you may be liable to be moved on, even if it takes some time, unless the owner of the land you are on is unknown.

What follows is a check-list to help you identify not only how much the right to stop has been reduced, but also which powers may be used against caravans or other vehicles on any particular type of land.

DESIGNATION

Your rights, if you are a gypsy, to be provided with a legal site will be dealt with later. We shall see how certain local councils have a duty to provide adequate numbers of caravan site places for gypsies who live in, or regularly come to, their area.

Once the Secretary of State for the Environment is satisfied adequate site numbers have been provided or has decided they do not need to be, the area of the county, district, group of districts, or London borough may be covered by a Designation Order.

This order gives extra powers to authorities and the police

against you if you are a 'person of nomadic habit of life' who is not on a legal site. It covers you if you are on highway land, occupied land (if there is no consent to your being there from the occupier) and unoccupied land. It is unlikely, though possible, that these powers would be used against you on your own land, although they could be used against those who stop without permission on a legal council or private site.

On land included within the three categories above, the local council or the police could prosecute you, and the local council could get a magistrates' court order which would allow them to tow off the caravans that belong to you and others on the land.

The police have powers to arrest anyone obstructing the legal eviction, and anyone doing so can be prosecuted separately.

If you or others wish to check the legal position of a group of caravans not legally on a site, you should check with the local council to find out if the area is designated. If it is, not only do the extra powers set out above apply, but also the general rights of landowners to evict trespassers through the civil courts.

OWN LAND

Whether or not the area is designated, if you live on land where you have freehold or leasehold title you may still fall foul of the law. If it is not a legal site and you do not have established use rights (see above) you *must* get planning permission and a site licence. If you do not seek planning permission from the local council, it may decide to take out an enforcement notice against you. If you do not appeal against this, or you are not successful with your appeal, you can subsequently be fined, face High Court injunctions to prevent the occupation of your land, and finally, in very rare cases, be imprisoned for contempt of court and have your land sold to pay unpaid fines.

If you apply for planning permission, the Race Relations Act could be used if your application was refused on racial or ethnic grounds. If this has happened to you, contact the Commission for Racial Equality at the address at the end of this chapter. Note also that in any planning appeal over a gypsy caravan site, the shortage of sites for travellers in an area is a 'material consideration' for the planning inspector to weigh up.

TYPE OF LAND

If you have no title to the land, the type of land may decide if and how anyone can be moved from it. Outside London, highway verges are both wider and more plentiful in rural areas, as is common land. In the first case, there are many powers to prosecute and move travellers on under the Highways Acts, but many councils, and the police, do not wish to make matters worse by using these powers, unless it is really necessary. In the case of common land, there may be legal complications about moving you on, unless that bit of common is already covered by an express ban on caravan parking. There should be a sign up saying so if it is.

WHO OWNS THE LAND?

If the land is neither highway verge or common land, and has a definite owner, the length of time you can stop on it will depend on a number of factors, including the number of caravans and the way that you and other travellers operate, as well as the level of complaint from others round about. Councils with too few sites and government departments may feel that it is unwise to evict you too quickly. Others may not feel limited by this. Action depends on the decision of the particular landowner.

IF THE LANDOWNER WANTS YOU MOVED OFF

There are now two methods that a landowner can use. The more important one has only been in use since 1 April 1987. It is Section 39 of the Public Order Act 1986. Under it, if certain conditions are satisfied, the police may direct any or all of the people on the land to leave it, and you may be prosecuted if you fail to do so, or if you return within three months, unless (in either case) you have a legal defence that you did not go on to the land as trespassers, or reasonable excuse for failing to leave the land quickly when directed.

Before a senior police officer can use the section he or she must reasonably believe that two or more people entered the land as trespassers with the intention of living there for a time, and that the occupier has taken reasonable steps, directly or through someone else, to ask you to leave.

If you and others have more than twelve vehicles (including caravans) between you, there are no further conditions, and the most senior police officer present may direct you to leave. If there are less than twelve vehicles, the police officer must also reasonably believe that there has been damage to property on the land by one or more of you, or that threatening, abusive, or insulting words or behaviour have been used against the occupier of the land, a member of their family, or their agent, or employee, by any of you.

In addition to the above, the landowner may use the civil courts to get a possession order against those of you who are on the land. You need only have two days' notice of such a county or High Court application.

IF THE LANDOWNER WANTS TO LET YOU STAY

In this case, unless you are a seasonal worker or a very short-stayer on open land, the landowner may be pressed by planning officers (see 14.2, p. 301) to move you and, if you have gathered for a festival or other event, you may be prosecuted for unlawful assembly.

14.3   The right to a site

Local authorities of all types (apart from the former GLC) have had the *power* to establish caravan sites since 1960. County councils and London boroughs have had a special *duty* to provide all travellers with sites, in some cases since 1970, but in others, as a result of the reorganization of local government, since 1974. The duty extends towards those who are gypsies as defined by the Caravan Sites Act 1968: these are 'persons of nomadic habit of life, whatever their race or origin . . .'.

The general duty on those who have it, is to provide 'adequate accommodation' for gypsies 'residing in or resorting to' their area, 'so far as may be necessary'. In London boroughs and Metropolitan Districts the legal duty is limited to provision for fifteen caravans 'at a time'. Elsewhere, there is no legal limit.

But this general duty gives no particular right to any traveller to claim a site place from a particular authority. What dissatisfied travellers have had to do is to take individual councils (and sometimes the Secretary of State for the Environment) to court for their failure to provide adequate sites, or the Secretary of State's failure to direct the council to provide them, as he has power to do.

This has resulted in a number of councils being found in breach of their duty, and, in one case, being told that their decision to evict a group of travellers from their land was 'unreasonable ... and a void decision'.

If you are seeking a site place (see below), you should keep in touch (preferably in writing) with the local council you have most connection with, hold on to evidence of your continuing stay in the area, and keep pressing for the building of a necessary site.

14.4   The right to housing

It is obviously very difficult for any nomadic people to secure rights to housing. It is hard enough if you are not nomadic and settle in an area with some legal accommodation. Some areas have large numbers of families in hotels or bed and breakfast accommodation. If you are single or childless and neither elderly nor handicapped, it will be difficult for you to get council housing, whether or not you are a traveller. All housing authorities have their own distinct rules for acceptance on to their housing lists and for deciding who gets priority once they are on the list.

If you are a traveller, you face daily difficulties if you have no legal accommodation to stop on or in, and these are dealt with elsewhere in this section. But it is important for you to remember that you have the right to seek council housing and to be considered for it, just as much as anyone else. You may also have rights to be provided with accommodation, or assisted with getting it, by a local council housing department, if you are judged to be 'homeless' (for example, you are being evicted from a piece of land or a highway verge, and you have nowhere legal to go and live in your caravan), and have a 'priority need' for accommodation (if you have children living with you, or elderly or handicapped people). If it is decided that you are homeless and have such a priority need, then the council can avoid its duty to provide you with accommodation only by showing either that you have a 'local connection' with another council's area that is stronger than your connection with them or that you made yourself intentionally homeless (for example, you were in housing or on a legal site, perhaps even some time ago, but left this legal accommodation for no good reason).

It is important to note that there is no duty on any council housing authority to provide you with a site for your caravan. In London boroughs and Metropolitan District Council areas the duty to provide sites is still on the council, but it is separate from the duty to provide for homeless people. In shire counties, the duty to provide accommodation for homeless people rests on the District Council, while the duty to provide caravan sites for travellers is on the County Council.

If you are looking for settled accommodation, or even if you want to put your name on a waiting-list for a possible caravan site, you should visit the local council housing offices, preferably in the area that you have most connection with, unless there is a good reason (risk of violence from another member of the family, or someone else, for example) for selecting another area. When you visit the housing offices, ask them what sort of provision is available. Do they have a site for travelling people? Does it have spare places on it? Where is it and how do they decide who goes on to it? If you have no interest in such a site, give the housing officer all the details about your living arrangements in your caravan. Remember that there are two separate ways of getting council accommodation, and that you can apply to be put on a council house waiting-list, without being homeless. Before you leave the council office, make sure that you have got a decision from them both about your application to go on to the council house waiting-list, as well as any decision about whether you are 'homeless'. Ask them to give you a written note of those decisions, or of when they will be made. Keep that record in a safe place.

If you apply to be dealt with as homeless, the council housing department should give you a quick answer. If necessary, visit them every day and find out the name of the housing officer or other person that you need to speak to, and try to speak to the same person each time.

If you are applying for a council house, make sure you keep in contact with the housing department, by telephone or letter (get a teacher or somebody else to write this for you, if you need to) as the council house waiting-lists are revised every six months or year in many areas, and you have to make sure that you stay on the list each time until they make you an offer. It is possible to be on more than one council house waiting-list at once.

Finally, you have the right to see all the information that the housing department keeps on you, although you have to pay a charge if you want to keep copies of this. If you do not read, or feel more confident with somebody assisting you, then ask a sympathetic councillor, council traveller's officer, teacher, health visitor or some other person that you trust to go with you on those visits, who could not only give you assistance, but also act as an independent witness.

14.5   The right to education

Traveller children aged between five and sixteen have the same legal right to education as anyone else. Other travellers who are not of compulsory school age have the same right to seek state education as anyone else of comparable age.

It is obviously difficult to claim or seek these rights if you do not have a legal place to stop. If you are a parent of a school age child, then you should simply take the child (or children) to the nearest school to where you are stopping, and ask them to provide education. It will be very helpful, both for the child and the local education authority, if you present children at school at age five, or even before. But if there have been great practical difficulties in getting your children to school earlier, do not hesitate to take them at *any* age. You have a legal duty to present them at school, and the local education authority has a legal duty to provide them with appropriate full-time education.

Once you have met the school secretary, headmaster or another teacher, it may be that all sorts of difficulties about admitting one or more of your children will be mentioned. It is important for you to stand your ground. Those practical difficulties are for the school or the local education authority to work out. If they ask you to go away for a few days, ask them exactly why you are being asked to do so. Be firm but polite.

If one or more of your children is refused education at a school, or there are many obstacles put in front of her or him, then you should approach the Chief Education Officer for that council, by going to the local Town Hall – ask at a Post Office or Police Station how to find your way there if you do not know it.

Many traveller children start school late, and attend only from time to time. If you keep moving because of work or other reasons, then you only have to make sure that your children are in school for 200 half days (100 full days) during the September to July school year. If your children have started late or attended irregularly, they may be judged to have special needs, which may include remedial help with reading, or even the necessity for them to go to a special school. There are rules about the way in which this decision on special needs is made, and you will almost certainly need the assistance of a literate friend to help you through this process.

In conclusion, remember that your school age children have a *right* to be educated, and a right to have their needs considered in the same way as any other child. If the school or education department is planning to make decisions that you do not understand or disagree with, keep asking them detailed questions at every stage, so that they tell you exactly what they are doing, why they are doing it, and what the likely result will be. What is most important is that you do not give up and withdraw your child or children from school if you do not understand what is happening. Taking a child away from school is likely to damage the child's education more than it challenges the local authority over the decisions they have made about that child's education.

14.6   The right to health care

Everyone has a right to health care from the National Health Service. What this means in practice is that no hospital should ever turn away someone who is the victim of accident or illness, whoever that person is and whether or not they have paid any National Insurance contributions. When you go to a dentist or take a prescription to the chemist, however, you will only get certain benefits free or at a reduced price if you are a child, someone who suffers from a long term illness or disability (for example, diabetes), or you receive income support or a pension or family credit.

Although many travellers go to casualty departments when they have an accident or illness, it is much more sensible to register with a local doctor, if you are in an area, or expect to be, for more than a few weeks. Lists of doctors should be available at main Post Offices, and the best way is to visit the doctor you pick from the list, and give her or him the exact details (dates of birth and so on) of those members of your family who wish to register with them. Some doctors are prevented from taking extra people on to their list if it is already too long, and so you may have to go to several doctors before you find one that will allow you to register with her or him. If you are turned down by all the doctors, whether or not it is because you are a traveller, then look up the address and phone number of the Family Practitioner Committee in the local telephone book (get somebody to help you with this, if necessary). Contact them (if possible in writing, after a telephone call) telling them that you have been turned down by the doctors concerned, the reasons you have been given by the doctors and any other reasons you believe may have affected the decision.

If there is an accident or illness within your family and you believe it may be unsafe to move the person concerned you can telephone any local doctor and ask them for emergency help. Try to make sure that there is somebody else with you when you make that call, so that there is no doubt that you made it.

In practice, Health Visitors may have more contact with your family and friends, especially around the time that any children are born. Ask a Health Visitor for advice about registering with a doctor and for help with getting your rights to health care, even if you are regularly being moved from place to place.

14.7   The right to welfare benefits

It is commonly believed that if you do not have a settled address then you are not entitled to welfare benefits. This is untrue. You are as entitled to welfare benefits if you move around as if you stay in the same place. But it is obviously more difficult to claim them; you may get long delays while the papers relating to you go from office to office of the DSS, and it is also likely that fraud, or the intention to defraud, will be assumed against you more easily than against other people.

If you and any members of your family that you live with do not have any income, or only a very small one, then you can apply for income support on form B1, which you can get from a Post Office. If you are on a site or in a house, you may be able to claim housing benefit, and for this you approach the local council housing department. If you have children under sixteen living with you, you are entitled to child benefit, whatever income you have. If you do not have a settled house or site to stop on, your child benefits may be paid at the end of each three months, unless you can make an arrangement for it to be paid through a close friend, relative or council officer, or it can be added to any income support that you are receiving each week.

You may also be entitled to other benefits, such as extra heating allowances, as caravans are probably more difficult to keep warm than houses. In addition, there are other benefits for the handicapped and those who look after them and you can get leaflets about all these from main Post Offices, or discuss them with the local DSS office. At the end of this chapter, there are details of a guide to many of these benefits and how to claim them.

Particular difficulties often arise with lost birth certificates, or with people proving their identity. These two issues may well be linked. If you have difficulty with either of them, approach your local Advice Centre, Citizens' Advice Bureau or local Social Services Department, to help you get your money, especially if it is an emergency.

14.8   The right not to be discriminated against

The National Union of Teachers has recently described the prejudice against travellers as being similar to that suffered by many other ethnic minorities, and sometimes as fierce.

For many years, it was said that the Race Relations Acts covered gypsies as much as any one else, but no one was ever prosecuted for incitement to racial hatred against gypsies, and there were only two notable cases that the Commission for Racial Equality dealt with concerning travelling people.

Recent changes in the law and practice now mean that a gypsy applicant (and not all travellers will come within the racial or ethnic definition 'gypsy') for a planning permission, or a council house is covered by the Race Relations Act. If someone produces material, including a leaflet, book, play, film, television or radio programme, which is likely or intended to stir up racial hatred against gypsies, then they can be criminally prosecuted, providing the Attorney General consents to the prosecution.

The Court of Appeal decided in the summer of 1988 that gypsies were one or more ethnic groups and were protected by the Race Relations Act. A 'No Travellers' sign on a public house could indirectly discriminate against gypsies, as they would be a large proportion of the group 'travelling' (that is, caravan-dwelling) who would be refused service. Unless, therefore, there is justification for the sign, it is in breach of the law.

If you have been refused service in a shop or a pub, or been prevented from entering premises normally open to any member of the public by an objectionable sign, or you know of planning policies which ban all gypsy caravan sites being approved in an area, or in some other way you suffer discrimination in treatment by virtue of your origins as a traveller, then it is extremely important that you complain, rather than expecting that it is something you have to put up with. Complain to the local Community Relations Council for your area, if you know where it is, or complain direct to the Commission for Racial Equality in London, whose address is at the end of this chapter.

14.9   More information

USEFUL ORGANIZATIONS

The Advisory Committee for the Education of Romany and Other Travellers (ACERT), c/o Keepers, High Wych, Sawbridgeworth, Herts (0279 722704)

Commission for Racial Equality, Elliott House, 10–12 Allington Street, London SW1E 5EH (01-828 7022)

National Gypsy Council, Greenhills Caravan Site, Greengate Street, Oldham, Greater Manchester OL4 1DQ (061-665 1924)

The Romany Guild, 50–56 Temple Mills Lane, Stratford, London E15 (01-555 7214)

Save the Children Fund, Head Office, Mary Datchelor House, Grove Lane, London SE5 8RD (01-703 5400)

BIBLIOGRAPHY

C. Brand, *Mobile Homes and the Law*, Sweet and Maxwell, 1986.
B. Forrester, *Travellers' Handbook*, Interchange Books, 1985.
R. Lister (ed.), *National Welfare Benefits Handbook*, Child Poverty Action Group, 1988 (updated annually).
T. Viney, *Benefits for Travellers*, Travellers & Benefits Working Party, 1988 (From: Tony Viney 56 Downhills Park Road, London N17).
Travellers on the Road, NCCL, Factsheet, June 1987.

15 Rights in Northern Ireland and Scotland

This chapter looks at some of the differences between the law and your rights in England and Wales and those in Northern Ireland and Scotland.

Although the countries which comprise the United Kingdom – England, Wales, Scotland and Northern Ireland – form one entity for certain legal purposes (for example, in the definition of territory for the purposes of the Prevention of Terrorism Act – see 6.7, p. 153), only England and Wales share the same laws. Northern Ireland and Scotland have their own legal systems. The other chapters in this guide deal exclusively with the law in England and Wales.

15.1   Northern Ireland

Created at the time of partition in the 1920s, the devolved government at Stormont had responsibility for much of the legislation introduced in Northern Ireland for the first five decades of its history. Stormont was dissolved in March 1972, amidst increasing unrest, and control over Northern Ireland reverted to the government at Westminster. Apart from a brief period in 1974, when responsibility for non-security matters was devolved to a short-lived power-sharing Executive, 'direct rule' has been unbroken. Despite direct rule, however, a number of important differences remain between the law in Northern Ireland and the law in England and Wales, the most important being the existence of the Northern Ireland (Emergency Provisions) Act.

THE NORTHERN IRELAND (EMERGENCY PROVISIONS) ACT 1987

The Northern Ireland (Emergency Provisions) Act (EPA) was first introduced in 1973. This Act was repealed and replaced by the Northern Ireland (Emergency Provisions) Act 1978, which was amended in 1987. It is subject to renewal by Parliament every twelve months and has a life of five years from 1987. Its most significant powers are as follows:

Powers to enter and search

The police may enter and search your home in order to arrest someone if they have reasonable grounds for suspecting them of committing an offence under the Act and if they have reasonable grounds for suspecting the person is there.

Powers to enter and search any premises are also available to the police or any member of the army on duty if they believe that there is someone unlawfully detained whose life is in danger (special authority is needed to enter your house); or to discover whether there are munitions unlawfully held or if there is a transmitter or a receiver that enables a range of transmissions to be detected or intercepted. These may be seized and any munitions unlawfully held may be destroyed.

An authorized explosives inspector also has the power to enter anywhere other than your home to discover whether there are unlawfully held explosives, which can be seized and destroyed.

Remember, always ask the police or army what authority they have to enter and/or search; that these emergency powers only allow searches to be conducted for people or munitions (arms, explosives etc.); and that any other search, for example, through papers or books, requires a warrant.

The police and any member of the army on duty also have a general power to enter anywhere, including your home, if they consider this to be necessary in the course of their operations or if authorized to do so on behalf of the Secretary of State. This does not provide them with a general power to search or to question.

If the police or army search your home you should:

- accompany them during the search. Do not provide any

opportunity for anything to be left behind or taken without your knowledge;

- insist that any damage done or items taken are listed in writing on a sheet provided by them which you should sign. Write that this is 'with reservations' if you are not sure that everything has been listed or if you could not watch the search all the time. If you are not happy, make your own list as soon as possible and contact your local Advice Centre or a solicitor who will forward a copy of this to the authorities. You have a right to compensation for any damage caused. If no damage is done nor anything taken you do not have to sign any form;

- make a record of any conversation or search as soon as possible afterwards, as you may wish to use this later in evidence.

Powers to arrest and question

The army: You can be arrested without a warrant by any member of the army on duty if they reasonably suspect you of committing any offence. There is no requirement that the offence should be connected with terrorism, it could be any offence at all. You may be detained for up to four hours; after that you must be released or transferred to the custody of the Royal Ulster Constabulary (RUC) or military police.

This power originated at a time when the police were effectively barred from entering certain areas. It was not meant to provide the army with a power to interrogate you. However, the law still does not make this clear despite evidence that the army has used it in this way.

While the army has no authority to question you about general terrorist matters when you are under arrest, they can stop and question you in the street about your knowledge of recent explosions or any other incident endangering life, as well as your identity and recent movements. It is an offence not to stop when required to, and to fail to answer questions. This does not provide the army with a general power to stop and question you.

If you are arrested by the army you do not have the rights which are available to persons held by the police (see below).

NCCL considers that the army's policing powers should be repealed.

The police: You can be arrested without a warrant by a police officer if he or she reasonably suspects you of committing an offence under the Act.

You are obliged to answer questions about:

- your identity (name and address);
- your recent movements (where you were coming from and where you were going to at the time of your arrest); and
- recent explosions or other incidents.

You are not legally obliged to answer any other questions and otherwise have the right to remain silent, although the court may be invited to draw adverse inferences from your silence (see 6.5, p. 150).

Ask the questioner to be as clear and precise as possible; do not repeat gossip or rumours. Unless you know anything as a fact from your own personal knowledge say, 'I don't know anything about it'. You do not have to sign any document or medical certificate. Do not believe everything the police tell you; it is better to say nothing than to say something you do not want to say.

If you are arrested and detained by the police you have the right to:

- legal advice – if possible, give the name and address of a solicitor;
- have a third person informed about your arrest. Make sure that someone in your family, a friend, a local community leader or someone you trust is contacted as soon as possible.

Under certain circumstances the police can prevent you from exercising these rights for up to forty-eight hours and an Assistant Chief Constable can insist that you consult your solicitor only in the sight and hearing of a police officer. These rights are the same as those provided for people held under the Prevention of Terrorism Act in Britain and derive from rights generally available in Britain under the Police and Criminal Evidence Act (see 6.5, p. 145).

The majority of the provisions of the Prevention of Terrorism (Temporary Provisions) Act 1989 apply throughout the UK and the Act is therefore covered in a separate section (6.7, p. 153). Part 1 of the Act, relating to the banning of organizations, does not apply to Northern Ireland, where a greater number of organizations are banned under the Northern Ireland (Emergency Provisions) Act.

If you are released:

- see a doctor immediately if you have been ill-treated, even if your injuries seem minor. It is important that a record is made in case you make any claim for damages and for your own protection in the future;
- contact your local Advice Centre. It is important that a record is made of every arrest to help prevent harassment;
- contact the Police Complaints Authority if you feel you have been maltreated.

RIGHTS IN THE CRIMINAL COURTS

In Northern Ireland you may be charged with a scheduled offence. This is an offence listed as such in the Northern Ireland (Emergency Provisions) Act and includes such offences as murder and robbery with firearms.

If this happens you may be tried by a judge sitting alone without a jury. The Director of Public Prosecutions (DPP) may, however, decide to 'certify out' your case from these Diplock courts, allowing it to be tried before a jury. Only certain types of scheduled offences may be 'certified out' by the DPP.

If convicted of a scheduled offence in a Diplock court you have the right of appeal to the Court of Criminal Appeal where your case will be heard by a panel of three judges.

EVIDENCE

The EPA allows any involuntary confession you may give, other than one shown to be obtained by torture, inhuman or degrading treatment, violence, or threat of violence, to be heard in a Diplock court. These courts retain the discretion to rule such a confession inadmissible if this seems appropriate to avoid unfairness to the defendant or to be in the interest of justice.

In Northern Ireland, as in the remainder of the UK, the law

provides for the use of uncorroborated accomplice evidence. In Northern Ireland, however, you can be charged and convicted on such evidence in a court with no jury.

BAIL

If you are over the age of fourteen and charged with a scheduled offence which is not certified out by the DPP the judge has a greater discretion to refuse bail than in England or Wales.

If you are charged with a scheduled offence and denied bail you may be remanded in custody for a maximum of twenty-eight days without any intervening court appearance.

BANNED ORGANIZATIONS

The Act bans a number of organizations in Northern Ireland and provides the Secretary of State with the power to delete organizations from this list or to add other organizations to it. It also provides for a number of related criminal offences.

It is an offence to belong, profess to belong, support or subscribe to the following banned organizations:

- The Irish Republican Army
- Cumann na mBan
- Fianna na hÉireann
- The Red Hand Commando
- Saor Éire
- The Ulster Freedom Fighters
- The Ulster Volunteer Force
- The Irish National Liberation Army

INTERNMENT

There is still a power that provides for the internment without trial of anyone suspected of being a terrorist. This power has not been used since 1975 although it can be introduced at any time without the approval of Parliament. It removes the rights to liberty, to a fair trial and the presumption of innocence until proven guilty.

THE USE OF TROOPS

The army remains operational in Northern Ireland and has, since 1973, had special powers to stop, question, search and detain you there under the Northern Ireland (Emergency Provisions) Act (see p. 314).

THE USE OF FIREARMS

There is no statutory provision in the UK that defines the circumstances under which lethal force may be used by the police, a member of the army, or any other person. In Northern Ireland the use of force is governed by Section 3 of the Criminal Law (Northern Ireland) Act 1967 which states:

A person may use such forces as is reasonable in the circumstances in the prevention of crime, or in effecting or assisting in the lawful arrest of offenders or suspected offenders or of persons unlawfully at large.

This provision was passed before the present deployment of British troops, and is identical to the provision that applies regarding the use of force in the remainder of the UK. It is not designed to cover the existing situation in Northern Ireland, where the police and army are permanently armed.

There are internal instructions that govern the use of firearms by the police or army but these are not publicly available. You do not, therefore, have the right to read and understand the circumstances which serve as guidelines on when they are and are not allowed to open fire.

However, certain of the principles that govern the use of firearms by the army are clear:

- minimum force should always be used;
- shots should be aimed at a particular target;
- precautions should be taken against injuring anyone other than the chosen target;
- no more shots should be fired than is necessary;
- a warning should be given unless this would increase the risk of injury or death; *and*
- firearms should only be used if they are the only means to

prevent action likely to endanger life or if there is no other way to arrest someone who has killed or injured someone else.

The internal instructions given to the police and army appear to place greater restrictions on their use of firearms than those which exist under the ordinary law. A number of unarmed civilians have, however, been killed by the police and army in circumstances which seem to have been in breach of their instructions but which were not considered to be unlawful. These instructions do not therefore appear to have the force of law.

COMPENSATION FOR CRIMINAL INJURIES

The system of compensation differs significantly in Northern Ireland from the rest of the UK (see 5.8, p. 119). In Northern Ireland you apply for compensation for criminal injuries or for criminal damage to the Criminal Injuries Division of the Northern Ireland Office. Applications for compensation should be made with the assistance of a solicitor.

In order to apply for compensation for criminal injury you must:

- obtain a medical report on your condition and injuries;
- report your injury within forty-eight hours to the police or within a period which a court considers reasonable;
- send a Notice of Intention to apply to the Criminal Injuries Division within twenty-eight days (the forms are available from the Northern Ireland Office); *and*
- send your Notice of Application within three months.

If you are a dependant of a person who dies as a result of criminal injury you may claim compensation.

Compensation for criminal damage to property is paid only if the damage is inflicted by three or more people.

Applications for compensation for criminal injury or for criminal damage can be referred by the Northern Ireland Office to the courts for a decision on the principle of whether compensation should be paid.

You can lodge an appeal against the decision of the Criminal Injuries Division within six weeks of it being made.

The time limits outlined may be extended at the discretion of the court or Secretary of State.

PRISONERS

A prisoner in Northern Ireland is entitled to remission under licence of up to a half of the sentence, or up to a third for a scheduled offence (see p. 316). Remission may be lost through breaches of prison discipline.

The authorities have wide discretionary powers to grant parole for public holidays and special family occasions, but the parole scheme for England and Wales does not apply in Northern Ireland. There is, however, a special review procedure for life prisoners. A person sentenced to life imprisonment will have their case reviewed by the Life Sentence Review Board after ten years. In the case of someone detained at the Secretary of State's pleasure (SOSP) this review takes place after eight years. The Board can recommend a fixed release date to the Secretary of State or refuse to recommend a date for release and inform the prisoner of the date of the next review. No reasons for refusal are given. A lifer, or SOSP, is released on licence for the rest of their life; conditions can be imposed regarding supervision etc., and the licence can be revoked if the terms of the licence are breached or if the person commits a further offence or presents a danger to the public.

A prisoner, their family or friends may write to the Secretary of State at any time to say that they think the prisoner should be released. You can also consider writing to your MP, local councillor, or the judge who sentenced the prisoner.

PUBLIC ORDER

Shortly after the Public Order Act 1986 came into force in England and Wales, and after a review of the existing law in Northern Ireland, the government introduced a new Public Order (Northern Ireland) Order in 1987. Under this Order the law in Northern Ireland continues to differ significantly from the law in England and Wales.

Some of the differences in the law are as follows:

In Northern Ireland, open-air public meetings as well as public processions may be banned under certain circumstances. The Northern Ireland Office denies that this is contrary to Article 11 of the European Convention which sets out the right to peaceful assembly. A public meeting cannot be banned in England and Wales and conditions can only be imposed on assemblies of twenty or more people.

The powers available in Northern Ireland to ban public processions are much wider than in England and Wales. The exercise of this power can include factors such as undue demands placed on the police or army, or serious disruption to the life of the community. It is this section in particular that may be contrary to the European Convention on Human Rights.

Notice of a public procession must be given to a police officer of the rank of sergeant or above at a police station near the place at which the planned event is to commence not less than seven days beforehand or as soon as reasonably practicable. In England and Wales notice can be posted if the police receive it six days before the event.

If notice of a procession has not been given to the police, it is a criminal offence for anyone to organize, or take part in it. It is not a criminal offence to take part in such a procession in England and Wales.

Where the law is comparable with that in England and Wales the penalties in Northern Ireland (for example, for failing to comply with conditions imposed on public processions or public meetings), are considerably more severe.

ABORTION

The Abortion Act 1967 does not apply to Northern Ireland. A woman can, therefore, only have an abortion in hospital in Northern Ireland under the following circumstances:

- if she has serious medical or psychiatric problems which would jeopardize her life/health if she were to have a baby;
- if she is mentally subnormal;
- if she has been exposed to German measles (rubella) in early pregnancy; *or*

- if there is a substantial genetic risk of having a handicapped baby.

Only a small minority of women actually receive abortions in Northern Ireland and there may be long delays for an appointment.

If a woman seeks a legal abortion in Britain neither she nor anyone helping her will be committing an offence in Northern Ireland.

HOMOSEXUALITY

Under the Homosexual Offences (NI) Order 1982 the age of consent for homosexual activity is twenty-one. This must take place in private; any act where more than two people take part or are present, and any 'performed' in a place to which the public would normally have access, is not considered to be private.

DISCRIMINATION

The Race Relations Act 1976 does not apply to Northern Ireland. However, under the Public Order (Northern Ireland) Order it is an offence to incite racial or religious hatred. This is similiar to the provision that applies to racial hatred in England and Wales under the Public Order Act 1986.

The Fair Employment (NI) Act 1976 was designed to promote equality of opportunity in employment and occupations by the elimination of religious and political discrimination. It established the Fair Employment Agency with the duty of promoting equality of opportunity and working for the elimination of unlawful discrimination. If you believe that religious or political discrimination has prevented you getting a job or getting promotion you should contact the Agency whose services are confidential and free of charge. The Agency can normally accept your complaint only if you have made it within two months of the date you first knew about it or within six months from when it occurred, whichever is earlier.

At the time of going to press, new laws are proposed under the Fair Employment (NI) Bill. They include the introduction of contract compliance, a requirement to monitor the composition of the workforce, the outlawing of indirect discrimination, a new Fair Employment Commission to replace the Fair Employment Agency, and the setting up of a Fair Employment Tribunal to consider individual complaints.

The Equal Opportunities Commission for Northern Ireland has responsibility for overseeing the implementation of the law on sex discrimination and equal pay, which is virtually the same as that in Britain.

TRADE UNIONS, EMPLOYMENT AND THE LAW

The 1982 Employment Act became law in Northern Ireland in July 1987 through the Industrial Relations Order, which is yet to come into force. There is as yet no equivalent to the 1984 Trade Unions Act, although it is likely that there will be proposals to introduce an order that will make this law in Northern Ireland in the near future.

The law on unfair dismissal and redundancy is, in substance, the same as in Britain although the statutes are different.

LEGAL SERVICES

The green-form scheme was introduced in Northern Ireland in 1978 and operates on a similar basis to the present scheme in England and Wales (see 5.6, p. 99).

If legal aid is granted for criminal cases in Northern Ireland no contribution is required. If legal aid is not granted there is no right of appeal against this decision.

Solicitors in Northern Ireland belong to the Law Society of Northern Ireland.

15.2   Scotland

The rights of citizens in Scotland are quite different from those in England and Wales, especially those which concern police powers and the criminal law. The system of courts, prosecutors and prisons is also markedly different. Scottish law, along with most European countries, is based upon Roman law as opposed to the common law of England and Wales. There is also less statute law in Scotland, made by the Westminster Parliament.

The responsibility for the administration of justice rests with the Scottish Law Officers, the Lord Advocate and the Solicitor General, while other responsibilities, such as for prisons and mental health, rest with the Secretary of State for Scotland.

Police powers, the prosecution and public order are discussed briefly below as illustrations of the differences between the Scottish and English systems.

POLICE POWERS

The principal police powers to stop and question and to detain suspects and witnesses are governed in Scotland by the Criminal Justice (Scotland) Act 1980, whereas the Police and Criminal Evidence Act 1984 (PACE) is the governing statute south of the border (see chapter 6). The police have special powers in Scotland to require identification of possible suspects and also of witnesses and to detain them for verification of identity. Failure to provide details is an offence and may result in immediate arrest without warrant. There is no general right to stop and search persons or vehicles, but, as in England and Wales, specific Acts of Parliament give specific powers. A refusal to be searched is an offence.

The Scottish 'sus'

In England and Wales the offence of being 'a suspected person' was abolished in 1981. In Scotland, a similar offence of being found without lawful authority 'in or on a building or other premises, whether enclosed or not, or in its curtilage or in a vehicle or vessel so that, in all the circumstances, it may reasonably be inferred that he intended to commit theft' has been retained and extended (Civic Government (Scotland) Act 1982).

Detention for questioning

In England and Wales the police cannot detain a person against their will for questioning without first arresting them. In Scotland, the position differs. A police officer can detain any person reasonably suspected of having committed an imprisonable offence for *up to six hours' questioning*, without arrest or charge and without any right to legal advice. The suspect may also be searched and fingerprinted without his consent. But, unlike the powers in P A CE, the police in Scotland have no power to hold the suspect beyond the six-hour period or to 're-detain' them for the same offence.

Arrest powers

In England and Wales an arrest may be made simply on reasonable suspicion that the suspect has committed an offence. In Scotland, an arrest can only be made when there is enough evidence to charge. Hence the wider power to detain for questioning, above.

PROSECUTION

Once the suspect is charged the local prosecutor, known as the *Procurator-fiscal*, takes over the prosecution. Minor offences are tried without a jury in the sheriff or district courts.

In more serious cases involving trial by jury, known as solemn procedure, the accused must first be brought before a sheriff for 'judicial examination', when the Procurator-fiscal is entitled to ask any questions for the purpose of obtaining 'any denial, explanation, justification or comment' from the accused about the offence, or any confession made by the accused in police custody. Although the accused does not have to answer the questions, his right of silence is weakened by the right of the judge or prosecution to make adverse comment upon it to the court of trial (see 6.5, p. 150).

The most serious cases, such as murder and rape, can only be tried in the High Court of Justiciary in which the cases are presented by barristers called advocates-depute.

The 110-day rule

A unique feature of the Scottish administration of justice is the use of time limits in criminal cases. A prisoner committed for jury trial must receive the indictment (the formal court document setting out the charges) *within eighty days* and the trial itself must begin *within 110 days*. If the eighty-day limit is breached the prisoner must be released but can still be prosecuted. If the 110-day rule is breached the prisoner must be released unconditionally and the proceedings are at an end.

Corroboration

In contrast to the law in England and Wales, the rules of evidence in Scotland require that evidence of certain important facts must be corroborated by a second witness. This means that if the prosecution case rests on an alleged confession made to a single witness it must be dismissed.

Verdicts

The Scottish system of jury trial is unique in having three possible verdicts: guilty, not guilty and *not proven*. The not guilty verdict applies to the defendant whom the jury believes to be innocent. The not proven verdict is reserved for the case where the jury is not satisfied beyond reasonable doubt that the defendant is guilty. Both the not guilty and the not proven verdicts amount to an acquittal.

PUBLIC ORDER

Marches and demonstrations

The principal difference between English and Scottish law is that controls imposed upon marches and demonstrations in Scotland are imposed by the local authority, whereas in England and Wales they come from the police (see 1.1. p. 1). The Civic Government (Scotland) Act 1982 gives district and city councils in Scotland the power to impose conditions on, and even to ban, public processions.

The police have only an advisory role. The council is required by the Act to send a copy of all applications to hold processions to the chief constable, and the council must consult the police before imposing conditions or a ban. But in the end the responsibility for the decision rests with the council. They have no statutory guidelines for exercising their powers; they must only act 'reasonably'. This gives councils a broad discretion. On one occasion, a council issued an order banning a march of the Orange Lodge through Inverness because it was 'contrary to the Highland way of life'.

At least seven days' written notice of a procession must be given in Scotland (as in England), but to the local council not the police. The council must be provided with all the details and arrangements for the procession. If the council decides to ban a procession the organizers have a right of appeal to the sheriff. If a procession is held without permission or in breach of the council's order, both organizers and participants will be guilty of criminal offences.

The new provisions of the Public Order Act 1986 (see 1.1, p. 1), which empowers the police to impose conditions on processions and assemblies, also apply to Scotland.

Public order offences

There are a number of old public order offences which are still quite widely used. In particular, it is an offence to commit a breach of the peace, whereas in England and Wales breach of the peace is not a crime in itself (see 1.3, p. 25). Another offence unique to Scotland is 'mobbing and rioting', sometimes used for behaviour committed in prison disturbances.

Most of the provisions of the Public Order Act 1986 relating to offences do not apply to Scotland, except the new racial hatred offences.

15.3   More information

NORTHERN IRELAND

Useful organizations

Belfast Law Centre, 62–6 Bedford Road, Belfast BT2 7FH (0266 659137)

Cara-Friend, (Northern Ireland Gay Rights Association), PO Box 44, Belfast BT1 (Belfast: 0232 32023; Derry 0504 263120)

Committee for the Administration of Justice, 45–47 Donegall Street, Belfast BT1 2FG (0232 232394/243920)

Equal Opportunities Commission, Chamber of Commerce House, 22 Great Victoria Street, Belfast BT2 2BA (0232 242752)

Fair Employment Agency, Andras House, 60 Great Victoria Street, Belfast BT2 7BB (0232 240020)

Northern Ireland Association for the Care and Resettlement of Offenders, 22 Adelaide Street, Belfast BT2 8GD (0232 30157)

Northern Ireland Association of Citizens Advice Bureaux, Regional Office, Newforge Lane, Belfast BT9 5NW (0232 681117/8/9)

Prison Regimes Dept of the Northern Ireland Office, Dundonald House, Upper Newtownards Road, Belfast BT4 3SU

Bibliography

S. Bailey, *Human Rights and Responsibilities in Great Britain and Ireland: A Christian Perspective*, Macmillan, 1987.

S. C. Greer and A. White, *Abolishing the Diplock Courts*, Cobden Trust, 1986.

D. Walsh, *The Use and Abuse of Emergency Legislation in Northern Ireland*, Cobden Trust, 1983.

SCOTLAND

Useful organizations

Scottish Council for Civil Liberties (SCCL), 146 Holland Street, Glasgow G2 4NG (041-332 5960)

Bibliography

K. Ewing and W. Finnie, *Civil Liberties in Scotland: Cases and Materials*, W. Green, 1988.

R. McCreadie and I. Willcock (eds), *You and Your Rights: An A to Z Guide to the Law in Scotland*, Reader's Digest in association with P. and G. Clark, 1984.

NCCL
Charter of Civil Rights and Liberties

We are committed to the defence and extension of civil liberties in the United Kingdom and to the rights and freedoms recognized by international law.

In particular, we are pledged to ensure and safeguard these essential rights:

1.

To live in freedom and safe from personal harm.

2.

To protection from ill-treatment or punishment that is inhuman or degrading.

3.

To equality before the law and freedom from discrimination on such grounds as disability, political or other opinion, race, religion, sex, or sexual orientation.

4.

To protection from arbitrary arrest and unnecessary detention; the right to a fair, speedy and public trial, to be presumed innocent until proved guilty, and to legal advice and representation.

5.

To a fair hearing before any authority exercising power over the individual.

6.

To freedom of thought, conscience and belief.

7.

To freedom of speech and publication.

8.

To freedom of peaceful assembly and association.

9.

To move freely within one's country of residence and to leave and enter it without hindrance.

10.

To privacy and the right of access to official information.

Table of Statutes

Index

The National Council for Civil Liberties is an independent organization committed to defending and extending the rights explained in this book. To do this it depends on its members and donations. Please help to maintain your civil liberties by completing the form below.

MEMBERSHIP OR AFFILIATION

INDIVIDUAL MEMBERS

Individual Membership £12
Two people at the same address £15
Students, OAPs, Claimants £6
Any two Students, OAPs or Claimants at the same address £10

ORGANIZATIONS

Under 100 members £17	**501–1,000 members £40**
101–250 members £20	**1,000–2,500 members £60**
251–500 members £30	**2,501–5,000 members £100**

Over 5,000 members: details on application

I/We enclose a cheque/PO for £ _____ membership/affiliation and £ _____ donation: total £ ___I/We* do/do not require a receipt. ☐

I/We accept the aims and the constitution of NCCL. *I/We* do not/Our organization* does not have objectives which are incompatible with those of the NCCL, nor am I/are we* members(s) or part of any organization whose objectives are incompatible with NCCL.

*Delete where applicable.

Signature _____ Date _____
Name _____
Organization (if affiliate) _____
Address _____
_____
_____

☐ Please send me details of direct debit payment
☐ Please send my/our details to a local NCCL group

A copy of the constitution is available from NCCL
NCCL, FREEPOST, 21 TABARD STREET, LONDON SE1 6BP

Give your support by way of a covenant and increase the value of your gift at no extra cost to yourself. By completing *both* of the forms below and pledging your support for at least four years, the tax rebate will enable the Civil Liberties Trust, the charitable wing of NCCL, to claim from the Inland Revenue and will give invaluable extra support to civil liberty work.

BANKER'S ORDER FORM
*Delete as required

Date _____ To _____
(Name of bank and branch address)

Please pay to the credit of the Charities Aid Foundation (D)
A/C No. 36880043 at National Westminster Bank plc 60-30-06,
126 High Holborn, London WC1, for the later credit of the Civil Liberties

Trust on the _____ day of _____ 19_____ the sum of
_____ pounds _____ pence and the same sum on the same
date annually/half yearly/quarterly* for the following six/three years*
and debit my A/C No. _____ accordingly.
(For a small amount we would prefer a yearly or half-yearly payment)

If you do not wish to make a covenant, you can still help with a donation.

I enclose a donation of £_____ to the Civil Liberties Trust.

Name _____

Address _____

_____ Postcode _____

COVENANT FORM

I _____
(Full name in capitals and address)

of _____

_____ Postcode _____

undertake to pay the Charities Aid Foundation of 48 Pembury Road, Tonbridge, Kent each year for four/seven* years (or during my lifetime if shorter) from today the sum that will after the deduction of income tax at the basic rate be £_____ per year/half year/quarter to be paid to the Civil Liberties Trust.

Given under my hand and seal this _____ day of _____19____

Signed _____

Witness's signature _____
(Please get a friend to witness your signature)

and address _____

_____

Please complete both forms and return them to us, not your bank, at the following address:

CIVIL LIBERTIES TRUST
21 TABARD STREET
LONDON SE1 4LA

FOR THE BEST IN PAPERBACKS, LOOK FOR THE 🐧

In every corner of the world, on every subject under the sun, Penguin represents quality and variety – the very best in publishing today.

For complete information about books available from Penguin – including Pelicans, Puffins, Peregrines and Penguin Classics – and how to order them, write to us at the appropriate address below. Please note that for copyright reasons the selection of books varies from country to country.

In the United Kingdom: Please write to *Dept E.P., Penguin Books Ltd, Harmondsworth, Middlesex, UB7 0DA*

If you have any difficulty in obtaining a title, please send your order with the correct money, plus ten per cent for postage and packaging, to *PO Box No 11, West Drayton, Middlesex*

In the United States: Please write to *Dept BA, Penguin, 299 Murray Hill Parkway, East Rutherford, New Jersey 07073*

In Canada: Please write to *Penguin Books Canada Ltd, 2801 John Street, Markham, Ontario L3R 1B4*

In Australia: Please write to the *Marketing Department, Penguin Books Australia Ltd, P.O. Box 257, Ringwood, Victoria 3134*

In New Zealand: Please write to the *Marketing Department, Penguin Books (NZ) Ltd, Private Bag, Takapuna, Auckland 9*

In India: Please write to *Penguin Overseas Ltd, 706 Eros Apartments, 56 Nehru Place, New Delhi, 110019*

In Holland: Please write to *Penguin Books Nederland B.V., Postbus 195, NL–1380AD Weesp, Netherlands*

In Germany: Please write to *Penguin Books Ltd, Friedrichstrasse 10–12, D–6000 Frankfurt Main 1, Federal Republic of Germany*

In Spain: Please write to *Longman Penguin España, Calle San Nicolas 15, E–28013 Madrid, Spain*

In France: Please write to *Penguin Books Ltd, 39 Rue de Montmorency, F-75003, Paris, France*

In Japan: Please write to *Longman Penguin Japan Co Ltd, Yamaguchi Building, 2–12–9 Kanda Jimbocho, Chiyoda-Ku, Tokyo 101, Japan*

FOR THE BEST IN PAPERBACKS, LOOK FOR THE

A CHOICE OF PENGUINS

Beyond the Blue Horizon   Alexander Frater

The romance and excitement of the legendary Imperial Airways East-bound Empire service – the world's longest and most adventurous scheduled air route – relived fifty years later in one of the most original travel books of the decade. 'The find of the year' – *Today*

Voyage through the Antarctic   Richard Adams and Ronald Lockley

Here is the true, authentic Antarctic of today, brought vividly to life by Richard Adams, author of *Watership Down*, and Ronald Lockley, the world-famous naturalist. 'A good adventure story, with a lot of information and a deal of enthusiasm for Antarctica and its animals' – *Nature*

Getting to Know the General   Graham Greene

'In August 1981 my bag was packed for my fifth visit to Panama when the news came to me over the telephone of the death of General Omar Torrijos Herrera, my friend and host . . .' 'Vigorous, deeply felt, at times funny, and for Greene surprisingly frank' – *Sunday Times*

The Search for the Virus   Steve Connor and Sharon Kingman

In this gripping book, two leading *New Scientist* journalists tell the remarkable story of how researchers discovered the AIDS virus and examine the links between AIDS and lifestyles. They also look at the progress being made in isolating the virus and finding a cure.

Arabian Sands   Wilfred Thesiger

'In the tradition of Burton, Doughty, Lawrence, Philby and Thomas, it is, very likely, the book about Arabia to end all books about Arabia' – *Daily Telegraph*

When the Wind Blows   Raymond Briggs

'A visual parable against nuclear war: all the more chilling for being in the form of a strip cartoon' – *Sunday Times* 'The most eloquent anti-Bomb statement you are likely to read' – *Daily Mail*

A CHOICE OF PENGUINS

Trail of Havoc Patrick Marnham

In this brilliant piece of detective work, Patrick Marnham has traced the steps of Lord Lucan from the fateful night of 7th November 1974 when he murdered his children's nanny and attempted to kill his ex-wife. As well as being a fascinating investigation, the book is also a brilliant portrayal of a privileged section of society living under great stress.

Light Years Gary Kinder

Eduard Meier, an uneducated Swiss farmer, claims since 1975 to have had over 100 UFO sightings and encounters with 'beamships' from the Pleiades. His evidence is such that even the most die-hard sceptics have been unable to explain away the phenomenon.

And the Band Played On Randy Shilts
Politics, people and the AIDS epidemic

Written after years of extensive research by the only American journalist to cover the epidemic full-time, the book is a masterpiece of reportage and a tragic record of mismanaged institutions and scientific vendettas, of sexual politics and personal suffering.

The Return of a Native Reporter Robert Chesshyre

Robert Chesshyre returned to Britain from the United States in 1985 where he had spent four years as the *Observer*'s correspondent. This is his devastating account of the country he came home to: intolerant, brutal, grasping and politically and economically divided. It is a nation, he asserts, struggling to find a role.

Women and Love Shere Hite

In this culmination of *The Hite Report* trilogy, 4,500 women provide an eloquent testimony of the disturbingly unsatisfying nature of their emotional relationships and point to what they see as the causes. *Women and Love* reveals a new cultural perspective in formation: as women change the emotional structure of their lives, they are defining a fundamental debate over the future of our society.